Tools
for Food

The stories behind objects that
influence how and what we eat

Corinne Mynatt

Hardie Grant

BOOKS

Foreword

Tools for Food started in earnest in the autumn of 2018, when I decided to go out on my own with this idea strapped under my belt. Yet the instigator of the project goes back almost fifteen years, to a tool I acquired in a French flea market (the *presse-ail et dénoyateur* [garlic press and pitter]) that had piqued my interest in design, food and the stories behind *quotidien* objects. I began to recall countless curious mid-century aluminium kitchen utensils spotted in European flea markets, and realised that my passions for cooking, food cultures, design and aesthetics could all come together in researching these tools from around the world. My work began in the archives of the British Library in London, where I delved deep into sometimes strange and insightful books by impassioned, idiosyncratic people like me. This first research was followed by a trip to Japan that same autumn, where I continued to explore, discover and admire the craftsmanship behind unique utensils for preparing exquisite Japanese cuisine.

After stints as an artist and designer, I realised the constant was cooking. Especially in periods when I couldn't, or no longer was, making things with my hands, my energies went into elaborate dinners and multicourse menus. Looking back, I remembered that I held my first dinner party at the age of eighteen (for my birthday), and that this passion combined with design and research is something that will carry me through life. I was also influenced by moving to New York that same year and wandering the supermarkets of Chinatown; this opened my eyes to new worlds of ingredients, cooking and different cultures.

My attraction to generally odd objects – whether for the kitchen or not – came to the fore in this project, where I've had the chance to uncover stories of the maker, craftsman or designer, and the surrounding histories of culture, materials, and technical innovations. Throughout my research it has been a pleasure to cross paths with like-minded and enthusiastic food historians, antique dealers, designers and chefs. À la *A History of the World in 100 Objects*, these tools express political and social sentiments, reflecting particular momentary priorities, how, why and what people eat. Each day was – and still is – an adventure, discovering unknown objects, accompanied by wonder in the similarities of humanity across the world. I hope you will also be amazed by these peculiar objects created by our human race, that contribute to the complexities of international cuisine.

You can continue to follow my journey on: @tools_for_food.

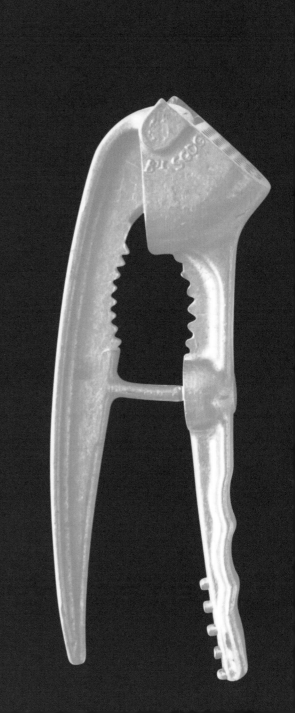

Turning Nature into Culture

'To acquire even one old kitchen utensil or implement is to possess a piece of local and social history, of craftsmanship and, often, of beauty.'
– Geoffrey Warren

Philosophers, writers and food aesthetes across the world agree that cooking food is what makes us distinctly man and not beast, human and not animal. Anthropologist Claude Lévi-Strauss observed that when man began to cook, we became cultured, left the world of beasts behind and began a new era; we opened possibilities for ingredients and flavours that were previously unavailable. Many foods conveniently eaten today could not be consumed until we developed stones to grind with, flints to cut with, and fires to roast upon. Food that is processed and cooked not only renders once poisonous or indigestible morsels edible (such as cassava, wheat and potatoes), but also makes it easier

to digest. Thousands of years ago, being able to cook our food gave us access to more calories than other species and allowed our brains to grow bigger; consuming food that was partially digested through the act of cooking freed up time for other activities besides chewing. As Claude Lévi-Strauss noted, cooking turns 'nature into culture' and is how we form bonds with new friends and old, strengthen community, celebrate love and family.

In one of food history's key written records, *Mrs. Beeton's Household Management: A Complete Cookery Book* (1861), she writes that the reasons for cooking are '... to render mastication easy; to facilitate digestion; to increase the food value; to eliminate any risk of infection from harmful bacteria; and to make the food agreeable to the palate and pleasing to the eye.' Her frank observation sums up the path of man and his transformation of food – from eating raw nuts, fruits, insects and animals, to slicing foods to the finest millimetre or moulding them into intricate forms, our tools for food are close to our hearts and contain a rich design and social history. Aristotle noted in Book One of *Politics* (4th century BCE) that the 'menial art' of cooking was something only slaves needed to know – a thought that is now ironic in the day and age of celebrity chefs. But it was only the evolution of tools and cooking processes, from labour-intensive to labour-saving, that allowed this transformation to happen. These utensils now hold within them a certain cultural

Poi Pounder (Pōhaku Ku'i Poi), Stone, 15.5 × 17 cm
(6⅛ × 6¹¹⁄₁₆ in), Brooklyn Museum, Gift of George C. Brackett and Robert B. Woodward, 02.258.2659

anthropology and are a demonstration of man's ingenuity in evolving designs to meet new needs. The tools presented here stretch from early man to contemporary life, from hand-crafted objects to the mass-produced, to coveted design objects. These tools for food show how design has influenced our eating habits, traditions and rituals, accommodating changes in food behaviour that show where we've been and where we're going.

The earliest refined cooking utensils, dating from around 7000 BCE, were discovered in Jericho and since that time we have advanced from cooking on fire, to cauldrons, to the stovetop range. Innovations such as heating stones to boil liquids and crafting knives made from metal rather than flint have refined the process of chopping that is necessary for preparing food. In the past 500 years, major developments were made in the designs of what we use to cook with today, most of which have occurred in the past two centuries. Incredibly, cooking tools were little more than knives, pots and variations on the spoon until the 16th century, and following this a more

diversified, specialist and mechanical range from the 19th century onwards. The Industrial Revolution and London's *Great Exhibition* of 1851 had a tremendous effect on accessibility to improved culinary tools, and these innovations transformed the landscape of the domestic kitchen. When production en masse began to take off, a *batterie de cuisine* – the name for the range of tools required in a professional kitchen, including utensils, pots and pans, as popularised by 19th-century French chef Alexis Soyer – became necessary for households and professional kitchens across the globe. Once this canon was established, in the 20th century more sophisticated designs appeared, taking into account kitchen science and ergonomics.

Distinctions in design vary by country, often influenced by the availability of natural materials, technological advancements or setbacks due to war. For example, Depression-era kitchenalia (reamers, bowls, ladles, storage containers) was made in glass because metal was diverted to the war effort, while earlier the Civil War in the United States (1861–1865) delayed progress in creating mechanical kitchen tools compared to that seen in England or Europe at the time. Yet just a century later,

Cooking pot, before 1613, Iron, 24 × 26.5 cm (9½ x 10½ in), The Rijksmuseum, NG-1977-195-W

Copper mould, since 18th century, Europe / UK, copper

after the Second World War, North America's industrial design output exploded when factories once used for producing weapons were put to new uses. This is when, in the 1950s, sensational and extraneous kitchen gadgets appeared, alongside developments in plastic and melamine. Each object tells a story about a time and place, a narrative revealed through design, showing the how, why and what people were eating, then and now. This space for preparing food embodies a complex social and political history – whether occupied by scullery maids and butlers, as the designated domain of a woman running the household or shouting celebrity chefs in professional kitchens on television.

Anthropologists compare learning to cook to learning a language – there is grammar, syntax and punctuation to master, but knowledge is also gained, through cultural osmosis. Indeed recipes, techniques and tools are passed down through generations, while chefs immerse themselves in other cultures to learn the tricks and tools of the trade. James Beard wrote in his *International Cook's Catalogue* (1977) that French cooks '... wouldn't dream of submitting their tender finds [from the market] to the mercies of inferior kitchen implements ... fine food demands respect at every stage of handling, from preliminary slicing to final presentation.' Using a well-designed or useful kitchen tool inspires 'aha moments', when you realise how easy the task could have been had the implement been introduced into life sooner. However, there is always a delicate balance to strike between the space something takes up in the kitchen, and its value in saving time and effort.

The kitchen, as we know it now, is the natural gathering place in the home, and regardless of time or place, food unites people across the world. Though each culture has its own rituals, tools, techniques and flavours, the act of eating is an everyday necessity and is therefore universal. *Tools for Food* considers the personal experience of food preparation, but also collective histories and futures. Writer Michael Pollan observed that not cooking is a loss of knowledge and a loss of power – cooking connects us to social and ecological relationships with the earth and each other. The landscape of food propagation, production and consumption has changed beyond recognition, and we must reclaim a closer

relationship to food. Perhaps the pleasure of using a well-designed tool, understanding its origins, cooking and enjoying meals together can somehow salvage a productive relationship with food, through an appreciation of design and our evolution from using just fire, knives and spoons to a *batterie de cuisine*.

Note to readers
Electrical appliances, kitsch items and extraneous gadgets have been excluded from the book unless of particular design interest. My apologies in advance to those who find their favourite utensil excluded – the journey started with many more tools which had to be whittled down to the small selection here. These objects only cover the kitchen and not the dining room, though there are a few exceptions I couldn't resist. Lastly, in the listings for each tool, it should be noted that some archetypes of form go back so far, the original designer can't be known. To acknowledge this fact, and distinguish between 'Designers' and 'Makers', such objects are listed as 'Maker Unknown' when the maker of the archetypal form is not traceable.

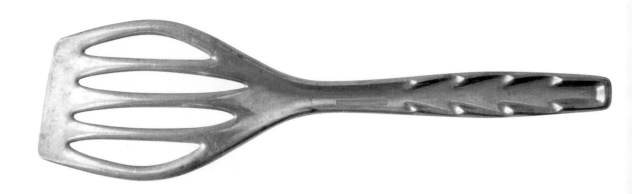

Spatula / Cake turner, mid-20th century,
Germany, Westmark, aluminium

Store & Contain

We have always needed to preserve and store food safely, whether for the winter months or due to uncertain times caused by climate or blight. Across the globe we have smoked, pickled, salted, spiced, dried and fermented foods to nourish ourselves over long periods of food uncertainty, and to add variety of flavour and texture to meals. Preserved foods bring unique flavour profiles to the table, whether tangy sauerkraut, kimchi or sweet and unctuous jams. As early as 2500 BCE, hominids were storing foods in gourds, ostrich eggshells, and coconuts until more hard-wearing clay vessels were created. Once basic storage was mastered, fermenting – usually by happy accident – was utilised and improved. In Ancient Egypt, Greece and Rome, the original larders were food chests crafted from hollow tree trunks. From bread-bins (bread boxes) to spice cabinets, these tools have always been essential equipment for any kitchen.

Though created out of necessity, objects that store food can be beautifully refined and sculptural: from undulating amphorae, the steamed bentwood boxes of the American Shakers, to the domestically efficient and modern Frankfurt Kitchen containers or skilfully woven baskets of Africa. As fixtures in the domestic landscape, the design and aesthetics of these objects are of serious consideration. Clay and earthenware are common materials for vessels such as Korean *onggi* or German *gärtopf* crocks; glazed or unglazed, the unique porosity – or controlled lack thereof – provides ideal insulation and temperature control for storing or fermenting food.

Storage doesn't always mean closed containers, however: wire baskets hung from the ceiling keep pests away from fresh eggs, and larger wirework containers keep air flowing through root vegetables and potatoes. Hooks hang and dry meat, branches thread through drying apples or mushrooms, and smaller containers of wood, metal and glass are required for storing grain and spices. Historically there was no 'popping to the shop' – chefs, servants and heads of households stored harvests or shopped in bulk at markets and therefore needed places and ways of storing food for long periods. Animals were typically slaughtered in the autumn, and along with fruits, vegetables and grains had to be preserved over winter.

Over the centuries our food cupboards tell a thousand stories about how we eat and cook – the way in which we store and contain these foodstuffs is of paramount importance for keeping food fresh and safe. Eventually 19th-century canning factories and domestic freezing changed what we could have at hand to cook easily, quickly and safely. It has been an extraordinary evolution from Greco-Roman amphorae to Tupperware parties.

Since the 19th century, each country across Europe and the USA has created their own brand of glass and rubber-seal preserving jars. These containers are some of the most familiar items in the landscape of our larders and pantries, filled with preserved fruits and vegetables from a summer glut; the process was once a necessity but is now an enjoyable pastime.

Prior to the rubber seal, wax was used to keep oxygen from spoiling preserved food in glass containers. This preservation method was pioneered by the French chef Nicolas Appert in the early 1800s. The evolution of designs using a rubber seal for this purpose date from the 19th century onwards: Kilner jars, 1842, UK; Mason jars, 1858, USA; Ball jars, 1886, USA; Weck, 1895, Germany and Le Parfait, 1930s, France. These innovations also coincided with developments in the more efficient mass-manufacturing of glass products. Each brand works on the same principle, though with different types of closures to make their hermetic seal effective. Kilner jars have a clip-top for the glass lid and rubber ring which is connected to the main container; Mason and Ball jars have metal screw-on lids with a rubber insert; Le Parfait have a clip-top like Kilner; and Weck uses spring-loaded clips that hold together the separate glass lid, rubber seal and container. The Kilner brand states that it is '… the original and best, [and that] all other brands are substitutes.' Though the use of these jars may have shifted to storing aesthetically pleasing beans and pulses for display, home preserving is still alive and well, with Le Parfait selling at least 20 million jars per year.

Storing and fermenting foods has always been a necessity for individual households – in the most basic sense, it is essential for survival. The tradition goes back thousands of years, especially when nomadic cultures began to settle in permanent dwellings. When trade systems developed, larger vessels, such as amphorae, were required for the transportation of mass-produced commodities. These strangely shaped terracotta vessels were used for olive oil, wine and sometimes grains. When it wasn't possible to produce one's own, households purchased these commodities and stored them in smaller vessels at home.

It's amazing to think that a single designer, maker or inventor came up with this typology of form, which went on to influence centuries of storage vessels across the cultures of Eurasia, China, Ancient Greece and Rome. Variations of the shape differ according to time period and location, but vessels with this basic structure are recognised as amphorae. Though they appear illogical to contemporary sensibilities, in ship galleys the pointed end allowed for easier stacking, while on land the amphorae could be stored upright by sticking the bottom in soft ground or sand. The peculiar shape also enabled easy lifting and pouring of the contents by grabbing the handle at the top and holding the opposite pointed end for stability. So common were the vessels in transporting commodities by sea that they are often used to help date centuries-old shipwrecks. The Celts eventually developed more lightweight barrels made of wood, which eventually replaced the heavier amphorae.

↑   **Onggi hangari, Since 4ᵗʰ–5ᵗʰ centuries BCE,**
    Korea, Various makers, Earthenware

Ancient food-preserving traditions remain strong, especially in Korea, whose culture is well-known for its spicy cabbage kimchi which ferments in large earthen-ware jars known as *hangari*. Food fermentation arose out of necessity, to preserve fruit or vegetables for the winter months, and these containers have been used since 4000–5000 BCE. This metabolic process is used to ferment rice, liquor, kimchi, soy sauce, gochujang and salted fish. This culinary technique has become hugely popular in recent years, used by famous restaurants such as Noma (in Copenhagen) and in domestic kitchens across the world.

Onggi means 'pottery', and craftsmen called *onggijang* create these earthenware vessels via the coil method and with a pottery wheel. *Hangari* vessels can be 1m (3ft)

in height or more, with diameters of 60cm (2ft), though the colour, shape and size vary according to the region of production in Korea. The clay used in *onggi hangari* contains a high percentage of iron, and its low firing temperature allows it to maintain the porosity that is necessary for the fermentation process. Some *hangari* are decorated with plant patterns or handles in the shape of lotus leaves; however, for the most part, the design is simple, due to their mass production for commonplace use. These jars are stored on purpose-built outdoor terraces known as *Jangdokdae /Jangttokttae* until the ferments are ready. Traditionally, *hangari* were kept outside in summer, and would have been buried underground in winter to prevent freezing. The design and function of *hangari* has hardly changed for thousands of years.

↓   **Gärtopf / Harsch crock, Since 19th century, Germany / Eastern Europe, Designer unknown, Stoneware**

The *gärtopf* crock is a water-sealed fermentation pot. The crock is made of stoneware rather than earthenware, meaning it is less porous, fired at a higher temperature, and long-lasting and robust. Though fermentation vessels have been used for thousands of years, this particular airlock crock was designed in the 19th century and comes with two half-circle weights that keep kraut (cabbage) or other vegetables underneath the brine during fermentation. The trough around the top of the jar is then filled with water, and when the lid is in place this creates a watertight seal. This technique can prevent unwanted yeasts and moulds entering the vessel, while allowing the gases of fermentation (hydrogen and carbon dioxide) to escape.

Preserving cabbage with rice vinegar originated in China thousands of years ago and was eventually adopted by cultures in Eastern Europe around the 16th century, using the lactic acid fermentation process. When cabbage is salted, the water is extracted and sugars transform into lactic acid, which is a natural preservative. These crocks originate in Germany and Eastern Europe, mostly for making sauerkraut (sour cabbage) and pickled vegetables. Sauerkraut contains live bacteria, probiotics, and is therefore touted as having many health benefits.

↓ **Food storage basket, Mid 20th century, Rwanda-Burundi, Tutsi, Straw, natural dyes**

Basketry and weaving natural fibres goes back thousands of years and is a practical way of making containers in places where grass, reeds, raffia (palm leaf) and rush grow abundantly. Exquisite specimens found in Ancient Egypt from the 15th century BCE demonstrate the sophisticated craft and use of these vessels, though the skill and tradition across humanity goes back even further.

There is a rich history and tradition of basket weaving in Africa and all over the world – from Japan to Native America – using skills that have been passed down through the generations. Different regions and tribes across the continent have their own techniques and variations, from coil-sewn baskets to woven styles. Patterns are created through colour, made with natural dyes from roots, flowers (such as banana) and seeds. These baskets are important objects for storing harvested roots, rice and grain, and hold symbolic significance as gifts when given or handed down at the moment of marriage. Shallow, unlidded baskets are also used to winnow rice and grains, or when inverted can be used as a food cover. The Tutsi basket pictured was typically made of sisal or papyrus. These baskets are now often exchanged or given as symbols of peace, since the end of the Rwandan genocide in the 1990s. Unfortunately, some basket-weaving traditions are dying out as a result of plastic replacing these containers, which are made from natural, sustainable materials.

↑ **Grain storage, Since 18ᵗʰ century, USA,**
Maker unknown, Stained pinewood

Attributed the the North East of North America, this grain storage bucket is akin to the style made by the Shaker community. Artefacts from the American Shaker culture are appreciated for their simplicity, use of natural materials and demonstration of traditional skills. The Shakers were a spinoff Christian sect of Quakers that originated in England before emigrating and settling in the USA in the late 18ᵗʰ century. Their legacy from a design perspective is of objects, furniture and architecture that embody a philosophy of harmony, order and utility, made with a dedication to craft and workmanship. They are well-known for their bentwood containers, which were used for storing grain and other dry items. This example has utilised the familiar Shaker-

style swallowtail bentwood straps that hold the circular form in place. Sometimes clusters of steamed bentwood boxes were crafted together in increasing sizes, so they could be stacked on top of one another or nest inside the largest box when not in use.

The Shakers lived simple, peaceful and communal lives, and their craft went on to inspire Modernists of the 19ᵗʰ and 20ᵗʰ centuries, who appreciated the direct relationship of form and function manifested in their objects. Though their community no longer exists, contemporary craftsmen across the world keep their legacy alive by producing containers and boxes using the same swallowtail bentwood forms and traditional techniques.

The Frankfurt Kitchen is an early example of household engineering and domestic science. Designed by Margarete Schütte-Lihotzky, this efficiently laid-out kitchen was a collaboration between the Viennese architect and the local city council. In the 1920s, Modernism was gaining momentum, and her effective design brought industrial rationalism (pioneered by Frederick Winslow Taylor) into the domestic sphere. Steps were calculated, necessities measured, ergonomics assessed, and the result was the ideally equipped kitchen, duplicated 10,000 times in the new housing being built in Frankfurt to address the shortage after the First World War.

Schütte-Lihotzky was influenced by the design of small cooking spaces such as those in ship galleys and railway carriages, and a recent publication of the time: *The New Housekeeping – Efficiencies in Home Management* by Christine Frederick (1913). Her goal was to make kitchen chores and tasks easier, and the Frankfurt Kitchen was the embodiment of the Bauhaus idea of a 'new life' for a 'new man' – or woman – of the 20th century. The kitchen design and built-in features eliminated the need for antiquated tools, excess space or furniture, where everything was within easy reach. These aluminium containers were part of the integrated storage designed for dry items such as rice, macaroni and sugar, with one even labelled with the Maggi brand of instant soup. This 'rational' kitchen was designed to fit into a space measuring 1.9 × 3.4 m (6 × 11 ft), and a replica of one can be experienced in the Museum der Dinge, in Berlin, as well as in other design collections around the world such as the Museum of Modern Art, in New York.

Spices brought from the East to the West were a valuable commodity, and in wealthy households they were kept under lock and key in cabinets such as the one pictured here. Even before 'exotic' aromatics made their way to Western kitchens via the Silk Road and the New World, herbs and spices were an essential commodity: their flavours elevate dishes or, in the time before refrigeration, mask the flavour of meat or seafood on the turn.

Although spices had already been circulating across the globe, new spices were brought to England in the 16th century and were highly prized – Queen Elizabeth I (1533–1603) had her own spice cabinet adorned with rubies, amethysts, garnets and turquoise. These cabinets held valuable ingredients for household chefs to transform food with new and unusual flavours. In line with their rarity and importance, furniture makers crafted elaborate boxes that folded out in radial forms and created various types of airtight containers. Specialist spice cabinets were still in use in the 18th and 19th centuries, and they were available for purchase from the very useful household resource of Harrod's catalogue. However, once trade routes were firmly established from the 18th century, spices were no longer an exclusive commodity. Ultra-secure cabinets were no longer required and are a far cry from the IKEA screw-top spice jars that are common today.

Earl Tupper was an in-house chemist and inventor at DuPont when he designed the famous airtight seal system for reusable plastic containers in 1946, pioneered by his new injection moulding process. Polyethylene – known as 'Poly T' – was a new thermo plastic of the time and dubbed the 'Material of the Future'. Inspired by paint tin tops, by pressing the lid down an airtight seal was formed through negative air pressure. This all started with his Welcome Ware series, which eventually led to his own successful company Tupper Plastics, and Tupperware. The marketing method of Tupperware parties was pioneered by Brownie Wise, the female lead behind the concept of selling by demonstration inside women's homes. From 1951 the products were removed from retail shelves and were sold solely via these social-networking Tupper-parties, which still take place today.

Though most well-known for storage containers, since setting up in the 1940s, the Tupperware brand seems to have made almost every useful kitchen object. From cups to jugs (pitchers), milk jugs (creamers), popsicle moulds, bowls, flour sieves and more, Tupperware constantly innovates with the new and very durable material of polyethylene. Although plastics are not an ideal material to use from a sustainability perspective, their reusable nature is a redeeming quality and why the containers are still widely used today. As an extremely successful product and company, Earl Tupper sold up in 1958 and retired to enjoy the tropical life in Costa Rica.

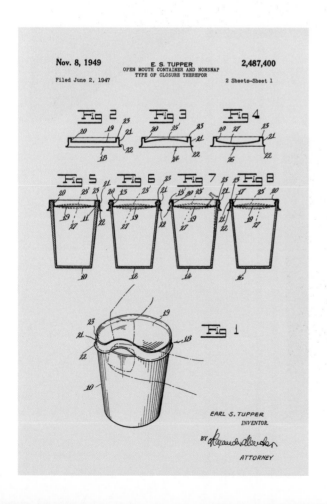

↑ **Kubus Stacking Storage, 1938,
Germany, Wilhelm Wagenfeld, Glass**

Wilhelm Wagenfeld was a German industrial designer who worked with the principles of the Bauhaus group, primarily using glass and metal in the objects he produced. Soon after being appointed Art Director of the glass manufacturer Lausitzer Glasverein in the mid-1930s, he designed these storage containers to be mass-produced. In line with Bauhaus ideals of form, function and utmost utility, these Kubus containers were intended for storing food, but their beauty and simplicity also allowed them to be used at the dining table. Their easy transference from refrigerator to tabletop encouraged households to use leftovers and avoid food waste. Prior to the advent of plastics

engineering and Tupperware storage, these easy-to-clean, modular and multipurpose containers could be stacked in the cupboard or refrigerator in a variety of ways.

Wagenfeld believed in good design for all (not exclusively the rich, for example), a principle that is often found in German industrial design and is known as 'democratic design'. He went on to work for the well-known German brand Braun, and created many iconic designs for kitchen items, lamps, typewriters and more that are still produced today. His works are held in design collections across the world.

Breadbins / boxes / tins were first made of wood, ceramic and tin, then enamelled metal. They were needed for storing bread, to slow down how quickly it dried out and became stale, especially before commercial baking and the Chorleywood method. From the 20th century – especially after enamelling had been made non-toxic in the late 19th century – this material was a popular choice for domestic kitchens. Enamelling techniques were used in jewellery by the Ancient Egyptians and Greeks, but domestic applications were not developed and applied until the 18th and 19th centuries. The process essentially fuses powdered glass to metal, fired at a high temperature; it allows for pattern and writing, and many breadbins bear a label indicating the contents inside. This style and material have now come to define much of vintage 'kitchenalia' and old utensils of a bygone era.

These boxes are common across the world where loaf bread is a staple food, differing only in shape material or ornamentation. Breadbins come in cuboid shapes with hinged tops and cubes with lids that lift off. They can be wooden with retractable doors, labelled, unlabelled, colourful, plain or decorated. Though plastic-wrapped loaves don't necessitate such a tool today, these boxes are still utilised for reasons of nostalgia, or where fresh daily bread is common (such as in France) for artisan loaves and baguettes.

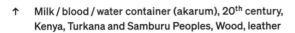

↑ Milk / blood / water container (akarum), 20th century, Kenya, Turkana and Samburu Peoples, Wood, leather

↑ Milk churn, 19th century, Denmark / Europe, Designer unknown, Aluminium

Though these containers look like gourds, this skeuomorph object is actually carved from wood, primarily by two different tribes in Kenya, the Turkana and Samburu. They are hand-carved from a log to the thickness of the gourds they resemble, then adorned with a leather strap for carrying. A circular woven mat accompanies the container, so the curved base can sit on flat surfaces. These jugs are 30–50 cm (12–20 in) tall, and usually have a detachable top which can be used as a cup.

The jug is used to collect and store milk or water, and also sometimes for ritual blood drinking as an initiation for young men. A yoghurt blend of milk and blood, a staple food of the Turkana and Samburu tribes, was also made and stored in these akarum. The jug was used on a daily basis to collect milk and would be cleaned regularly with ashes scrubbed with a whisk made from goat's hair. As with ancient metal tools in the West such as cauldrons, these akarum containers were mended and repaired so they could be used for generations.

The first animal milks to be consumed came from goats or sheep, before cattle breeding was developed. Although a 'milk churn' shares its name with a vessel used to churn butter, this is the word for the container used to transport milk. Before the milk churn, milk was transported in pails or buckets, often two at a time on either side of a carrying yoke or long piece of wood that lay across the shoulders of a dairymaid. When milk began to be transported across longer distances, the standard buckets had a tendency to spill and were no longer sufficient. Someone noticed that the tall form of a butter churn would be more suitable, hence the name-sharing of this container. Though the butter churn was innovative in form for this purpose, it was soon realised that wood was not the best material for transportation. From the mid-19th century, milk churns were made of steel, and eventually lightweight aluminium. A singular hinged handle on top or two handles on each side made them easy to load on and off transportation vehicles, often by rail. Though milk churns disappeared from use in Europe towards the end of the 20th century, they can still be seen strapped across bicycles in places such as India. Eventually milk churns were replaced for transporting milk by huge 150,000-litre (33,000-gallon) tanks.

Once people migrated to urban areas and cow ownership was less common, households were delivered smaller quantities of milk from the milkman's churn. The milkman would ladle out milk into any kind of containers the customer could provide. Eventually individual glass milk bottles were designed, around the 1880s in both the UK and USA. This allowed for a streamlined delivery, and to keep track of the amounts that customers were consuming rather than using estimates by the ladleful. The pasteurisation process that was developed in 1894 also helped grow this method of storage and distribution, and many customers had milk cubbies built into the outside of their houses to receive the bottles.

Glass was used to show the milk's purity, and many shapes were created until the pictured bottle form and 568 ml/pint size became most common. Some early bottle designs had porcelain, wood or cardboard closures, which were finally replaced by the most hygienic and practical material – aluminium. In the UK the glass bottles have colour-coded caps that indicate the milk type: red for whole homogenised; silver-red striped for semi-skimmed; dark blue and silver for skimmed. Confusingly, these codes differ to what is found on plastic bottles today, which have more or less replaced the sustainable glass version.

In the 1940s milk deliveries began to decline ever so slightly, due to advances in domestic refrigeration and the popularity of grocery shops. Though glass milk bottle delivery makes up a very small percentage of the business today, in the UK you can still spot milkmen in open-air electric vehicles in the early hours of the morning. They've been using these battery-powered vehicles called 'milk floats' since the 1930s.

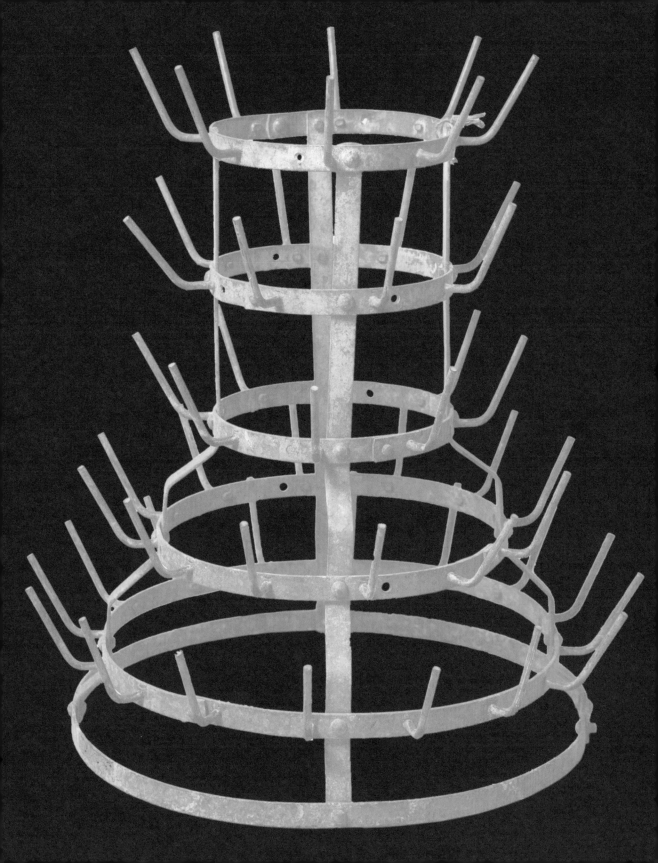

← **Bottle rack, 20th century, France,
Designer unknown, Galvanised iron**

This form is recognisable to some as Marcel Duchamp's readymade artwork, *The Bottle Rack/Hedgehog* (1914). By putting the rack in an art gallery, the Dada artist challenged conventional norms by elevating the status of this everyday object to that of an artwork. The original is in a private collection, but these bottle-drying racks can also be found in antiques markets, as they once served a practical purpose. Indeed, this early 20th-century rack is a lovely yet useful form and was ideal for drying wine or milk bottles ready for refilling. A series of concentric circles with pegs tilted at about 60 degrees allows liquid to escape from the bottles, which can then dry out effectively; its verticality was also a space saver. It is said that Duchamp purchased the rack from the French department store Bazar de l'Hôtel de Ville (BHV), which still exists today on Rue de Rivoli in Paris. The original égouttoir (rack) came in galvanised iron in 50, 100 or 150 bottle-drying sizes.

→ **Meat hook, Since 1st century CE,
Worldwide, Designer unknown, Metal/Iron**

Extraordinarily simple in form – generally an 'S'-shape – meat hooks were essential both for butchers and kitchens in the houses of large estates. Hanging meat encourages lactic acid production in the carcass as the haemoglobin breaks down the soft tissue and muscle. This acid helps prevent bacteria from forming but temperature and humidity must also be carefully controlled, otherwise the meat may spoil. Longer hanging times will give a better flavour, such as 30-day-plus aged steaks found in high-end restaurants and butchers. Cured meats such as saucisson or Parma ham must first be salted to extract moisture; they are then hung for a few weeks to lose a third of their weight before being ready to eat. French meat hooks have metal loops at the top of the hook, so the height can be adjusted on hanging rails. In contemporary domestic kitchens, S-shaped hooks are mostly used to hang utensils from railings.

↑ **Egg basket, 19th century,
France, Various designers, Steel**

Wirework egg baskets could be used when gathering eggs from hens and for storing them in the larder. The open structure keeps eggs cool, and the basket could be hung from the ceiling away from rats and other pests. Larger wirework baskets were also used to go to the market, collect berries or store vegetables such as potatoes that benefit from air circulation. These objects represent a certain time period from the 19th century onwards, when metal spun in thin threads became easier to manufacture; previously baskets were primarily made of natural fibres. In various designs of these tools, the opening at the top of the egg basket is slightly smaller than the bulk of the container – sometimes with wire tops that fold over like a lid – to prevent rats and vermin crawling inside. The size, shape, style and design of these egg containers is more or less interchangeable with salad washing baskets, and they were sometimes marketed as such a dual-purpose utensil.

↓ **Ham stand, 19th century, UK,**
Designer unknown, Ironstone

→ **Jamon rack, Since 20th century, Spain,**
Designer unknown, Wood, metal

These white pedestals were used to display hams in butcher's shops and grocers in Britain, and they were sometimes emblazoned with the name of the meat seller or the producer of the stand. The ham stand pictured here is made of ironstone, which was a cheaper alternative to porcelain. It gets its name from being strong as iron, though it doesn't contain any content of the ferrous metal. The bone end would be placed in the central hole, with the ham standing upright for easy display and slicing. Many of the ham stands that survive bear the names of butchers and meat sellers at Smithfield Market, in London, as this
was one of the premier spots for wholesale meat trade, running since the 14th century. Some show the name of the stand maker (in this case Glenhurst Equipment), often a shop outfitter or similar merchant. The original 'designer' of the stand pictured here is unknown, though logic suggests it was a simple commission for a display stand from a butcher to a potter, who turned a form on the lathe before making a slip-cast mould. These stands are 20–30 cm (8–12 in) high.

Most European countries have a tradition of cured and dried meats, particularly of pork; Spain and Italy are known for their whole legs of dried ham, which are held in specialist racks. The process is not exclusive to Europe, of course – curing and drying meat and fish has been done for thousands of years across the globe as a means of survival. Jamón Serrano, Parma ham, prosciutto and more, once the pork leg has been salted and cured, its final resting place is on the purpose-built jamon rack (ham rack). These objects can look extremely technical or remarkably primitive and have a ring- or U-shaped loop to hold the foot end, and a wider base for securing the ham with screws. More elaborate designs have a curved support at the bottom, which can be adjusted as your meat is sliced so that you have the best ergonomic angle for cutting millimetre-thin pieces.

↑ **Salt pig, Since 18th century, England,
Designer unknown, Earthenware**

Previous to these ceramic 'salt pig' forms, saltboxes
or salt kits, as they were known, were made of wood
and hung by the fire or hearth to keep salt dry (salt
cellars are for the table as opposed to the kitchen).
Centuries ago, salt was a precious commodity, not only
because of its flavour but also its ability to preserve
meat and food for the winter months. When salt was
difficult to procure, small dried fish were fermented into
a sauce – known as garum – used as an alternative to
season food. Garum was used by the Romans in ancient
times and is still commonly used in Asia today. When
Oliver Cromwell introduced a salt tax in 17th-century
England, the mineral became an even more precious
commodity. Housewives and heads of kitchens had
to determine which foods were 'worth their salt or not',

a well-known phrase today that describes if someone
is good enough for a job to be done. If the quality of the
food wasn't worth its salt, it was pickled with vinegar or
verjuice instead.

The design of this form keeps moisture out and makes
it easy to grab pinches of salt during cooking. Early salt
pigs of this shape date to the 18th century, and some
originals were actually glazed with salt. In salt-glazed
stoneware, the mineral is added to the kiln at its highest
firing temperature wherein the sodium reacts with the
silica in the glaze to give unique textures and colours
of sodium silicate. This object is called a salt pig due
to its resemblance to the snout of hogs and swine.

↓ **Garlic container, 21ˢᵗ century, UK,
Designer unknown, Earthenware**

Garlic (*Allium sativum*) is described as far back as 5,000 years ago by the Egyptians; the plant is used across the world in a multitude of cuisines and also has several medicinal purposes. Almost 30 billion tonnes of this allium are grown each year, mostly in China. Once picked and dried, garlic must be kept away from moisture and light to prevent germination. Sometimes it is strung together ornamentally and hung, otherwise it is kept in specially designed containers. These jars are typically made from various types of porous clay and have holes in the vessel to keep air circulating among the bulbs. Garlic containers are always recognisable by their holey appearance, no matter what time period they originate from – the garlic keeper pictured here has a particular affinity with Art Deco or even Post-modern styles, though it was made in the 21ˢᵗ century.

↑ **Cheese keeper, 19ᵗʰ–20ᵗʰ century, England, Maker unknown, Ceramic**

Form follows function in the cheese keeper, which is designed to house and keep fresh prized cheese wedges or wheels. In a similar way to butter dishes, ceramic helps to keep the contents inside cool, as it is generally lower than ambient room temperature. Most of these types of dishes were made in the 19ᵗʰ century, in truly eccentric Victorian style: decorated with elaborate floral patterns, designed in the style of Majolica Ware or blue and white Delftware, or made from pressed glass. This food-specific storage device would have been made by various makers of pottery as part of their range of products; the industry was mostly based in Stoke-on-Trent at the time. In France, the *cloche à fromage* was typically made of glass. English cheese keepers could be round and tall to hold whole wheels of Stilton, or large wedge shapes for portions taken from the main cheese. Often clunky and frankly garish, these objects are unique collector's items.

→ **Butter dish, Since 18ᵗʰ century, Europe / UK / North America, Various makers, Ceramic and glass**

Butter dishes were required to keep smaller quantities out for cooking and designed to keep the contents cool before the advent of refrigeration. The chef Samin Nosrat identifies two main types of culinary culture: those that cook with oil and those that cook with butter. Therefore, these objects are mostly found in locations such as Europe and North America where people like to cook with butter. Twentieth-century butter dishes incorporated materials such as glass, metal and plastic, and their designs embody the zeitgeist of place and time.

In the kitchen they were commonly made of ceramic, sometimes with ice chambers to regulate temperature. Early dishes are found in round shapes, but now they are designed to fit rectangular portions. Some French butter cloches submerge the dairy in cold liquid – the two-part structure has a cupped lid to hold the butter, which is placed upside down in a vessel filled with water. Incidentally, French butter is actually washed with water a few times before it is sold and has distinct flavours in each region of the country.

The discovery of butter was a happy accident: through the agitation of milk stored in sheepskin containers on the backs of animals while travelling across the plains. Evidence of its production and use goes back at least 4,000 years, and it was a valuable way to prolong the life of dairy and maintain its fats for nourishment and flavour. The Celts used to preserve butter by burying it in bogs. Known as 'bog butter', some of these treasures can still be consumed once discovered, even though their contents may be hundreds of years old.

1   Pressed opalescent glass, USA, 1888
2   Ceramic, UK, 21st century
3   Delftware, Netherlands, 1750

← Kendi, Since 13th century, Asia,
Designer unknown, Terracotta

Kendi were used for ceremonies and rituals as well as practically in daily life to store water or other liquids. The unique form lends itself to easy pouring for drinking directly from the receptacle without having to touch the mouth. They bear a striking resemblance to Spanish oil cruets and were made in various materials – earthenware, silver, gold, bronze and porcelain.

The *kendi* form is found across China, Indonesia, India and much of Asia, and is defined by a bulbous body, bulbous spout – sometimes described as mammiform (meaning like a breast) – and a narrow neck. Some kendi are shaped like animals or people in the body and spout. Highly decorated forms were used for ritualistic Buddhist or Hindu ceremonies, whereas the common earthenware or terracotta vessels would have been everyday kitchen or household items.

↑ Spanish oil cruet (aceitera), 19th century, Spain,
Designer unknown, Glass, cork & stainless steel

Centuries ago in Spain, olive oil was bought in pigskins, stored in larders and siphoned out into smaller containers to cook with in the kitchen or to dress vegetables. Like the *kendi*, the unique design allows for a steady and slow stream of oil, which is useful when mixing aïoli with a mortar and pestle. This form is also the basis of the famous communal drinking vessel – the *porrón* – the flow from which is remarkably and famously hard to aim into the mouth. Aceiteras, as they are known in Spanish, are usually made of glass, stainless steel or ceramic, and will always have a stopper / cork / covering for the opening into which oil is decanted from larger receptacles. This type of vessel has been used for almost a thousand years, likely originating in the Arab communities who occupied the area from the 8th to 15th centuries.

Original designs and traditional forms do have a problem – oil drips down to the base after pouring, leaving an oily ring mark on surfaces. In 1961, Catalan architect and designer Rafael Marquina set out to refine the function of this everyday object and created a glass aceitera that would not drip or leave marks behind. A central spout protrudes upwards from the middle of the vessel like a submarine periscope, and after pouring the oil returns back into the central cone which catches any excess fluid.

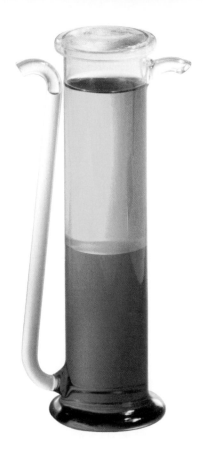

→ **Salad Sunrise, 1990, Netherlands,
Arnout Visser (for Droog), Glass**

The design of this vessel takes cues from cruets, *kendis*
and fat separators. With a spout for each material, the
Salad Sunrise allows you to control how much vinegar
or oil is poured on a salad. Using principles of polarity,
the polar vinegar sinks to the bottom while the non-polar
oil rises to the top; with some imagination, red wine
vinegar and olive oil, the interface of the liquids
resembles a sunrise. Contrary to the usual shaking of
salad dressings to emulsify the ingredients, this bottle
is meant to dose out each component one at a time.

The Salad Sunrise was created by Dutch designer
Arnout Visser and is produced by the Amsterdam-
based conceptual brand, Droog. Since 1993, Droog
has pushed the boundaries of form and function,
elevating the Dutch Design scene to one of global
recognition for its experimental products and beyond.
Droog was founded with a 'down-to-earth design
mentality' and often commissions young, international,
up-and-coming designers who push the boundaries
of what design can be.

↓　**Fat separator, 20th century,
Germany, trendglas Jena, Glass**

When making stocks or gravies, it is necessary to remove most of the fat produced during the cooking process. Scooping fat out bit by bit is tedious and inefficient, but these fat separators make light work of the task. As oil naturally floats above water or acid due to non-polarity, after settling in this container the flavoured liquid can be poured out until only the last layer of fat remains to be discarded. Several early 20th-century patents exist for fat separators, though the simple genius of a spout at the bottom of a vessel came in the latter half. Some fancy adaptations today allow fatless broth to escape from the bottom of a jug through the press of a button. The fat separator pictured is made from borosilicate glass which is heat-resistant and ready to receive and decant freshly made stock.

↑ **G-type soy sauce container, 1958, Japan, Masahiro Mori (Hakusan Porcelain Company), Porcelain**

This soy sauce container is a Japanese design icon and found in households throughout the country. It is still manufactured today, since its design and original production in 1958. The soy sauce container is a necessity in kitchens and on tables, and it comes in small or large sizes and various colours of glazed porcelain.

Masahiro Mori was a Japanese ceramic designer, and this everyday bottle has won many design awards across the world since its initial release. He designed many spouted vessels in his lifetime as a designer, often with a playful and accessible approach. Prior to the G-type bottle Mori created a few other soy sauce containers, but it was the timeless style of this form that became an everlasting icon. Its efficient, utilitarian and simple design encourages polite pouring of soy sauce: the forefinger rests on the lid to hold it in place while the body is gripped with the thumb and other fingers. The lid opening is large enough to comfortably refill the G-type container over and over again. The G-type joins a long list of Mori designs, including other ceramics and products labelled A-type, L-type, and more, which use the Latin-Roman alphabet for their titles. Later in life Mori designed collections for MUJI, including a round version of the G-type bottle.

↓ **Soy sauce dispenser, 1961, Japan, Kenji Ekuan (GK Design Group), Glass, plastic**

Almost as ubiquitous as the G-type, this soy sauce dispenser is known across the world. Most famously on Japanese restaurant tables but also in domestic kitchens, the Kikkoman glass soy sauce bottle is a fixture of Asian cooking. Though it looks as if the design is for single use, it can be refilled again and again.

Kenji Ekuan was a Japanese industrial designer, and though he created many other products, this soy sauce bottle was his lasting legacy. Ekuan's design challenge was to create a bottle to hold smaller amounts of soy sauce, which was usually sold in 1-litre (¼-gallon) quantities or more. The spout had to be efficient in pouring, but not drip, and feel comfortable in the hand. The hourglass figure with a larger bulbous base fits this purpose perfectly, and the famous red plastic lid – designed after about three years and 100 prototypes – is drip-free due to the 60-degree inward angle in the spout. Like the G-Type, the bottle also aids the delicate and polite pouring of soy sauce due to the ergonomics of its design. The Kikkoman dispenser holds a global, three-dimensional trademark which means it cannot be replicated without permission.

KIKKOMAN®
NATURALLY BREWED
Soy Sauce
150 ml ℮

↓ Jar tops, 2006, The Netherlands,
Jorre van Ast, Plastic (polypropylene)

→ Batter jug, 1882–1885, New York, USA,
Whites Binghampton, Stoneware

These universal jar tops allow one to transform ordinary glass jars into new useful kitchen items. Off-the-shelf jars can become water or milk jugs, syrup dispensers, flour dredgers, sugar casters, oil or vinegar containers. What were once passive food storage jars, become active utensils of the kitchen. Designed before apocalyptic climate change was firmly on our radar, these jar tops by Dutch designer Jorre van Ast contribute to the dialogue of sustainable design. As plastic packaging continues to plague our lives and our planet, intelligent design that promotes reuse and resourcefulness become increasingly more important.

This stoneware batter jug from the late 19th century is 22 cm (8½ in) tall and has an appropriately fat spout, so that thick batter can flow easily without being trapped by air. These jugs were used to prepare pancake batter the night before, mixing the meal or flour, yeast and water in advance to leaven in time for the morning. Whites Binghampton produced many stoneware crocks and containers in the 19th century, usually with hand-painted blue and white decorations. Similar kitchen tools morphed into bowls with handles and spouts, such as the melamine Margrethe bowl; Le Creuset produces its own version of a spouted 'batter bowl' today.

Pancakes have been around for centuries in many forms across the globe, and they hold a special place in the hearts of Americans. Pancakes (cakes cooked in the pan) have been known as griddle cakes, hoe cakes, johnny-cakes, buckwheat cakes or flapjacks, and in the United States were first made of cornmeal or buckwheat. Though yeast or natural leavens such as sourdough were used centuries ago, today American pancakes are made with baking powder to create stacks of the fluffy and thick breakfast food.

Measure & Weigh

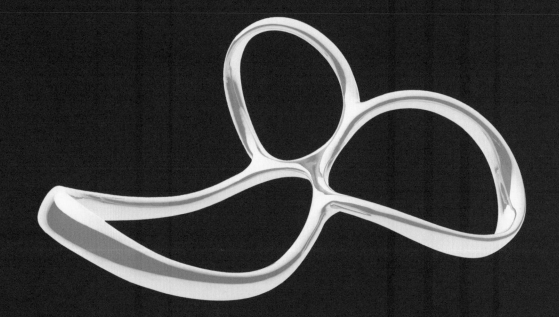

Precise measurements make or break a recipe, be they of time, temperature, weight or volume. We take for granted tools as simple as an oven thermostat, measuring jug or digital scales to determine accurate quantities of butter or sourdough starter, or whatever is needed to procure the correct proportion for success. Measurement is also essential before food even enters the kitchen – for the trade of goods between societies and from producer to consumer. Weights and measures have existed for thousands of years to facilitate fair trading, and evidence of an equal arm balance and fulcrum dates from Egypt around 5000 BCE. More exacting instruments eventually evolved from what were probably improvised equivalent weights and methods of balancing out quantities.

The raison d'etre for measuring lies in cooking recipes, which were not formally written down until the 16th century (and more commonly from the 18th); before this, cooking methods and 'recepts' were conveyed orally. Ancient recipes often referred to comparative quantities such as a goose egg, a nut of butter, a first joint of thumb or, in the past 100 years, 'the size of a US dollar bill' or a 10 × 23 cm (size 10) business envelope. Larger quantities in Britain were referred to as a pottle (½ gallon / 4 pints), firkin (9 gallons / 72 pints), kilderkin (2 firkins), runlet (1 kilderkin), a bucket (2 gallons / 16 pints) or hogshead (63 gallons / 504 pints). Now we go by ounces, pounds, kilograms, grams or pints. In the Middle East, a *ratl* was standard in medieval times (about a pint), and in Japan the square wooden *masu* box for measuring rice is still used today, though now more as a cup for drinking sake. Standardisation aside, some countries still rely on a pinch of intuition and the teacup, cup, soup spoon and other approximate units when cooking; given that gastronomic capitals such as France and Italy still use these references, we can hardly say it's to their disadvantage.

Eliza Acton was one of the first chefs to pioneer precise recipe instructions – her book, *Modern Cookery for Private Families* (1845, UK), gave ingredient lists, measurements, temperatures and cooking times to ensure culinary triumph. In 1896, Fannie Farmer from the USA decided that arbitrary terms such as a 'pinch of salt' or a 'nut of butter' were not sufficient for accuracy in the kitchen. This spawned an official level measurement system in her *Boston Cooking School Cook Book*. Try as you may, the weight-volume dichotomy has still not evaded us. Between continents, the volumes that recipes call for still vary greatly, and these imprecisions determine resounding success or discouraging failure when replicating a recipe from abroad. It's true that the only tried, tested and reliable method for full accuracy is using pure weight (grams) or pure volume (ml).

Before the thermostat, cookbooks suggested putting your hand inside the oven for a certain number of seconds until it burned to check the temperature. In medieval times and before, it was certain that your grand banquet could be grossly overdone or undercooked depending how accurately this was done. The science of assessing quantities also goes into realms beyond weights and measures, such as using density to calculate the salinity of brine for pickling or the parts per hundred of alcohol. All measurements aside, no meal will taste as good as any that has the right amount of love put into it.

A *masu* is a wooden measuring box from Japan. As with many ancient volumetric measures, it was primarily used to measure grains, in this instance rice. It is based on the Japanese units of measurement, known as shakkanhō, which derive from China and have been in use since the 8th century.

Masu come in many sizes; the most familiar boxes provide a measure of 1 *gō*, which is about 180 ml (6 fl oz). This measures out the optimal amount of rice or sake for one person. The use of *masu* for actual measuring has more or less fallen out of favour, and today they are mostly used for drinking sake. In fact, many sake bottles are bottled at an exact 1.8 litres (3 pints), known as a Sho, to provide a clean 10 *masu*'s worth of drinking. Another unit, the *Koku*, is 1,000 *masu* – the amount of rice needed for one person for one year. The measuring cup is constructed with a simple box joint made from hinoki, cypress or cedarwood, giving a fragrance that some say enhances – or distracts from – the drinking experience. From the 1868 Meiji Restoration the metric system then dominated, especially after Japan entered the Treaty of the Metre in 1885 which created the International Bureau of Weights and Measures.

Beyond its use in tea service, the teacup also evolved into a measuring tool in the kitchen. Although not a truly exact standard, it is a more or less similar volume universally found in households across the United Kingdom and throughout Europe. Its 'give or take' measurement allows home chefs to use intuition, estimate and improvise. The teacup averages about 175 ml, or a bit more than ½ cup by American standards.

The use of teacups-as-measures would have coincided with the European tea trade beginning its boom in the 18th century. Initially, when tea was exported across the world, tea caddies, teacups or full-service sets were sometimes sent with the product to the tea merchants who were selling on the goods. At first these teacups were sent to Europe without handles: in Asia, teacups (or bowls) are handle-less – if the vessel is too hot to pick up, then the tea is too hot to drink. After some time, cups without handles were no longer acceptable to the Western market, and they began to be added after 1750. Robert Adams is credited with having added the handle as well as refining the overall design for Western sensibilities, that were then manufactured closer to home. The teacup pictured was made by transfer printing under the glaze with cobalt oxide, a technique first developed in England.

→   **Weights and measures, Since 3rd century BCE,
    Worldwide, Various designers, Various materials**

Weights and measures came into use around the 3rd
to 4th centuries BCE and were essential to fair and
efficient trading. Though many of the weights and
measures pictured here would have been used in the
context of the marketplace, they show the beginning
of order being applied to quantifying foodstuffs, which
eventually made its way into the kitchen. In terms of
cooking, measurements were initially described by
comparison with objects or arbitrary statements such
as a pinch or 'nut size of butter'. Though reasonably
imprecise, this was a clever way to get around the fact
that the world was not yet beating to the same drum
in the land of standardisation.

Egyptians had kedets and debens, often used to compare
the weights of metals, whose value made its way into
trading consumable goods. In Britain, quantities such
as a bushel, quarter gill and noggin were used; a noggin
was a quarter of a pint, a wee dram you might drink
during a quick chat at the pub on the way home from
work. In the 15th century, standard Winchester measures

were established by Henry VII which rationalised
equality between volume and weight. The International
Bureau of Weights and Measures (BIPM) was founded in
1875 and controls intergovernmental standards across
the world. Across the Atlantic, Americans had English-
derived bushels and pecks: a peck is a unit of dry
volume equalling 2 dry gallons, 8 dry quarts or 16 dry
pints; four pecks make a bushel. For the kitchen, the
'cup' measure became standard in the USA at the end
of the 19th century. In the past, volume would be used
to measure liquid or grain, such as the American
quart (page 47, top left) or European decilitres (page
46, bottom right). Weight could be a 182-gram deben
(6½ oz) or the 19th-century standard kilogram (2 lb 4 oz).
In general, volumetric or weight measures are used
in the kitchen, and there are many ways, words and
implements for measuring used across the globe. The
International Bureau of Weights and Measures (BIPM)
was founded in 1875 and now controls intergovernmental
standards across the world.

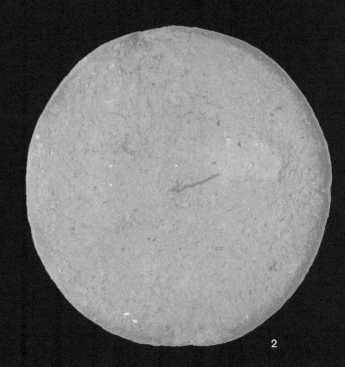

1 One kilogram weight, Dutch, 1798
2 Egyptian weight, pottery, 1295–1070 BCE
3 Quart measure, USA, 1835
4 Bull's-head deben, 182 grams (6.4 oz), Egypt,
   1550–1391 BCE
5 Seventy deben weight (1kg; 2.1lbs), Egypt,
   1850–1640 BCE
6 Six deben weight, Egypt, 1981–1640 BCE Egypt
7 40 Kedet weight (301 grams, 10.6 oz), Egypt,
   1981–1640 BCE
8 Pewter measure, Dutch, late 18th–early
   19th century

3

4

5

7   6

↑　**Measuring cups, Since 1896, USA,
Fannie Farmer, Stainless steel (modern day)**

To the annoyance of many residing out of the United States, the American measuring cup is a somewhat arbitrary volume that was 'invented' or standardised by Fannie Farmer in 1896. It does relate to the formerly used English gill, and two of these can be measured in one American cup. Fannie's innovation was mostly the concept of a 'level measure', which evolved into the cup, tablespoon and teaspoon units used today. The units make perfect sense to any American who grew up cooking with them but can prove less precise in some instances when exact ingredient *weights* are an important component of a recipe. Substitutions of teacups or glasses worth of measurements can cause frustration when following American recipes in other places in the world. Conversion charts exist, but it is a complicated dance to equate volume and weight with ingredients of varying densities such as flour, sugar or butter. An American cup is 240 ml, but this differs slightly in Australia, Canada and South Africa whose standard is a round 250 ml.

Teaspoons and the subsequent measurement (about 5 ml) emerged from the common teaspoon used in the home, for stirring tea. In France, they prefer to use the *cuillère à café*, or coffee spoon unit. Tablespoon measurements originate from apothecaries and are 15 ml (or three teaspoons). The name 'tablespoon' refers to the spoon you would bring to the table when personal cutlery sets were the norm. Confusingly, it also used to indicate the spoons used for *serving* at the table, which are much larger. There was good reason for all this standardisation; however, standard 'cups' and 'spoons' still vary by country.

↓   **Pyrex® measuring jug, Since 1915, USA / Worldwide, Various designers, Borosilicate glass**

The origins of Pyrex® lie in the invention of borosilicate glass for chemical uses in Germany in 1893. This new glass was remarkably heat- and shock-resistant. An engineer at Corning Glass Works in America discovered that it could be applied in the kitchen after his wife, Jessie Littleton, experimented using the material to cook casseroles and other high-temperature oven dishes. From the 1920s onwards companies in France and the UK began to manufacture Pyrex® glass, producing pie dishes, casseroles and measuring jugs, among other products. In the UK, the main factory was in the well-known glass manufacturing area of Sunderland, though production ceased in 2007 after 85 years of service.

The familiar red writing on these measuring jugs appeared around the 1940s and, depending on location, would feature metric or imperial standards for dry and wet ingredients. Some Pyrex® jugs from the 1980s onwards show both units, for international cooks of the world. These days, most European Pyrex® is manufactured in long-established factories in France.

↓   'Voile' pasta measure, 2004, Italy, Paolo Gerosa
     and Laura Polinoro (for Alessi), Mirror polished
     stainless steel

The 'Voile' pasta measure, designed by Paolo Gerosa
and Laura Polinoro, is an undulating steel object that
calculates portions for one, two or five servings of
spaghetti. A classic problem in the kitchen, this pasta
measure takes away the uncertainty by providing
approximate portion sizes for solo or more convivial
eating occasions. Here the designers have taken the
simple idea of measurement and turned it into an
intriguing yet useful form. Out of context the object's
function is abstract and unknown: a piece of jewellery,
a paperweight, perhaps a small sculpture. This design
was part of the Objet Bijou collection produced for the
Italian company Alessi.

→   Curry Measure, 2013, UK, Jasleen Kaur
     (for Tala), Enamelled metal

Tala is a long-standing British company that has been
producing homeware and kitchenware since 1899. Their
Tala Cook's Measure was developed in the 1920s, and
originally measured out standard British ingredients for
cooking at the time such as barley, groats and custard
powder. When measured out level, each line and section
of the cone assisted new modern chefs in completing
a recipe. A similar iteration, the Messbecher (measuring
cup), was made by German company Luch and worked
on the same principle.

In 2013, as a sign of the times with diverse societies
and diverse cuisine, Tala released their Curry Measure.
The same principle applies with this cone, so curious
British chefs can cook dishes such as chicken jalfrezi,
pakora, raita and rice steamed to perfection. Their
Cook's Measure cones are still produced by hand in
Liverpool, in the UK, today.

→ **Funnel, Various dates, Worldwide,
Various designers, Various materials**

Although not strictly for measuring, this tool is essential in the kitchen or marketplace for decanting bulk goods, whether grain or liquid, into smaller vessels. The etymology comes from the Latin *infundere* (pour in) and *fundere* (to pour). In English, funnels were originally called tunnels – tunnels were the pipes that drained from the tun that held wine or beer; the word also derives from the French 15th-century word used in the wine trade, *fonel*. In fact, some of the earliest archaeological finds of funnel-type objects were conical sieves for decanting wine – clearly the most important

and universal use of funnels. Over the centuries they have been made of every material imaginable: ceramic, wood, coconut shell, glass, aluminium, copper, tin, enamelware and more. Cultures across the world have created extraordinarily unique shapes and sizes of funnels, all with a reasonably similar purpose. These days, funnels are also used to make funnel cakes (batter is dripped from a funnel into frying oil), or even to drink beer quickly by attaching a tube straight into the mouth from the spout, both novel uses from the USA.

1   Aluminium funnel, USA, 20th century
2   Earthenware funnel, location unknown, 19th century
3   Wood funnel, Zambia, 19th century
4   Pottery funnel, Cyprus, 2000 BCE
5   Copper funnel, Sweden, 18th century

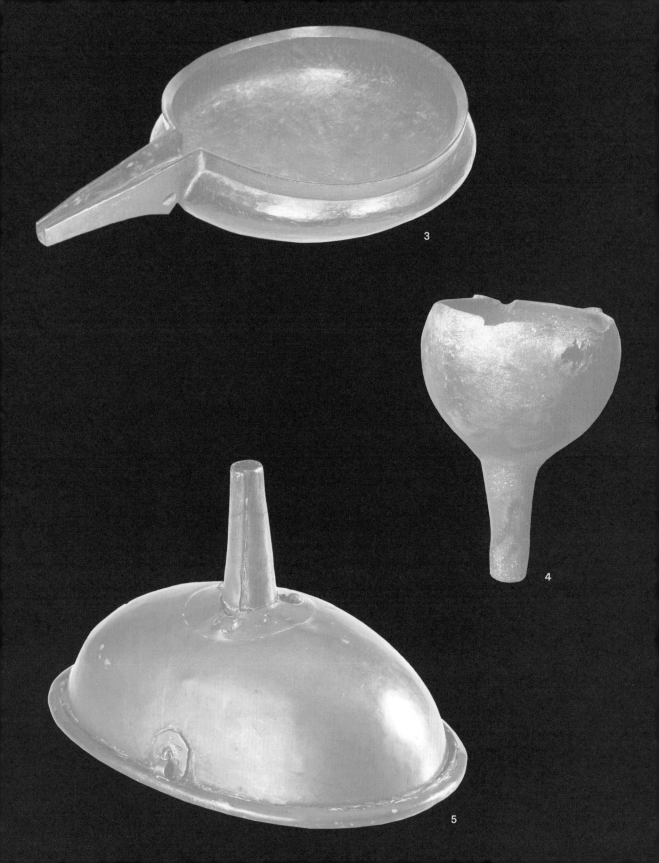

Modern ovens can be remarkably imprecise, though it is nothing compared to the chaos of cooking temperatures hundreds of years ago. Modern temperature gauges in cooking did not arrive until the 17th century, though these were hardly refined until more accurate measuring devices were developed in the 18th century. Prior to this, recipe books and culinary guides might suggest that you hold your hand in the oven for a certain number of seconds before it burned. Another method was to throw flour in the oven to see how fast it browned; a similar test was performed with baking paper for patisserie. Although gas and electric ovens were developed in the 19th century, thermostats didn't arrive until the 20th.

Thermometers are used for many precise culinary processes these days, including for dough, candy, meat and fruit. In the catering industry, temperature control is essential to ensure foods are cooked through (meat) or to achieve the correct shine or texture in patisserie (using candy thermometers). Just as there are unique scales for measuring the weights of different ingredients, so there are thermometers for specific foods – sugar melts and tempers at a very high temperature of 50–200°C (122–392°F), whereas meat requires temperatures of 50–80°C (122–176°F). The probe of analogue meat thermometers works by metal inside expanding and subsequently twisting, which turns the dial of the temperature gauge. In the absence of these tools, professional chefs can tell how well-cooked meat is through checking its springiness or the colour of its juices.

Hydrometers are used to measure the density of solutions, which can gauge alcohol content or determine the ratio of water to sugar. A similar tool, the salinometer, is used to measure the salt content in water. Hydrometers are used in brewing processes for wine, beer and spirits, and measure alcohol content. They do this by measuring the density of the liquid alcohol, which is less than that of water. Vinometers are used in the wine industry for low-sugar wines and measure alcohol by surface tension. Though often used in scientific laboratory settings or historically on naval journeys, salinometers are also useful for measuring the saltiness of your pickling brine or the salt content of cheese in the dairy industry. A light brine has a salt content of about 10 per cent, whereas a heavy brine – likely too salty – has about 80 per cent. Antique salt measures often have beautiful glass-blown, sometimes baroque forms whose bulbous end is filled with lead pellets to sink in saline solutions.

J. ELY.
HYDROMETER.
APPLICATION FILED AUG. 14, 1907.

964,628.

Patented July 19, 1910.

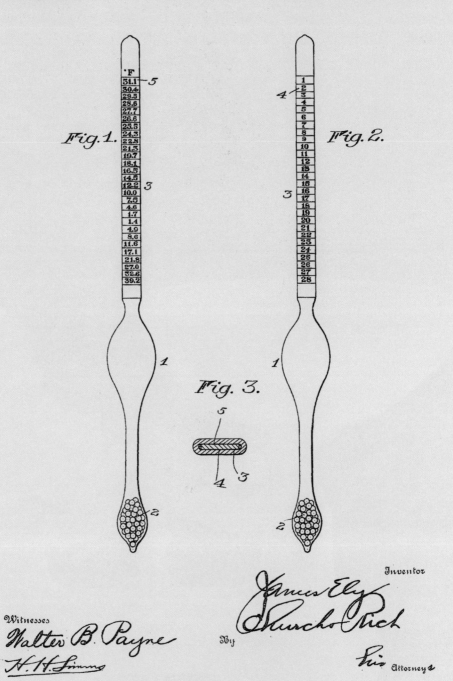

Fig. 1.

Fig. 2.

Fig. 3.

Witnesses
Walter B. Payne
H. H. Simms

Inventor
James Ely
Church Rich
By
Fin
Attorneys

← **Weighing scales, Since 2000 BCE, Worldwide, Various designers, Various materials (metal)**

Historically scales had an individual purpose, be it for weighing bread, butter or spices. Depending on the average weight of the food, different types of scales are required. They have been essential for efficient and fair-trading for centuries, and their use dates back thousands of years to Ancient Egypt, Pakistan and beyond. Before convenience food and packaging, balance scales were used for weighing goods out from sacks or barrels, using flour scoops, sugar scoops, tea scoops and more. Most scales worked on the basic principle of balancing weights from a fulcrum, until Richard Salter invented a spring-based weighing device in 1770. Spring scales measure the tension on the spring to determine the weight of the object placed on it. In 1980, the digital scale was patented and is most common in contemporary homes and supermarkets today.

↑ **Kitchen scale BA 2000, 1969, Italy, Marco Zanuso (for Terraillon), ABS plastic**

Before digital scales became available in the 1980s, most domestic scales worked via the spring method invented by Richard Salter. Marco Zanuso's design of 1969, for the Italian company Terraillon, is a true zeitgeist that speaks of Modernism, simplicity and 'good design for all'. His design very cleverly encases the spring-scale mechanism in a unified form, with a lid that can be flipped up to be used as a container or kept flat for a bowl to sit on. The scale is also compact for easy storage. The viewing window showing the weight is visible when it sits on the countertop below eye level, yet otherwise appears minimal when stored on a shelf. The BA 2000 scale came in a series of colours besides red such as white, yellow and blue and can measure up to 2,000 grams.

Marco Zanuso was an Italian architect and designer, part of the postwar design set of Milan that carried on and developed Modernism and the concept of 'good design for all' or democratic design. His work was minimal in aesthetic and mirrored his experience and work in architecture. He often collaborated with the designer Richard Sapper who also designed a few kitchen items; together they designed a minimalist knife sharpener and various audiovisual pieces of equipment in the 1970s.

We can't get into the whole history of time here, but
as with temperature and weight, it is as an important
component in the culinary arts. Overdone, and your
meat or cake is dry and tough; undercooked, and it
can be inedible or dangerous to consume.

Moving on from 1000 BCE, Egyptian shadow clocks,
sundials, water clocks and even measuring burning
candles, the hourglass form and method of measuring
time has been around since the 8th century and remains
a reliable cooking companion to this today. Though
longer amounts of time could be measured by following
the sun, moon and seasons, it wasn't until the 14th century
that we had more precise time-keeping clocks in households, which were definitively refined in the 18th century.
Once time was harnessed, a baker's pocket watch
was a prized possession and indicated a high level
of professionalism and accuracy.

The hourglass was designed by a French monk and
measures specific units of time through its precise
manufacture. They've survived into contemporary life
as egg timers, which typically come in units of three,
five or ten minutes. Now egg timers are mostly rotary
clocks that you spin in the hand to buzz after the
desired cooking time, though it's certain the iconic
hourglass will never leave this earth.

↑ **Minitimer Kitchen Timer, 1971,**
Italy, Richard Sapper, Plastic

Though designed in the 1970s, the minimalist and modern style of the Minitimer Kitchen Timer is almost … timeless. It could comfortably sit in a contemporary kitchen today, although the iPhone has taken over for recording cooking times. Similar to Marco Zanuso's Terraillon scale, Richard Sapper's Minitimer hides the components of the time-keeping mechanism for a streamlined finish that 'fuses technology and style'. It really is mini, measuring about 7 cm (2¾ in) across, and was produced in various colours. The product was originally manufactured by Ritz-Italora in Milan but was licensed to Terraillon shortly after.

Richard Sapper was a German industrial designer who settled in Milan – he was a close collaborator of Marco Zanuso and other Modernists who contributed to the changing aesthetics of our daily lives. Sapper simplified and concealed the emerging complex technologies of the 20th century in his product designs, as with this timer. A design icon by maker or form, the Minitimer is in the collections of the Museum of Modern Art, in New York, and the Pompidou Centre in Paris.

Prep & Wash

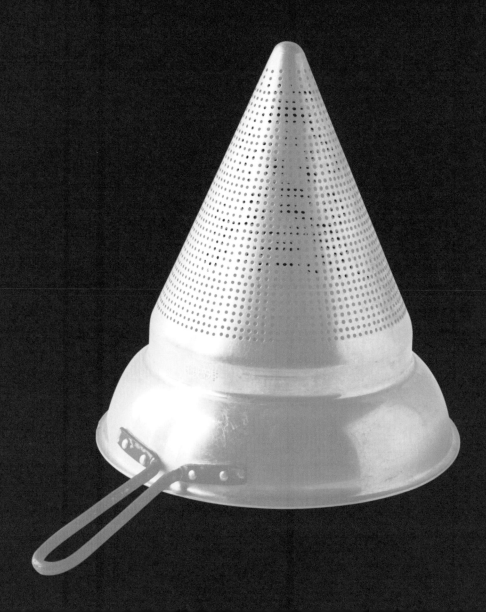

Once your food has been gathered, stored, maybe weighed and measured, the chef must wash and prepare it. Before chopping commences and ingredients are amalgamated, fruits and vegetables must be washed clean of insects, modern-day pesticides or lurking bacteria. Preparing food for cooking (or eating raw) can entail washing, peeling, pitting, proving, basting, brushing, straining, sifting, draining, larding, coating, scaling, piercing or deveining. A myriad of dedicated tools is required for these specialist activities.

Though some processes such as washing can be done by rinsing ingredients in flowing spring water, even the Romans in Jericho had colanders to aid this cleaning task as far back as 4500 BCE. Peeling vegetables or pitting fruits isn't strictly necessary – yet in the former case it can improve flavour and in the latter the eating experience is less fraught with the possibility of choking to death. Necessity or not, what stands true throughout this exploration of tools for food, is that when you use a well-designed or useful utensil, such pleasure is gained in the time saved and ease with which you can perform the task. In this section in particular, many objects have truly intriguing forms, such as intricately woven baskets for extracting poison from cassava or minimalist piercing devices for eggshells, which were created because of obscure and specific needs. And before refining our tools we innovated with what was at hand, such as a bone to core an apple or a jawbone to remove corn off the cob.

Over the past two hundred years, a few key moments definitively influenced the development of these utensils and their subsequent everyday use in the kitchen. Following the Industrial Revolution (1760–1840), the *Great Exhibition (of the Works of Industry of All Nations)* of 1851 in London was a worldwide occasion for demonstrating the possibilities of new materials and manufacturing processes. After this world expo – exhibiting items from telescopes to toilets to ceramics – mechanical, labour-saving kitchen tools flooded the market. There was a remarkable explosion of peeling, slicing and grinding devices created around this time, with the new use of cogs and wheels being exploited for purposes from small to large scales. By the beginning of the 20th century, mass-produced products were firm fixtures in the domestic landscape. Many innovations were spawned from these moments, whose influence can be seen throughout the book.

Preparation takes places at many stages of the cooking process, as the first thing the chef does, but also the last. You may need to remove inedible parts of food to start with, oil your pan with a brush, baste food to keep it moist while cooking or end with egg-washes to create sheen. Some single-purpose prepping tools are unnecessary, drawer-crowding gadgets that are mostly excluded from *Tools for Food*. But some of the utensils here, which aid the simplest processes, do what design is intended for – to 'solve a problem' efficiently and make light work of a task with the right tool.

Dough bowls like these were also referred to as kneading troughs, due to their trough-like shape. The sloped sides prevented flour or dough falling out when kneading, and dough could also be left to prove in these hand-carved containers. This particular example has had its cracks repaired with metal.

A larger version of this type of tool is the dough bin. Lidded bins kept flour and dough safe from pests and provided a warm place for dough to rise or prove. They were often made of elm in Europe (until the decimation caused by Dutch Elm Disease) and pine or poplar in America. The bin was divided by a partition to provide one side for flour and another side to knead dough, which would then be left to prove inside.

The flat surface on top was used to shape loaves ready for baking, or even for ironing and other domestic purposes. It was a mobile item in the household – during the winter months it could be moved to warmer places in the house, such as near a fireplace, for the dough to prove. These large containers were used in households, but also in bakeries and boulangeries. Made for daily use, surviving dough bins mostly lack extravagance of decoration, though some French examples are ornately carved out of oak or walnut wood.

↑　**Banneton, Since circa 17th century and earlier, France / Europe, Various makers and designers, Rattan / Cane**

Historically made of rattan, many bannetons are now made from cane, with a hypnotic spiralling shape like a clay coil pot that hasn't been smoothed. These baskets are used during the dough-proving process for bread, to keep the shape of the dough before baking. Without a banneton to support the loaf, the gluten that relaxes as the dough rises causes it to flatten like a pancake. Bannetons can be directly coated with flour to prevent the loaf sticking, or they may come lined with linen fabric (again coated with flour) for easy removal when the bread is turned out before baking in the oven. Their shape is usually circular or oblong and over years of use the inside becomes more and more resistant to sticking. Made from

a natural material, bannetons allow an ever so slight amount of air to reach the dough, which improves the quality of the crust as it proves.

Most bannetons are designed for loaves weighing 500 g (1 lb 2 oz), though the largest can hold loaves of up to 8 kg (18 lb), with diameters of almost 50 cm (20 in). Long and thin bannetons are used for making baguettes, though more often these days this bread is risen in long, metal, zigzag structures or even just long pieces of linen cloth, which help the elongated sticks to keep their shape while proving.

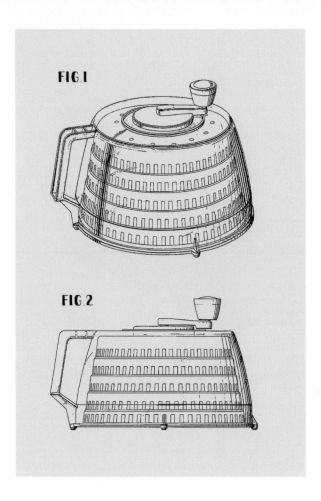

FIG.1

FIG.2

↗ **Salad spinner / Salad baskets, 1971 / 1973; 1963,
Jean Mantelet; Gilberte Fouineteau, France,
Plastic, metal**

The salad washers and dryers pictured come from a
long line of utensils designed for this purpose. The tool
on the right was patented in 1963 by Gilberte Fouineteau,
noted as a 'collapsible walled basket capable of being
stiffened'. The origin of this salad dryer lies with the
Parisian designer and inventor Henri Gautreau, who
registered many patents for kitchen items, stoves and
lamps, including a two-sided folding basket for washing
salad in 1923 (Le Restreint); a collapsible basket was
the second iteration of this design for washing fruit
and vegetables, and marketed as 'Solid, Light, Practical'
(Solide – Léger – Pratique). These metal wire woven
baskets were submerged in flowing rivers or under
the tap, and if out of doors, swung in a circular motion
like a baseball pitcher until water retreated from the
leaves. This process makes perfect sense when you
fast-forward to the 'salad spinner' of 1971, also invented
by a Frenchman.

Jean Mantelet, who founded Moulinex, a company that
produces various kitchen utensils, registered his patent
for a 'Salad Dryer' in the early 1970s. In 1974, salad
dryer rival Fouineteau trumped Mantelet's design by
creating a similar tool with a removable basket and no
central core to interrupt the flow of salad washing and
drying. Some contemporary salad washer-dryers these
days require no spinning of the handle, and instead
have a button that when pushed up and down creates
the familiar centrifugal motion. Although incredibly
useful and almost essential, there's no denying these
devices take up a substantial amount of space in
kitchen cupboards.

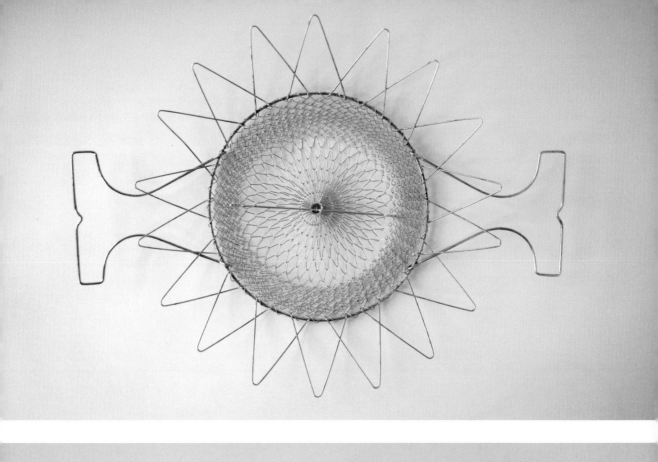

Across Asia there are many ways of rinsing and polishing rice, depending on the type and for what purpose it will be used. It is an important ritual in the process of cooking Thai, Korean, Japanese food and more, eaten with almost every meal across South and East Asia and is also used to make desserts, sushi and wine.

Rice can be rinsed between three and four times in these bamboo baskets strainers before being cooked. After being used the natural fibre container is hung to dry; through years and decades of use the object takes on a natural amber colour.

Contemporary strainers can be made of plastic or steel mesh; however, rinsing rice in the natural-fibre colanders creates a more pleasant sound and is less likely to damage the rice than man-made materials. Although they are mass-manufactured, craftsmen still produce hand-woven strainers throughout Asia.

The pictured strainer with a handle is useful for rinsing rice but also to lift vegetables, noodles or anything that needs collecting from a pot of water. Some of these types of strainers are made with one piece of bamboo, like the familiar Japanese tea whisk. The handle merges with the scoop, which is cut into strips to support the weaving of the main form (the warp of the weft). Strainers similar to these, smaller than a fist, are used to strain loose-leaf tea across Asian countries.

↑ Horsehair sieve, Since 1st century CE, Worldwide, Designer unknown, Horsehair, wood

These tools have been around for thousands of years: Pliny the Elder (the Roman author of the first 'encyclopedia' called *Naturalis Historia*) recorded the use of horsehair sieves by the Gauls between the 5th century BCE and 5th century CE. Horsehair was a versatile material, used for textiles, upholstery, wall insulation, violins and sieves. The fine weave of a horse-hair sieve can be used to strain liquids, make berry coulis or extra-smooth potato or vegetable purées. Foods can be pushed through the horsehair with a *holzstampfer* (wooden masher), or by hand. Across the world different types of fibres were encased within steam-bent wood: papyrus in Egypt, flax in Spain, palm fibres in Latin America, fish skin in Siberia, though now the mesh is usually made of metal or nylon rather than natural materials. In France, this drum-shaped sieve is known as a *tamis*, and in Japan as a *uragoshi*.

These types of bentwood sieves with textile strainers have been and still are used the world over – for puréeing fish or miso in Japan, straining coconut in Thailand or Indonesia, extracting poison out of cassava in Latin America, or sifting flour. The Shakers in America also made horsehair sieves, adapting their technique for steamed wooden boxes to accommodate the fine weave for puréeing foods.

The chinois gets its name from its shape, which is similar to the conical woven hats worn in 20th-century China and before. There are two versions – one with a fine mesh sieve and the other with larger holes. This icon serves many purposes in one: it can be used like a colander or filter, but also like a food mill – chefs can rinse fruit and vegetables, strain pasta, rice and broth, yet also purée velvety sauces when the tool is used with a counterpart cone-shaped pestle to grind food through the holes in the metal. Its handle allows for the processing of hot foods and liquids at arm's length, and some have a smaller handle on the other side so the chinois can be mounted in a bowl. The chinois predates food processors and is preferred by professionals for this purpose.

The chinois is a must in French households or in a professional chef's *batterie* de cuisine, and it defines the French kitchen almost as much as the copper pot. The tool holds a special place in the hearts of Francophone cooks, with its unique shape that provides an efficient flow of foods and liquids through perforated holes. The exit of liquid or purées through the holes has even been described as 'flowing like the fountains of Versailles'. This example was manufactured in the USA and comes with a stand to hold the strainer while purées or jellies are pulverised through.

Washing and straining food is a necessity the world over, and ancient specimens of these tools exist from every culture of the world. Before the advent of metallurgy thousands of years ago, these devices were made of ceramic, natural materials and animal skins. Clay colanders were moulded in bowl forms and pierced with holes; sheepskin was stretched over a hoop and punctured with a hot iron, or they were woven with natural fibres.

This tool is used for bigger pieces of food, with its cousin the sieve or horsehair tamis being reserved for puréeing and fine sifting. Now colanders are made of a myriad of materials such as plastic, silicone, aluminium, enamelled metal or stainless steel, with hardly any fragile ceramic versions on the market. Metal colanders are manufactured by puncturing small holes in flat sheets before being spun into their bowl shape on a lathe, with the handles spot welded on at the end; plastic colanders are produced by injection moulding. The material, pattern and colours of these tools reflect a zeitgeist throughout history: made of colourful plastic in the 1960s and '70s, futuristic-looking UFO shapes from outer space in the 1990s; 21st-century collapsible designs made of silicone; or new metal colanders with thousands of patterned holes, created using new technologies. The tool also finds multiple purposes as a stand-in for a spaetzle maker, or a steamer over boiling water.

Cassava squeezer, 20th century, Guyana
(pictured) & South America, Various makers,
Palm fibres (arumã or jacitara)

Cassava (also known as manioc or yucca) is poisonous until processed to remove the hydrocyanide toxins. These extraordinarily beautiful tools for squeezing out the poison originate in South America and are known as *matapi*, *yuro*, *tipití* or *sebucan*. Though today most processing of cassava is done industrially, or with tools that have not been handcrafted as such, some indigenous tribes still create and use these woven *exprimidores de yucca*. Once cassava is peeled and grated, it is put into the *matapi* to extract the poisonous juice. The tubular basket is quite large at 1.5 m (5 ft) long by 12 cm (5 in) wide and is hung by the handle at the top with the loop at the bottom pulled down with a branch like a lever to squeeze the contents inside. This action works just like a finger trap toy: when pulled, pressure is exerted and tightens the middle of the squeezer. Once removed, the cassava has a snakeskin-like texture from the crisscrossed imprint of the basket. It is then processed into its final state of flour, porridge or the other myriad forms in which this starchy root vegetable can be eaten. This staple is consumed in vast quantities across South America and Africa, and it can also be processed to make tapioca starch or flours for West African gari.

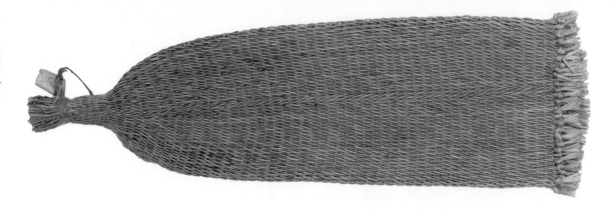

↑   **Intluzo / Ivovo (beer filter), Since 17th / 18th centuries, Various makers, Sedge grass**

Intluzo are used to strain the South African beer known as umqombothi. The beer is made with maize, corn malt, sorghum malt, yeast and water; it is opaque once the brewing is complete, with a creamy consistency and sour taste. These conical woven funnels have been made for hundreds of years to strain beer made from local ingredients, and they have a loop at one end for hanging them up to dry once used. This beer and the corresponding filters are made by various tribes in South Africa such as the Xhosa people, Mpondo, Hlubi, Zulu and more. Each filter is unique to its maker in pattern and shape, though the function remains the same – to filter grain and sediment in the beer-making process. The loop at the top forms the warp for weaving, which can be in straight patterns, diagonals or zigzags, often ending with a fringed edge at the opening. These tools are woven by both men and women from twisted, grass-like sedge stems; the traditional craft is slowly dying out, and today it is mostly the elderly members of the tribes who weave these traditional beer filters.

↑ **Flour dredger, 19th century,
UK, Designer unknown, Metal**

Flour dredgers were used for adding thickening agents to sauces, covering the countertop before rolling or kneading dough, or to coat meat and vegetables before frying or braising. The holes were suitably large enough to control flow without clogging – not too big, not too small. These tools closely resemble sugar dredgers, which were used at the table to sweeten food and drinks to personal taste. Antique dredgers have various dents and scratches from being used well and often in the kitchen, and were usually made of brass, copper or tin. Twentieth-century versions were made of aluminium, ceramic or plastic and today they are made of stainless steel with a finer mesh top, used to dust cocoa onto coffee or icing (confectioner's) sugar onto cakes. In the UK, fish and chip shops have appropriated the tool for shaking salt onto large quantities of chips. Although you can use your hands to sprinkle flour where needed, the dredger is cleaner, easier and more efficient.

→ **Flour sifter, 1819, USA,
Jacob Bromwell, Aluminium**

The flour sifter came after the flour dredger, with a distinct purpose in the art of baking. Remarkably simple in its mechanical function, the various types of flour sifters that were invented in the 19th to 20th centuries work on the same principle – to aerate flour and remove any lumps that could create an unsatisfactory result in fine baked goods. The original sifter was created in 1819 by the kitchenware producer Jacob Bromwell, though it was not registered in the US Patent Office by one of his descendants until 1930. Many old sifters bear the Bromwell name, pressed in relief in the main body of the tool; the company still manufactures them today. Some sifters operate by rotating a handle to agitate the flour over the fine mesh surface within the cylindrical container; others evolved a lever that is depressed by the thumb to rotate a blade over the sieve. This utensil is ubiquitous in the kitchen, sometimes with squeaks and creaks from many turns over the decades, and often looks pretty worn after being passed down generation after generation.

April 8, 1930.   T. G. MELISH   1,753,995

FLOUR SIFTER

Filed June 18, 1926

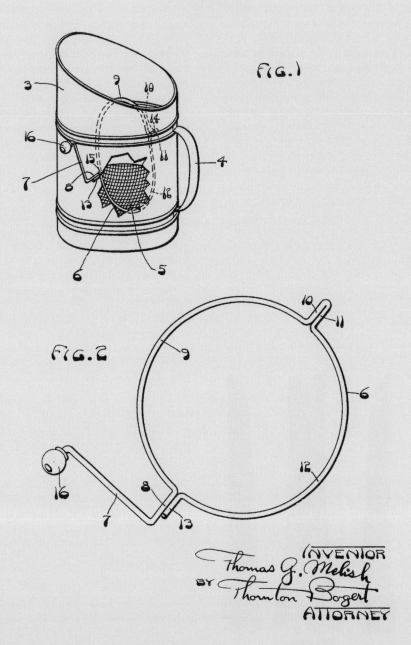

FIG. 1

FIG. 2

INVENTOR

Thomas G. Melish

BY Thornton Bogert

ATTORNEY

Some of the earliest apple corers ever found are made from the metacarpal bone of sheep. Many early culinary tools would have been carved from animal bones, and this post-medieval (after 1485) scooper and apple corer is no exception. The natural hollow of the bone made it easy to carve and adapt into a tool for food. Archaeologists believe these tools would have helped those without teeth to eat raw apples by scooping morsels out bit by bit; these tools could also be used to test the ripeness of cheese or to remove marrow from larger bones for eating. From the 17th century more elaborate apple corers were carved from animal bone, and they even became treasured 'love tokens' or special gifts for lovers. The 'X' form often seen on these bone apple corers was a symbol for luck, but also a symbol for a kiss, as in contemporary life. Over the centuries, apple corers have been made from sheep bone, ivory, boxwood, sycamore, lignum vitae hardwood, coquille nut and silver. Contemporary apple corers are usually metal or plastic, a simple sharp cylinder with a toothed end which is pressed directly through the middle of the fruit to remove undesirable bits.

At the end of the 19th century, inventors were two a penny, and peeling machines were big business at the time. In the 1850s, when cast-iron gears became readily available, inventors went mad for applying their function to multiple uses – the zeitgeist was everything mechanical. During this time, changes in society as well as the Industrial Revolution had an extensive influence on the domestic landscape. Labour that would have previously been undertaken by servants and helpers eventually transferred to the head lady of the household. Before this social change, there was no need to use 'labour-saving' devices, because labour was cheap or, unfortunately, free. Concurrently, the Great Exhibition of 1851 in London was a world showcase of the new innovations a modern world had to offer, and the world was ready to accept and develop them.

This peeler was part of the beginning of a shift in new social structures, as well as the soon-to-come onslaught of kitchen gadgets and time-saving tools. It was mounted on the countertop and used to peel potatoes, apples or whatever hard vegetable or fruit of suitable size and texture needing its skin removed. Made of iron and wood, it was built like a brick house, and would last hundreds of kilos worth of apple- or potato-peeling tasks.

American. Apple Peeler, 19th century; Iron, wood, 10¾ × 8 × 6½ in. (27.3 × 20.3 × 16.5 cm). Brooklyn Museum, Gift of Fred Tannery, 82.112.10a–b

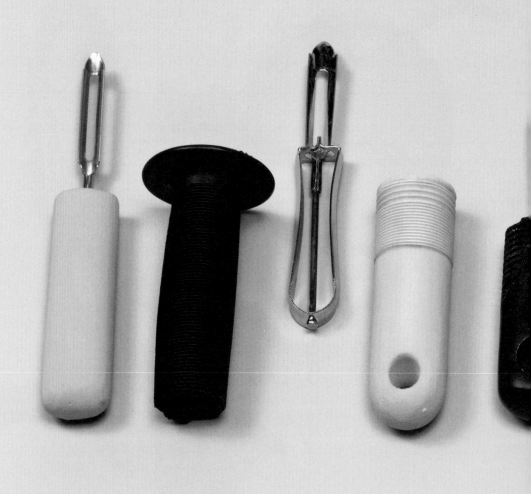

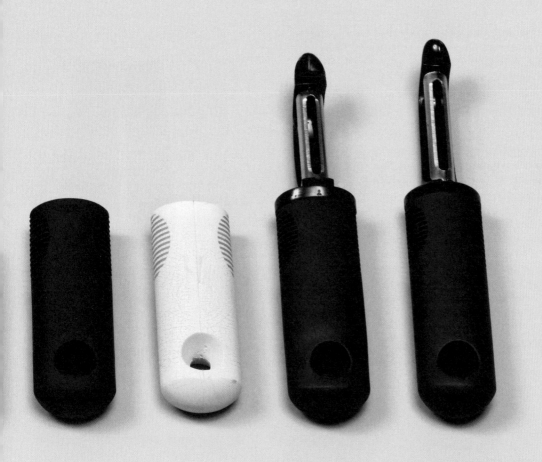

← **Good Grips peeler, 1990, New York, USA,**
Davin Stowell, Daniel Formosa, Tucker Viemeister
(Smart Design, Inc.), Rubber, metal

The Good Grips peeler marks a point of design history and development where considerations of ergonomics and 'universal design' finally met the end user in mass manufacture. Although the concept of ergonomics was developed in the 1920s, it took many decades to infiltrate everyday objects and households.

Universal design takes into account those with different abilities or limited movement, and in this case, arthritis. Sam Farber, of the kitchen tools brand Oxo, was spurred on by his wife's impairment to develop utensils that were easier to use for sufferers of this condition. Tasked with the challenge, Smart Design Inc. worked by modelling possibilities in three dimensions rather than drawing on paper. Early prototypes were adapted from existing objects, such as inserting a peeler into a rubber bike handle. Through field research working directly with individuals with impairments and designing-by-making, they evolved the universal, ergonomic Good Grips peeler. The handle's large oval shape avoids straining or having to rotate the hand, and the material is soft to handle and dishwasher-safe. This image shows the development of the handle, non-slip grip, proportion and the placement of the hole which can be used to hang the tool. Oxo have applied this 'good-grip' handle to many of their products; they manufacture many arthritis-friendly tools such as scissors, pizza cutters and tin openers.

→ **Peeler, Date unknown, Asia,**
Designer unknown, Steel, wood

This trowel-shaped peeler used in China, Thailand, Vietnam and Southeast Asia differs from the Y-shaped Rex Peeler. It has a fixed blade, rather than a swivel, and is made of two pieces of steel or iron with the cutting edge set at an angle. The construction is very simple: made of two pieces of metal hinged at the top that slot into the wooden handle. It is easy to assemble and disassemble to stretch out 180 degrees for sharpening; in a pinch, the unhinged blade can be used as a knife. These peelers vary in size from about 10 cm/4 in blade (pictured) to at least 25 cm (10 in). The V-shaped angle of the joined metal helps to peel fruit or vegetables more effectively than a flat shape would – the flat style is what necessitates a swivel blade. This type of peeler is very useful for peeling or slicing carrots, green papaya, sugar cane, banana blossom and more.

↑   **Rex Peeler, 1931, Switzerland, Alfred Neweczerzal (ZENA made), Aluminium**

The Rex Peeler is a true example of reductive design: the object is both efficient for use and for manufacturing. In Germany the tool is known as a *sparschäler*, which translates as 'saving peeler'; its design avoided the food waste that a deep-cutting paring knife might cause. The Rex Peeler is made up of six parts: a bent aluminium strip, the indents of which fit the thumb and forefinger, a blade that swivels, a crossbar for structure, and an extra loop at the top to remove potato eyes / stem buds – the remaining parts are fixings. Here function has been reduced to its simplest form of only the most essential elements, and the tool is well-designed to fit in the hand.

Working with the businessman Engros Zweifel, Alfred Neweczerzal designed the peeler and they started producing it in 1931. The patent was officially registered in 1947. Subsequently, the ZENA Produkte company was formed; they still produce the peelers, about 3 million each year. In 1984 they began manufacturing colourful plastic versions to keep with the trends, but the original aluminium style and design has remained unchanged for almost 100 years and is still a popular favourite and design icon.

↑ **Citrus peeler, 20th / 21st centuries, Location unknown, Designer unknown, Plastic**

Out of context, the purpose of this tool is perplexing – even in a kitchen drawer, its form is abstract, though pleasing in proportion and geometry. To use the tool, you place your fingers inside the loop and score wedges into the orange or citrus peel. By carving sections the peel is easier to remove, finally revealing a naked orange to eat with wild abandon.

→ **Cherry pitters, 20th century, USA, Various designers, Stainless steel / aluminium**

Cherry and olive pitting is a laborious task, but greatly improves the eating experience. In the mid-19th century, after the Great Exhibition of 1851, a slew of cherry pitters came on the market. The 20th century was not much different, with at least one hundred versions registered in the patent office since 1900. Antique mechanical cherry pitters were table-mounted, cast-iron devices in which the fruit was fed through a funnel whose narrow passage forced the seed out, slightly crushing the cherry in the process. Most 20th-century domestic versions are handheld tools that eject the seed by puncturing or pressing a levered device through the middle of the fruit. These pitters are most common to places in the Northern Hemisphere, where most cherries grow: Turkey is the world's largest producer of cherries, followed by the USA and many countries in Eastern Europe and Eurasia. These pitters are prevalent throughout the USA and Europe.

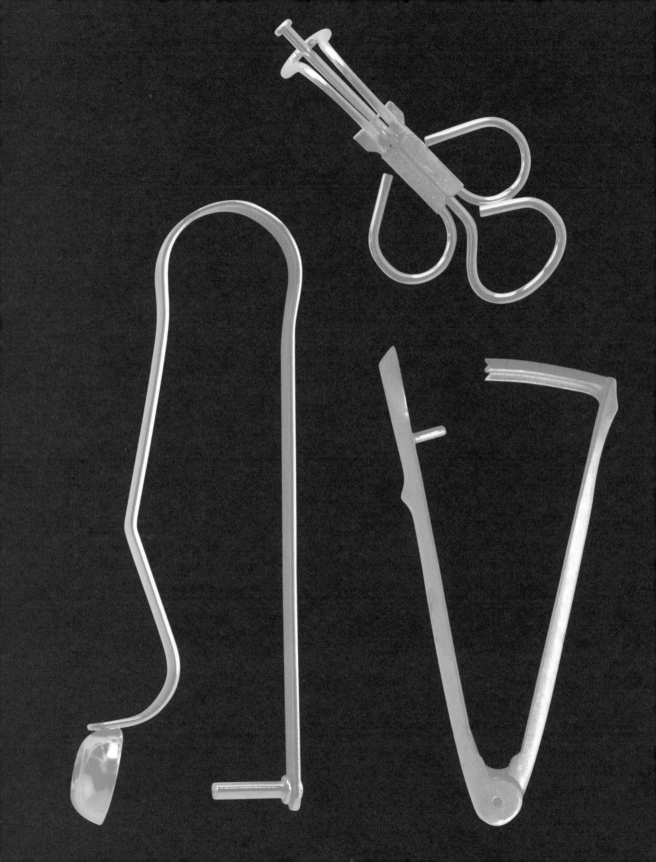

↑ **Shrimp cleaner, 1954, USA,
Irwin Gershen, Plastic, metal**

This object, with its striking form, is used for cleaning
and shelling prawns (shrimp). The curve of the tip mirrors
the sea creature it is intended for, with an ergonomic
handle that is pleasing to the eye in shape and colour.
It was designed by Irwin Gershen in 1954, was featured
in the Museum of Modern Art's exhibitions that surveyed
'Good Design' (2019, 2011), and is part of their permanent
collection. 'Good Design' isn't just an exhibition title;
it was a term and moment of time in postwar USA
and Europe which defined design that was modern,
affordable, useful and made to high standards. The
Museum of Modern Art, in New York, featured this
shrimp cleaner – or Shrimpmaster as it was marketed
– alongside various useful and well-designed kitchen
utensils and consumer goods. The tool is simple, beautiful
and effective, and claims to make 'no drudgery, no tired
fingers, and no ruined shrimp!' To use the tool, the tip
is inserted through the head end of the shrimp all the
way through the body to the tail. Then when the handle
is depressed, it shells and deveins the crustacean.

↓ **Fish scaler, 20ᵗʰ century, Japan,
Designer unknown, Brass, wood**

The fish scaler pictured here is common in Japan and known as an *urokotori*. The sawtooth head is made of brass and attached to a wooden handle. This design closely resembles that of an American patent of 1894 by W. J. Ruedisale of Detroit, Michigan, though the added gaps in the head of the Japanese version allow scales to fall away more easily. These tools and their varieties of design tend to originate in water-locked countries where fish is a primary source of nutrition in the diet. Older fish scalers from Scandinavia were made of a single piece of cast iron, with numerous protruding, circular teeth to descale the fish. Though a knife can be used to remove the scales from fish, this runs this risk of damaging the flesh or cutting the hand. To use the urokotori, fish are held by the tail end and scraped gently up towards the head to remove the tough armour. In the USA, this tool has a dual purpose: it is also used to scrape corn off the cob for the dish of Southern creamed corn.

D7-667
D9532

EX

OR   D 28,876

DESIGN.

B. F. MACY.
EGG SEPARATOR.

No. 28,876.   Patented June 14, 1898.

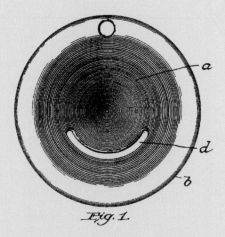

Fig. 1.

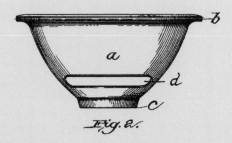

Fig. 2.

Witnesses: Inventor:
Arthur H. Randall   Bernard F. Macy
Annie J. Darley   by Crossley & Goddard
                                        Atty's.

← **Egg strainer, Since 19th–20th centuries, Europe / USA, Various designers, Various materials**

There are endless tools for prepping eggs, from separating to whipping, boiling, coddling, frying and poaching. To keep eggs from touching the hands of the chef or to quicken the process of separating the whites from yolks, a strainer is a helpful tool. This task would have been essential, commonplace and frequent in kitchens of yesteryear, when egg whites were the prime leavener of cakes before baking powder was created in the mid-19th century.

Antique egg strainers made of ceramic have a small slit in their form to let the white escape from the yolk. Postwar they were made from colourful plastic (Tupperware) using the same principle: a bowl-like shape with small slits; simple, cheap-to-produce forms are made of stamped sheet metal. Wire strainers consisted of a single piece of metal, spiralised at the bowl end of the spoon-like shape to let the white drain out. Contemporary 'life-hackers' today use plastic water bottles as suction devices to suck out the yolk from a cracked egg, leaving the white for whipping or low-cal omelettes.

↑ **Egg piercer, 1966, USA, Paul Pelzel, Plastic, metal**

The number of tools for preparing and eating eggs is endless. For pernickety egg boilers, this egg piercer is an essential tool. Piercing one small hole alleviates the pressure of the sulphur pocket inside the egg, preventing the shell from cracking when boiling. If crafting Easter eggs is the end goal, two holes can be made to allow the contents to be removed. A push down on this device exposes the pin that gently punctures a hole in the shell of the egg. This minimalist egg piercer is reminiscent of many tools and design objects of the 1960s, sleek in its form with the casing concealing the mechanics of its function.

The concept is simple – multiple sharp points depress into pastry for pies, crackers or biscuits. These small holes prevent dough rising where it needs to remain flat, sometimes under other ingredients such as in a pie or quiche. Early pastry prickers or dockers were rudimentary devices: multiple thin metal rods sharpened at one end and inserted into a wooden handle. Antique wooden versions from the 19th century have a beautiful simplicity in their primitive necessity, and some were crafted to create ornamental patterns through their punctures. Innovation produced rotary dockers in the 20th century, where a quick rolling action pricks the dough and prevents rising or blistering.

Rotary dockers for focaccia and pizza are found in metal, with repeated pyramid forms on the wheel that leave the necessary dents in the dough before baking. Pizza Hut patented their own rocking, curved pizza dough docker in 2008 to allow steam to escape, prevent 'unwanted damage' and keep their products consistent.

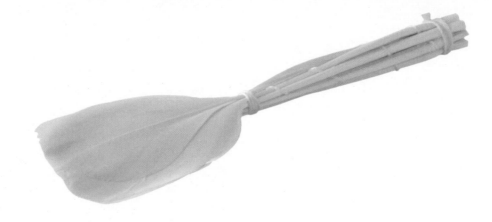

↑   **Pastry brush, Since 19ᵗʰ century, Eastern
    Europe, Maker unknown, Goose feather**

Goose feather brushes are mostly found in Eastern and
Northern Europe, traditionally in the Czech Republic,
Hungary and Austria. They are extraordinarily simple,
effective, long-lasting and beautiful to look at and use.
As an innovative tool made from natural materials, it's
quite possible they have been around for hundreds of
years, contributing to glossy glazes on elaborate spreads
of foods for medieval banquets. Due to the natural
degreasing qualities of goose feathers, these brushes
only pick up a small amount of liquid, allowing for a
thin layer of egg glaze, butter or oil where required.
This kind of delicate finish is often necessary to
complement the art of Viennese pastry (from where
the term 'Viennoiserie' derives). About 18 cm (7 in)
long, these brushes are formed of eight goose feathers
braided and tied together at one end to form a handle,
sometimes in contrasting red twine, almost reminiscent
of Czech traditional folk dress. After China, Hungary
has one of the largest industries of goose rearing for
meat and feathers and is where many of these brushes
are made today.

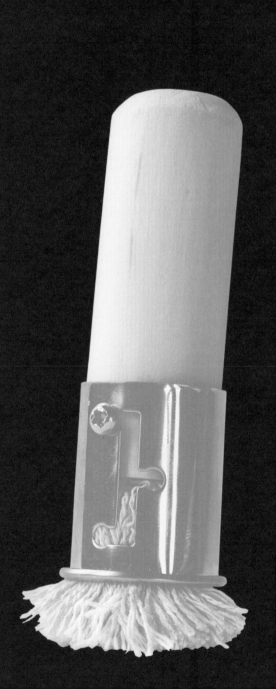

← **Takoyaki brush, Since 20th century, Japan, Designer unknown, Cotton, metal**

Takoyaki is the famous street food eaten in Osaka, Japan (where it was originally created). It is made with diced octopus, pickled ginger, spring onions (scallions) and tempura scraps held together in a wheat-flour batter. The small, pan-fried balls require a custom-shaped griddle (*takoyaki-nabe*) of half spheres, whose cooking batter is rotated with a long metal pin by street food vendors to make perfect three-dimensional shapes. Before the batter is poured in, a *takoyaki* brush is used to grease the pan and provide the right amount of oil to create a crunchy outside texture. The bristles must be able to absorb and distribute a fair amount of oil, so they are usually made of cotton with either a short wooden or metal handle. This popular street food was invented almost one hundred years ago in the 1930s and is eaten all over Japan and even in Taiwan. This brush could also be useful to grease your *ebelskiver* or *poffertje* pan (for making sweet spherical Norwegian or Dutch pancakes), which has a similar shape to the *takoyaki* griddle.

↑ **Mushroom brush, Since 20th century, Germany / Europe, Bürstenhaus Redecker, Beechwood, horsehair**

This mushroom-shaped brush is used for cleaning grit out of the delicate gills and caps of fungi. The brush's function is particularly essential for cleaning as this task should be performed without water to preserve the flavour and amino acids of mushrooms – the tool is used to remove the dirt instead of water. The process is especially important for commercially bought mushrooms, which are grown in compost containing manure. Though mushroom cleaners such as these are made across the world, one of the foremost producers is Bürstenhaus Redecker, in Germany, who have been crafting a huge range of natural brushes since 1935. This tongue-in-cheek brush in the shape of the vegetable it is intended for, is made of oiled beechwood and traditional horsehair.

There is a myriad of brushes for particular vegetables, especially for tubers such as potatoes: the tool is essential for removing dirt and pesticides from skins and crevices. They come in a variety of shapes and textures, from natural fibres to plastic, soft or hard bristles, depending on the food to be brushed.

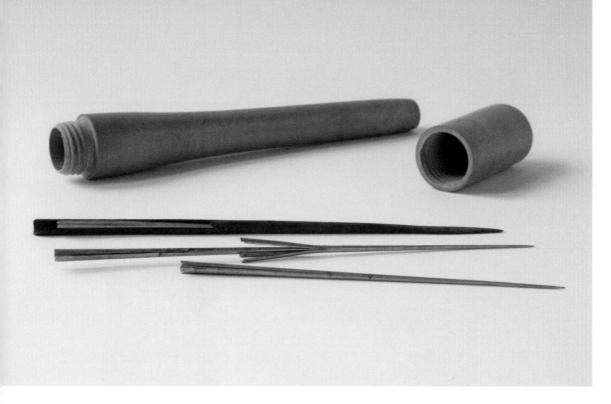

↑ **Larding needles (lardoir), Since 19th century,
France, Designer unknown, Metal**

These tools work like any sewing needle but are used
to thread lard through cuts of meat to keep them moist
while cooking. This is especially useful with meat that
is low in fat such as venison or hare – the lard woven
through the meat prevents it drying out and becoming
tough. To use the needle, a piece of pork fat or lamb
caul is clasped in the end of the needle, then woven
through the meat in the direction of the grain. Once
threaded through the meat, the clasped end is released
and then the needle is pulled out. The fat melts and
distributes moisture and flavour to the meat as it cooks.
Larding needles come in various sizes up to 50 cm (20 in),
and traditionally had their own case to house the various
sizes and protect the sharp tools in the kitchen drawer.
Now they are produced in stainless steel, or steel with
a wooden handle.

The infamous turkey baster, known throughout the USA as the fat-picker-upper-and-dropper, keeps Thanksgiving turkeys from drying out. The enlarged eyedropper easily sucks up roasting pan juices and squirts them back out onto the roasting meat. The tool is efficient, but this basting method, which requires constant opening of the oven, has in some instances been replaced by the turkey bag. Roasting bags are made of un-meltable plastic and allow moisture to rise to the top, condense and fall back onto the meat. One of the first basters for the domestic kitchen, made of glass and rubber, was produced by the Artbeck company in 1946 (with heat resistant Pyrex glass), though most know the iconic plastic versions with their orange or red tops from the 1960s and '70s onwards. The latter design is iconic, in that the plastic tube and orange top are unmistakably recognisable as a tool that might possibly be used only once a year.

Cut & Chop

The most important tools in every cook's cabinet are their own two hands. After that follows the knife or other sharp implements for cutting, perhaps a grinding device, and the various types of mixing tools that were originally improvised and later designed into precise forms. Even before fire, flint and other knife-like tools were some of the first used for preparing food, and remain the most essential implement in kitchens across the world.

From the prehistoric Stone Age 2.5 million years ago until the Bronze Age of 1700 BCE, cutting tools were made of cryptocrystalline materials such as flint, chert or obsidian; these sedimentary rocks were chipped to form a sharp edge for hunting, defence, removing flesh from animal bones or harvesting plants. Eventually the Bronze Age introduced a range of versatile tools using a mix of 10 per cent tin and 90 per cent copper, with more robustness to follow during the Iron Age. In fact, archaeologists analyse chipped animal bone fragments to ascertain whether stone or metal was used, and therefore can estimate specimen date ranges. In medieval kitchens, 'chopping, pounding, and pulping' were the main methods of preparing food for cooking. While elaborate moulds and displays were key features of a medieval banquet, the kitchen tools available to create these feasts were hardly refined.

Across the world, diverse foodstuffs require their own shape of blade and chopping movement to suit the shape or texture of the food being cut. Cutting doesn't just involve knives – there are also curved choppers and mezzalunas, wheels for pastry, razors for rising bread, taut wires for eggs and cheese, mandolines, plier-like sugar cutters, scissors and more. In the world of knives, comparing forms across cultures demonstrates a particular consideration for ergonomics: how our hands and joints need to move and be positioned when chopping meat, fish, vegetables and fruits. Western blades enable a rocking motion while cutting; Japanese knives a straight, precise, 'push and pull' cut; and when using a South Asian boti/pirdai the *food* is pressed over the blade rather than the other way around. Confucius said that you 'must not eat what has been crookedly cut', and thus the Chinese cleaver provides the tool to meet this need.

James Beard suggests that the 'wardrobe of knives' needed by chefs should include a chopping knife, butchering knife, slicing, blooding and skinning knife. Others suggest you can get away with a chef's, paring and bread knife; in China they may propose that a cleaver will meet all needs. Knives also need their counterpart – a chopping board, which has evolved from a basic chunk of wood to those made from high-tech materials. Cutting processes in the kitchen eventually applied to more than just food – once food was tinned, we also required effective tools to open metal cans. Although there are 'a thousand ways to skin a cat', design developments have improved the tools, methods, processes and end results in the kitchen.

↑ **Mezzaluna, Since 16ᵗʰ century, Italy / Europe,
Designer unknown, Steel, wood**

Moving on from ancient utensils, the mezzaluna has
been around for hundreds of years, and would have made
light work of chopping before mechanical machines
were invented in the 19ᵗʰ century. The word mezzaluna
translates directly from Italian to 'half moon'. This is
exactly the shape – perhaps the inspiration – for this
rocking, chopping knife. Similar to Inuit ulus and Western
choppers, the mezzaluna is an efficient and quick tool
for chopping herbs and other foods that need a fine
mince. This utensil is distinct from its forebears in that
it has two handles which allow for a gentle, or vigorous,
rocking back and forth of the blade. Some contemporary
versions have double blades in parallel, for even quicker
chopping actions. Examples of these types of knife were
cited in Bartolomeo Scappi's infamous cookbook *Opera
… The Art and Craft of a Master Cook* (1570), one of the
earliest records of food preparation and instruction. The
tool was also recorded as being used to chop some of
the first pizzas in the 19ᵗʰ century.

→ **Choppers, 18ᵗʰ / 19ᵗʰ centuries, USA/Europe,
Makers unknown, Wrought iron, fruitwood**

Variations of choppers have been used all over the world
for thousands of years. Before the endless varieties of
kitchen knives that we have now, these were practical
and robust tools which could mince numerous foods
quickly and easily. Most choppers were hand-forged in
wrought iron, but they were also made of cast steel or
tin. Their forms show a clear evolution from primitive
tools like the ulu and resemble familiar knives today
such as mezzaluna or cleavers. The earliest choppers
would have been forged and finished by metalworkers
or sword smiths, and often handles were adapted from
common tools such as handsaws.

A tiller-style chopper handle rose up from one top
edge, the hand holding it directly above the blade; this
allowed for a push-pull motion, much like soba noodle
knives. Other styles had a curved blade (or two) to be
rocked back and forth – some had an accompanying
bowl to match the curve and keep ingredients together
while chopping, which is particularly helpful for herbs.
As utilitarian aspects were refined, some highly decorated
choppers were crafted – uniquely shaped blades with
patterned piercings and elaborately carved handles.
Surviving examples in the best condition, whether plain
or decorated, are from the 18ᵗʰ and 19ᵗʰ centuries.

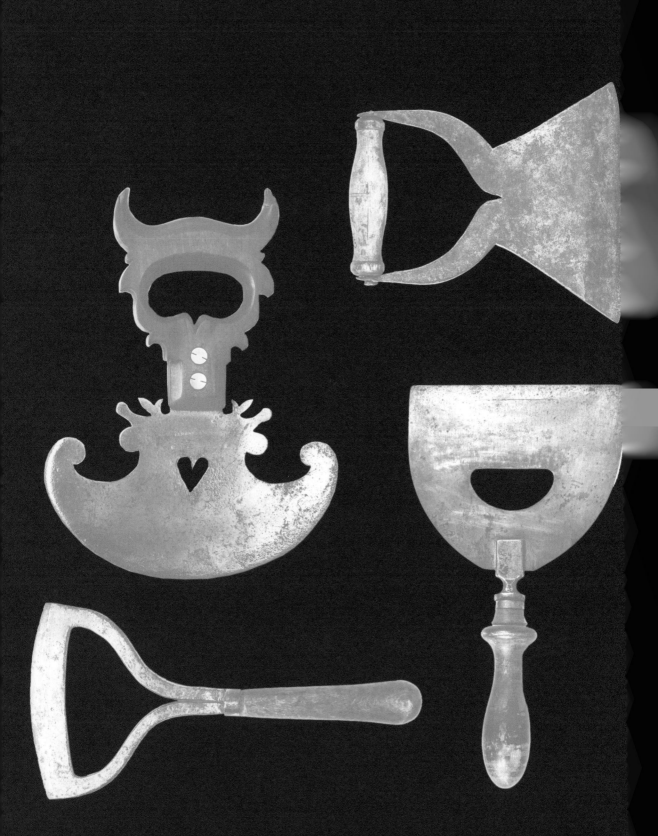

The *boti* / *bnoti* / *dao* / *pirdai*, and its many other names in the various languages of India and South Asia, is especially common to the Bengal area, but can be found throughout the country and nearby regions. This cutting device is used while sitting on the floor, with the user sitting over the base to hold it steady. Both hands are used to easily control and guide food over the curved blade to slice vegetables, fruit, fish and meat into small pieces. This motion allows for quick preparation, especially for items that are difficult to cut with a hand-held knife such as pumpkins, or other foods with hard skins and shells. A dish or newspaper is placed under the blade to collect the food that is being sliced, peeled or grated. Originally *botis* were all metal, whereas now you can find the blade mounted on wood, or a blade that folds away for safer storage. Some blades can be mounted on tabletops to work while standing, as opposed to sitting on the floor.

Some *botis* have a *narkel kuruni* at the top end, a round and spiked implement which is used for grating coconut or fruit flesh. This specific addition is more common in areas where coconuts are grown and used in the local cuisine such as Kerala, Tamil Nadu, Karnataka, Gujurat or Goa. A similar handheld tool that resembles the *narkel kuruni* implement can be found in the West Indies where it is used to grate coconut used in Caribbean food.

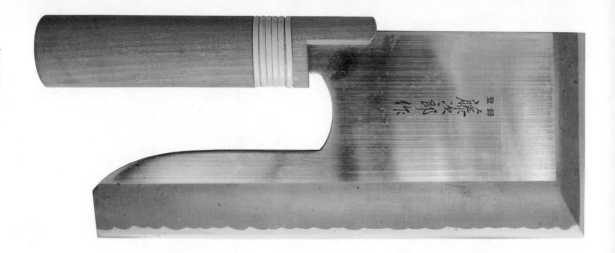

↑   Soba kiri, Since the Edo Period (1603–1868),
Japan, Designer unknown; Pictured: Tojiro,
Magnolia wood, carbon steel

The specialised knife known as a soba kiri is used for
cutting soba noodles. A soba kiri differs slightly from
the udon kiri, whose blade runs the length of the handle
whereas for the udon it just falls short. This single-
bevelled knife is heavy in form to aid the cutting of
the noodles in a forward motion, and when gripped in
the hand the index finger is used to stabilise the blade.
On the non-bevelled side, a wooden stick laid on top of
the folded dough allows for precisely measured cuts.

Soba (buckwheat) has been eaten in Japan since the
Jomon Period (14,000–300 BCE), mostly in dumpling-
like form until the Edo Period when cut noodles were
created in the Nagano Prefecture. Soba noodles are
typically 2–3 mm (⅛–³⁄₁₆ in) thick, while wheat-flour udon
noodles are a meatier 5 mm (¼ in). To make these noodles,
flour is mixed with water to make a dough, which is rolled
out and layered over itself to be cut into fine strips in a
rhythmic motion. This blade is made from molybdenum
vanadium steel, which is easier to maintain than carbon
blue or white steel, which are common materials for
Japanese knives. This knife has a wood handle, though
some soba or udon kiri come with a corded grip, or
none at all, so that the chef can customise their own.

1	Chinese cleaver, carbon steel	7	Santoku knife, aogami steel
2	Chef's knife, Robert Herder	8	Petty knife, aogami and stainless steel
3	Deba knife	9	Nakiri knife, aogami steel
4	Paring knife, Robert Herder	10	Bread knife
5	Paring knife, Sabatier	11	Gyuto knife, shirogami 2, Damascus
6	Paring knife, Opinel		1, 4, 7, 8, 9, 11 courtesy of Kitchen Provisions, London

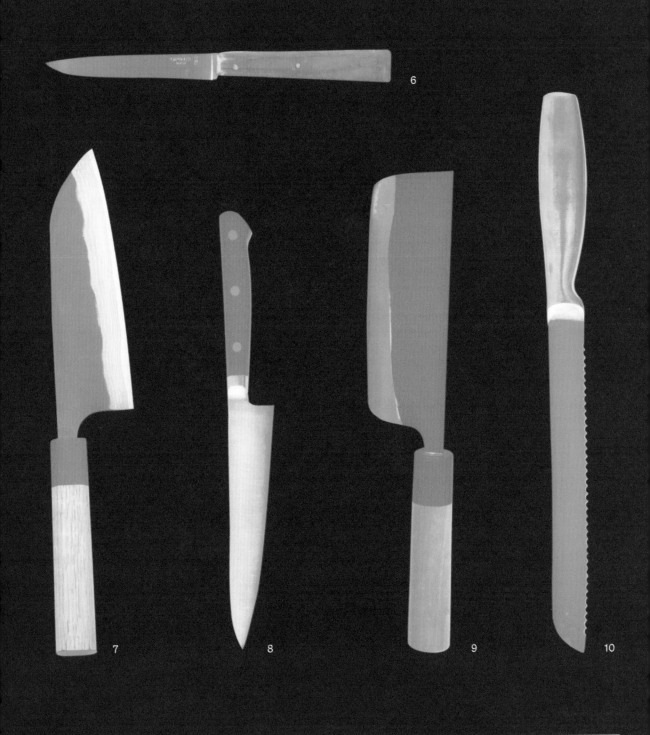

There are hundreds of shapes and sizes of knives, each performing different functions, and they really haven't changed a great deal since early illustrated records such as Bartolomeo Scappi's food reference book *Opera … The Art and Craft of a Master Cook* (1570). Since they have been made of metal as opposed to flint or stone, the essential structure and assembly have remained the same – all derivations of a sharp edge with a handle to hold it. They're made specifically to peel fruit (paring knife, fig. 5), bone or fillet fish, cut bread (fig. 10) or soba noodles, open oysters, carve meat, slice cheese or saw through frozen food. The different shapes and functions of knives tell us as much about ergonomics and design as they do about differences in culture. For example, in East Asia (primarily China, Japan and Korea), many knives function with a push-pull action rather than the up-and-down rocking action that many Western knives encourage. Rectangular, cleaver-type knives (fig. 1) are more common as an all-purpose tool in the East, whereas in the West knives have a curved shape at the tip rather than a square one.

In recent years there has been more crossover between 'Eastern' and 'Western' knives, with companies from both locations producing both types to meet the demands of their globalised market and customers. For example the German company Wüsthof began making Japanese style santoku knives in the 1980s; Japanese company Yoshida began to make their well-known Global knives for the West in 1983. Wüsthof were the company to introduce oval 'kullens' on the side of the knive to prevent food sticking to the blade. Japanese knives are especially well-known for being some of the best in the world (deriving from centuries-old, razor-sharp sword manu-facturing), and can be forged in stainless steel, carbon steel, and white or blue steel (which differ in carbide size and corrosiveness). Although it is possible to survive with just one knife, most chefs agree that the essentials are a chef's knife, paring knife, cleaver and bread knife; sharpening regularly is essential.

If you are too impatient to wait for food to defrost before cutting it, or if the bread wasn't sliced before you put it in the ice-cold storage box, a frozen food knife may be required. Once modern refrigeration was standard, food-freezing techniques were developed, and by the 1930s it was usual to purchase and store such things in a domestic kitchen freezer. The frozen food knife was invented for items frozen in large blocks that needed portioning before defrosting. This absolutely brutal-looking knife was patented in 1954 and dubbed the 'Freez Cut' that 'never needs resharpening' – possibly because it wouldn't be used that often. The objective was to prevent food waste, by being able to portion out what you needed rather than defrost an entire package. The designers noted in the patent that a wood saw could be used for the task, but would clog with food or cardboard; therefore, this design has unique gullets in the blade that allow contents to fall away when cutting. Though possibly just a novelty item for your *batterie de cuisine* in the mid-20th century, frozen food knives are still sold today. This particular and uniquely shaped frozen food knife is in the collection of the Museum of Modern Art, in New York.

Aug. 3, 1954 **F. B. SEEBERGER** **2,685,131**

FROZEN FOOD CUTTER

Filed June 2, 1953

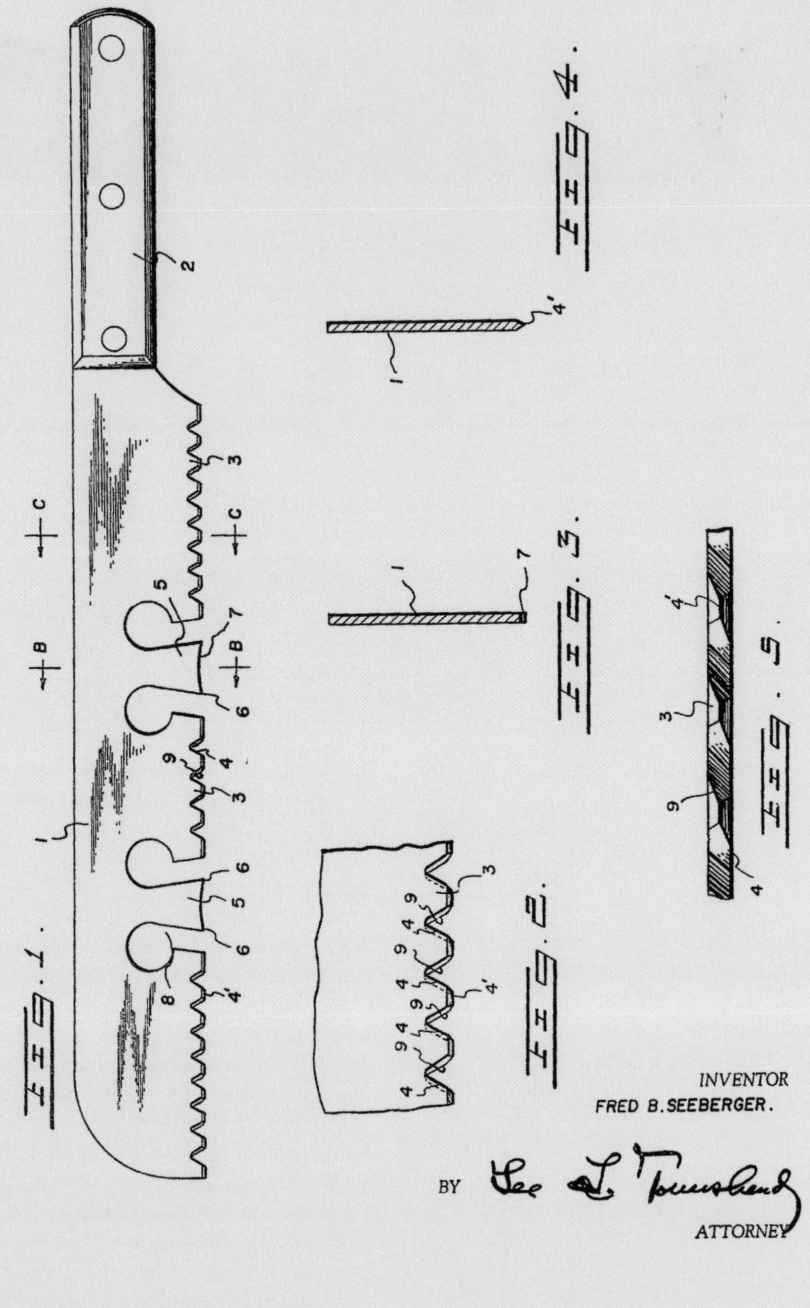
FIG. 1.
FIG. 2.
FIG. 3.
FIG. 4.
FIG. 5.
INVENTOR
FRED B. SEEBERGER.
BY
ATTORNEY

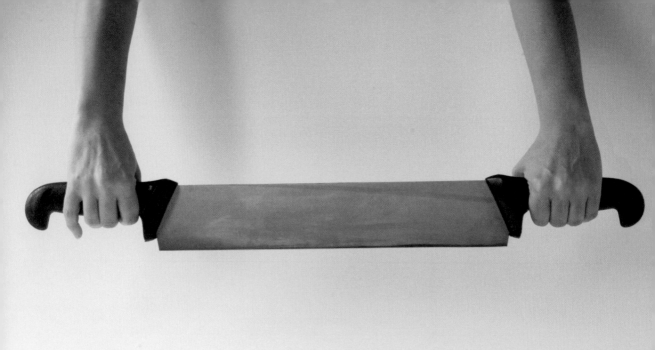

↑   **Double-handled knife, 20th century, Europe /
Japan, Designer unknown, Steel, plastic**

Double-handled knives like these are found in the East
and the West, though are used for different purposes.
It looks like you might cut some food with a friend with
this super-strong knife, though it is designed for one
person to cut particularly hard or large foods. It is similar
to the mezzaluna in that it has two handles, though in
this knife the handles remain in line with the blade, so
the user can get leverage on the item being cut. In Japan
they use this knife to cut squashes, pumpkins and
watermelons with hard rinds; in places such as France,
Switzerland or Spain, it is used to cut large wheels of
cheese where a single-handled knife isn't strong enough.
These double-handled knives can also be used to cut
pizza, pastries, frozen food and slabs of fudge, or even to
shave large sheets of chocolate when copious quantities
are required to cover cakes and pies. Most of these
types of knives are manufactured in France or Japan.

← **Lame, 20th century, France, Designer unknown, Pictured: Breadtopia, Metal**

As with all clever inventions that are the result of a happy accident or ingenious shift of context or purpose, so it is with the bread lame (pronounced *lahm*). Perhaps a clever baker, with his shaving razor nearby, realised that such a sharp blade was just the tool needed to make essential slits in bread ready for baking. Most examples of this tool allow for the blade to be replaced over and over again with a common shaving razor. The best-designed lames allow for the blade mounted on the tip to be curved ever so slightly: this means the razor can make an even finer slit on the surface of doughs about to be baked in the oven. This process is essential for artisanal loafs, to let the steam escape as the bread expands when baking – without these slits the bread crust can tear in all manner of unsightly directions.

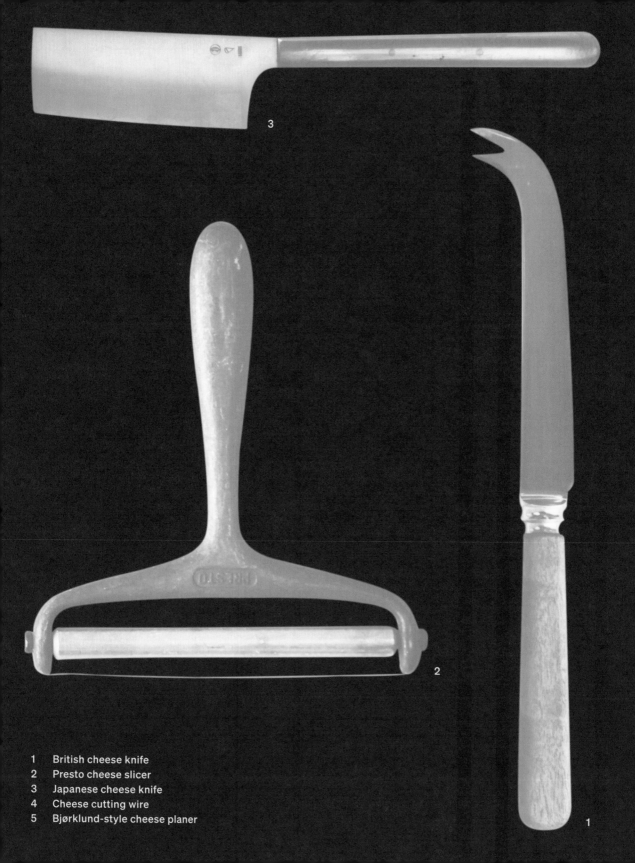

1　British cheese knife
2　Presto cheese slicer
3　Japanese cheese knife
4　Cheese cutting wire
5　Bjørklund-style cheese planer

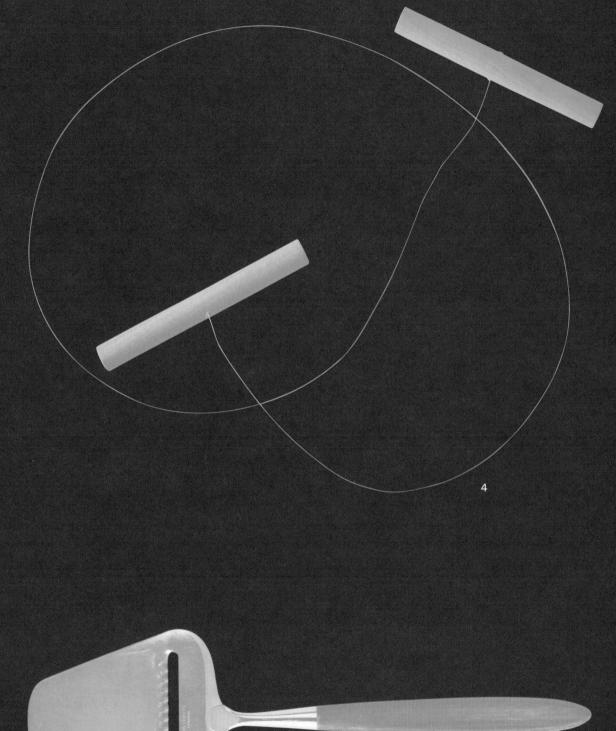

4

5

← **Cheese knives, cutters, slicers,**
Since 19ᵗʰ century, Europe & Japan,
Various designers, Various materials

106

There are many types of knives for the different kinds of cheese to be cut, whether hard, soft, round or square. The numerous forms have been designed to cut most effectively through the dairy for serving, and to keep the shape of the cheese intact while doing so. They can have off-set handles, holes in the blades to prevent soft cheese sticking, be shaped like a small butcher's knife (for harder types) or have two prongs at the tip of the blade to pick up a piece of cheese. Cheese cutters can be as simple as a guillotine wire, or as specialised as the Northern European pie-cutter-shaped slicer with an integrated blade. In Switzerland, there is the specialist cheese 'girolle' which is especially made for shaving wavy pieces of *Tête de Moines* (Monk's Head) and mounted on the cheese itself. For super-hard cheeses like Parmesan, an almond-shaped knife – which resembles an oyster shucker – can be used for gauging out hunks of cheese. All of these tools help with cheese-cutting etiquette, involving certain angles and slices that should be made in order to cut cheese for yourself or a guest in a polite manner. Though in use before the 19ᵗʰ century, most antique examples are from this time period onwards.

There is a story of a Norwegian carpenter called Thor Bjørklund who became peckish while working away in his carpentry workshop; he fancied a sandwich, took his wood planer to some cheese for slicing and realised how nicely and efficiently it cut the food. Bjørklund developed the blade, function, form and style into a cheese-sized, stainless-steel cutter with a teak handle in 1925. He finally patented the design in 1930, and many have copied it since. The blade is arranged 'to the longitudinal direction of the handle … like of the planing type … [and is] for cutting cheese and the like.'

The Presto cheese slicer was America's answer to Bjørklund's tool, an aluminium utenstil with 10 cm (4 in) of taut steel wire for slicing, a miniature version of guillotine wire. This tool was designed by John R. Carroll in 1944 for the Presto company. Presto originally sold pressure canning devices before expanding their range of kitchen tools. Though this slicer was designed in 1944, production would not have taken place until 1945 when aluminium stocks could be used again in industry as opposed to for the war effort.

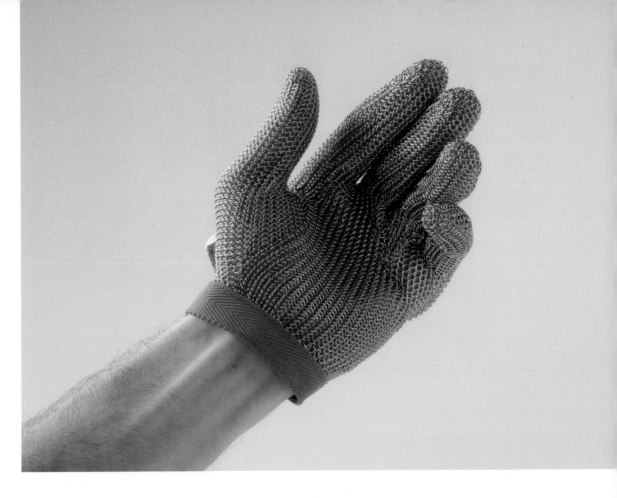

↑   **Oyster glove, 20th century, Germany / France,
     Various designers, Stainless steel**

Shucking oysters is a tough and dangerous job, requiring
a second skin. For the hand that holds the oyster – the
other holds the oyster knife – serious protection is
needed, not only from the sharp shell, but from slips
of the knife when prising it open. Originally very thick
leather gloves were used, but the fine weave of metal
shown here is even more effective in preventing mishaps
from occurring. Though the chain-mail oyster glove is
passive rather than active in its 'tool' function, it's an
essential part of opening and preparing this food.
These gloves are also sometimes used by butchers,
who slice and cut all day long. Patents were registered
by both French and German inventors in the 20th century.
A particularly beautiful chain-mail oyster glove by
German manufacturer Carl Mertens sits in the Museum
of Modern Art, in New York, though many standard
metal or carbon gloves are easy to find to protect the
hands while shucking.

↑ **Whetstone, Since 1st century CE and
earlier, Worldwide, Various makers,
Stone / Ceramic / Composites**

Though it appears modern due to its shape and colour, the whetstone and its function is thousands of years old. The sharpening stone has been used in one form or another since metallurgy and the use of knives for culinary purposes, agriculture, shaving, hunting and warfare. Pliny the Elder cited the use of such stones in his *Naturalis Historia* encyclopedia from the 1st century CE. Depending on the location, these sharpening tools would have been made of the best local abrasive stone; a common natural mineral used for this purpose is the microcrystalline and super-hard novaculite. Whetstones come in different grits like sandpaper, starting rough, then becoming finer. This is why contemporary stones have two colours: one side is coarser to start with, the other fine for finishing the process.

The etymology of 'whet' is to sharpen, but this has nothing to do with wetting the stone for sharpening, although lubrication is part of the process to allow 'swarf' particles to fall away so they don't clog the tool. Today these tools are made from various materials, including natural stone, ceramic, oil stones and Carborundum. The combination whetstones pictured here areis synthetic, which is generally regarded as the best material for sharpening with water;. these are made by Suehiro, one of the best whetstone makers in Japan. A grit of 320 is used to first bevel or fix blades (foreground, made by Shapton); the red and white whetstone shown has both 1000 and 6000 grits, for everyday sharpening and finishing respectively. Otherwise, ceramic or natural stones are used to sharpen antique or valuable blades. Carborundum stone is silicon carbide, a very hard stone found naturally, but more often than not man-made. Oil stones are manufactured with oil inside the stone, which lubricates the blade as it is drawn across the surface.

Sharpening takes place on the whetstone by removing metal to create a new fine edge, first coarsely and then refined with a smaller grit. To complete the process the edge is straightened and then 'stropped' on a leather strap to give the edge a final reshaping. There is nothing more unsatisfactory than a dull knife in the kitchen, and nothing more gratifying than a clean and easy cut with the sharpest of tools.

**Knife sharpener, 1963, Italy, Marco Zanuso and
Richard Sapper, ABS plastic, grinding stone**

This sharpener is a far cry from the original sharpening
processes using stones or elongated butcher's steels.
In large households or those of the gentry, the carver
was an important person, responsible for dishing out
portions of meat at the table. They carried their 'steel'
with them hanging from their belt, ready to sharpen
their knife for carving. Fast forward hundreds of years
to this futuristic grinding stone, which hides rather than
shows off its functional components, leaving only clean
lines and shapes.

This knife sharpener from Marco Zanuso and Richard
Sapper is another example of their modern designs.
The product was commissioned by the Italian company
Necchi, who originally produced sewing machines but
diversified their output to other products in the 1960s.
The product is electric, the grinding wheel turning
as the user puts the blade in the slit for sharpening.
Though most of the function is hidden in the casing,
the designers left a hint of the top of the wheel showing,
so that the user can see when the grinding stone is
spinning. Aficionados prefer to do the job manually,
as electric knife sharpeners are known to be too harsh
on the blade.

Ever since knives have been used to prepare food, we've required a reliable surface on which to cut and prep. In China, where large cleavers are used in everyday cooking, thick wooden blocks were needed to withstand blunt force. Blocks were usually basic, as is the case with this slice of tree trunk, seasoned and oiled, though these rounds had a tendency to crack and could be secured with leather or metal straps as a preventative measure.

In the West, big chunks of wood were mostly used by butchers, but the 'chopping block' slowly crept its way into domestic kitchens, especially after modern milling techniques and circular saws could be used to produce a flat plank of wood. Though butcher's blocks were huge, stand-alone chopping stations, the portable boards were much more practical for everyday use. They not only provide protection for the surface underneath, but also prevent damage to the knife or tool being used. Some medieval blocks had wrought-iron handles, whereas more elaborate Victorian English breadboards are carved around the edges with wheat sheaves and mottoes. Plastic eventually emerged as a malleable and useful material for cutting on; however, wood remains preferable due to its naturally antiseptic properties. Some modern-day blocks have channels for juices and crumbs, but all that is really needed is a simple slice of wood.

↑ **Breadboard, Early 19ᵗʰ century,
UK, Maker unknown, Wood**

These carved breadboards were very popular in Victorian times, often featuring wheat sheafs, useful mottoes and sometimes coats-of-arms. Some have inscriptions such as 'Our Daily Bread', 'All with one Accord in one place' or just 'Bread' and organic decorations around the edges. These boards were particularly popular with the aristocracy, who were always looking for new ways to spend money on uniquely crafted products. Originally hand-carved out of sycamore, and sometimes oak or beech, workshops in the 1860s soon caught on to mechanised carving techniques to produce boards for a mass market. There is an enthusiastic breadboard-collecting community, and even a breadboard museum in Putney, London.

The No-spill Chopping Board, or Chop2Pot as it is also known, was a revelation at the time. Designed by Mark Sanders in 1988, this chopping board finally solved the problem of scraping things into the pot from your board, preventing the contents from spilling off the sides. At the time of its design the Chop2Pot won many awards, including for 'Innovative Use of Plastics', and is in the Museum of Modern Art collection, in New York. It is manufactured with a one-piece mould whose built-in hinges of thinner plastic allow for folding in seven places. This process was developed with special injection-mould flow techniques to produce the board in one piece. Joseph Joseph now manufacture the official product and it is available in many colours.

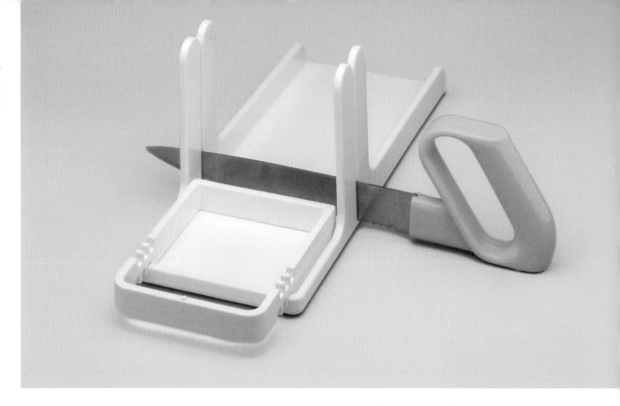

↑   **Kitchen knife and cutting board, 1973, Sweden,
Maria Benktzon and Sven-Eric Juhlin, Plastic, metal**

Although designers are known for problem-solving,
they don't always think of the less able, the elderly or
those with arthritis or other ailments that would prevent
someone from using a tool or object in a 'normal' way.
Aesthetics – which are important – are often at the
forefront, but sometimes function and accessibility
come second, or are forgotten. This is not the case with
Ergonomi Design, founded in 1969 in Sweden, who
specialise in meeting the needs of people besides those
who are fully 'able'. Ergonomi is now known as McKinsey
Design, and the company's products from their earlier
days are still manufactured, alongside new ones that
embody 'people-driven design'. This kitchen knife and
cutting board is one such example, an object which
makes it easier to slice foods safely and with control.
The food is kept in place with an adjustable piece, while
the knife is supported vertically to cut with a back-and-
forth motion. This tool, along with similar empathetic
designs, were featured in the 'Designs for Independent
Living' exhibition at the Museum of Modern Art, New
York, in 1988, which highlighted products for the elderly
and people with physically challenging abilities.

← **Mandoline, Since 16th century, Europe, Designer unknown, Wood, steel**

The name of the mandoline comes from the movement of the hand when slicing, which is like strumming the instrument of the same name. The tool has been around for a while, as it features in Bartolomeo Scappi's cookbook *Opera … The Art and Craft of a Master Cook* (1570). The board is constructed with a raised blade parallel to the surface creating uniform slices when strummed upon, or julienne strips (a style of cut named after a chef Julien) when perpendicular blades are added to the tool. For repetitive slicing and consistent size, this tool is quick and efficient. Precision-driven Japanese mandolines are favoured by professionals today, and styles with V-shaped blades also claim superior cutting.

In Northern and Eastern Europe, the mandoline is a familiar utensil for cutting cabbage for preserving, and is sometimes referred to as a *krauthobel* or 'cabbage slicer'. Some rumours suggest it was modelled after the guillotine – and, indeed, the mandoline is a sharp and dangerous tool if used without care. It is rumoured Marie Antoinette had miniature guillotines that resembled mandolines in her Petit Trianon palace at Versailles, for executing dolls.

→ **Katsuobushi kezuriki, Since 16th/17th centuries, Japan, Designer unknown, Wood, metal**

The speciality of bonito or *katsuobushi* (dried tuna flakes) has been consumed in Japan for over 500 years. After refining drying techniques and smoking and fermenting methods, a tool was required to shave the delicacy into fine slices for garnishing and making dashi stock. The unique sound of dried skipjack tuna being grated is familiar and comforting across Japan, a sign of a delicious meal to come. Like many tools for food, the kezuriki was probably a result of a shift in context that resulted in this specialised utensil. The *katsuobushi* grater does resemble a wood planer, and indeed carpenters are some of the craftspeople that make these kitchen utensils in Japan today. The box is crafted in wood such as oak, chestnut or magnolia, with a precision blade mounted within the removable lid. With a pushing action of the dried tuna on the blade, wafer-thin slices waft like delicate feathers into the container below which is pulled out like a drawer. If your piece of dried tuna is small enough, it can be stored in the box when not in use. Today, *katsuobushi* is well-known in the West as one of the final toppings for *okonomiyaki*, but is also an essential ingredient for dashi, the base of many soups, sauces and dishes in Japanese cuisine.

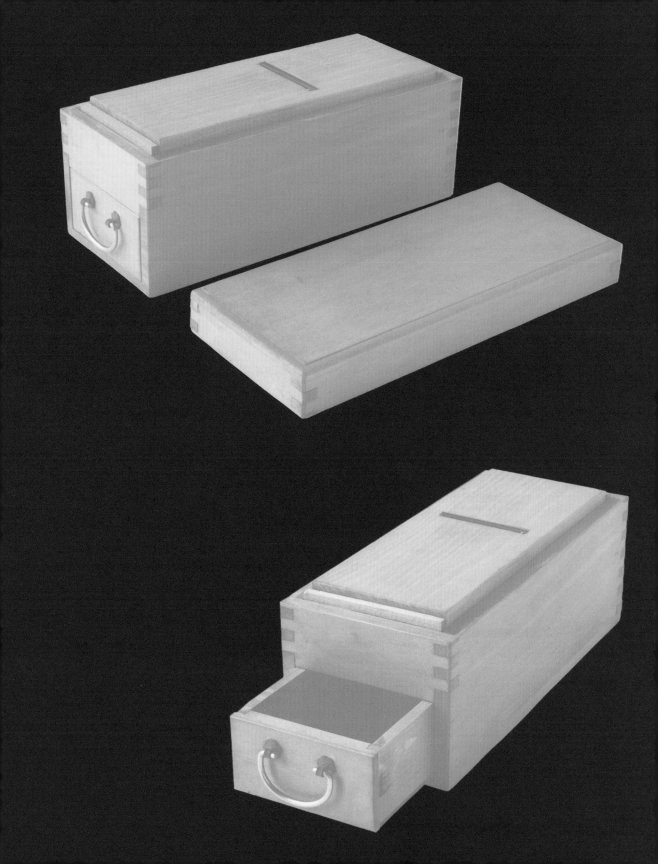

↓ **Egg slicer, 1940s, Germany,
Westmark, Aluminum, steel**

Westmark manufactured (and still do) a number of
aluminium tools, especially prolifically during the postwar
period when metal was reintroduced to manufacturing
rather than only being used for ammunition and weapons.
Their range of utensils were called *küchenhelfers* or
'kitchen helpers'. These tools made easy work for
new modern women who wanted to spend less time in
the kitchen, and this aluminium egg slicer speaks of
that moment.

The first designs for this function were registered in the
early 20th century, a few by the German brand Westmark
in the late 1940s. In the UK, egg slicers such as these were
produced in parallel with a high-profile postwar campaign
that advocated eating eggs as a source of protein and
energy. The 'Go to Work on an Egg' promotion was driven
by the British Egg Marketing Board and included TV
adverts and publicity posters promoting the food for
breakfast. The Duplex cutter *für runde und ovale* (UK /
Germany 'for round or oval foods') or 'Rond y Oval' (France)
by Westmark allowed you to easily cut uniform slices of
eggs for sandwiches or salads, and even mushrooms and
other round foods. The tool uses a taut metal wire that
cuts through soft ingredients, a method also used in
foie gras cutters, cheese and avocado slicers.

↑   **Vegetable holder / slicer, 1957,
Germany, Westmark, Aluminium**

This tool promotes limited contact of the hand with the
food being prepared. That, however, is its secondary
function, as its primary one is to hold round foods while
they are sliced, so that equal pieces may be cut. It can
be used for tomatoes, eggs, and soft spherical fruits
and vegetables, especially onions, which can even be
held at arms length to mitigate the risk of crying during
cutting. This tool was patented in the 1950s by the
kitchen tool manufacturer Westmark, whose description
of the utensil bemoans the difficulties of cutting round
items in a flat world. The patent notes the 'gripping
shells … provided with a plurality of parallel slots …
[guide the] knife to be cut by hand into slices.' Though
similar tools were around before, their new clamshell-
like handheld utensil 'eliminated [the] disadvantages'
that others had. Primitive versions of this tool are a
series of long parallel pins mounted on a handle that
both spear the food being sliced, but also provide
a guide for the knife to make even cuts.

↑ **Egg topper, 1911, Birmingham, UK,**
Hammond, Turner & Sons, Silver

Boiled eggs have been eaten for at least 5,000 years,
once pottery was developed for cooking in. The Romans,
who often ate eggs as an appetiser, coined a phrase
ab ova ad mala, meaning 'from egg to apple', to describe
the entirety of a meal. This silver egg cutter, also known
as a topper, was made in the early 20th century during
Edwardian times, a peak moment in the development and
distribution of gadgets and serving tools for food which
had begun flooding the market in Victorian England.
This delicate and at the same time terrifying machine was
used to cut the top off a soft-boiled egg, to be scooped
or dipped into with a spoon or soldier of toast.

The modern version of this tool looks much less
intimidating. Registered for a US Patent by Ferdinand
Fleischmann in 1907, retractable teeth are hidden inside
a circular metal casing that are only seen when the
handles are brought together to cut a precise line
across the top of the egg.

← **Eierschalensollbruchstellenverursacher
(CLACK! Egg Opener), 1999, Germany,
Take2 Design, Stainless steel**

Perhaps an equally violent-looking machine for a
reasonably delicate job, the Clack! Egg Opener creates
a perfect cut at the top of the egg through force and
friction. To open the egg, the silicone ball handle is
lifted up the 16-cm (6-in) shaft, which exerts a force
of .6867 Newtons in 0.181 seconds. Through precise
German engineering, the vibration and sharp edge
around the bottom of the dome cuts a perfect line
through the top of the shell which is then lifted away.
The manufacturers state: 'This is just the right amount
of force to cut a perfect ring around the top of the egg,
without damaging the rest of the egg shell.'

Soft-boiled eggs are a popular item for *frühstuck*
(breakfast) in Germany, and the *Eierschalensollbruchstellenverursacher* allows Germans across the country
to enjoy their eggs to perfection. The name translates
as *Eierschale* (eggshell) + *Sollbruchstelle* (predetermined
breaking point) + *Verursacher* (causer). Though the
force for the egg is 'perfect', the manufacturer does
warn against using the Clack-er on eggs in fragile egg
cups such as filigree or porcelain. Rösle produces a
spring-loaded version of this type of egg opener, using
the same principle of force and friction.

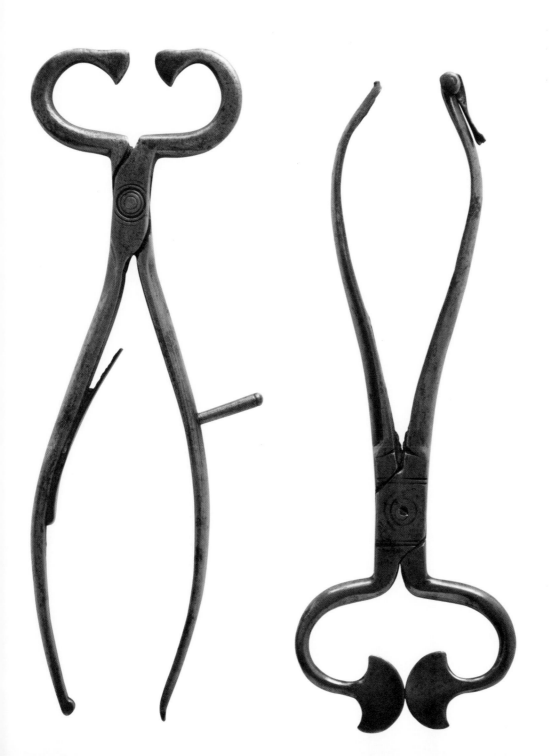

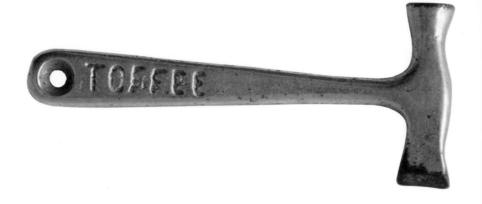

← **Sugar nipper, 18th century, England, Designer unknown, Steel**

The discovery, cultivation, processing, distribution and consumption of sugar has a long and complicated history. It was originally used in medicine and eventually in food. Sugar and sugar cane were brought to Europe from India by Alexander the Great around 325 BCE, then was propagated around the world in tropical zones. Sugar cane needs fertile soil and sun, and is labour-intensive, and so it was not feasible to grow this crop in Northern Europe; therefore, the commodity was mostly traded, and such records exist from the 11th century.

Once trade routes were established, processed sugar came in large cone shapes, and could weigh up to 6 kg (14 lb). The rich would buy whole cones, but the less well-off would ask the grocer to cut off a few ounces. Whether at the grocers or in a stately kitchen, a sugar nipper was required to nip off smaller pieces for cooking and baking. Sometimes the cone would first be hacked at with a sugar axe, with the nipper making smaller pieces. These tools were made of iron or steel and work just like pliers or forging tongs, with circular blades at the end to snip off portions. Some sweet (candy) makers used to give nippers to their clients, and the tool was in use even in the 21st century. Though mostly plain and utilitarian, some sugar nippers are decorated with engraved designs. They vary in size, with smaller cutters made for the dining table.

In the 19th century, Germany developed sugar beet, a tuber that grows easily in European climates, which is refined into granulated crystals. This type of sugar soon gained popularity as it was less expensive than importing labour-intensive sugar from the tropics and is common today, though sugar cane still holds the majority of the global market.

↑ **Toffee hammer, 19th century, England, Edward Joseph Walker, Aluminium**

Like the sugar nipper, toffee hammers were sometimes included as gifts with the product sold, so it could be used to break sweet slabs into bite-size pieces. These cast aluminium hammers were cheap to manufacture and reasonably light to include with toffee. Officially, toffee is the tough kind of processed sweet or sugar, heated to a 'hard crack' stage that makes it brittle once cooled; caramel is the softer type of heated sugar or processed sweets (candy). Many of these small sugar hammers still exist – possibly lying around at a grand-parent's house – often emblazoned with 'Toffee' and the name of the manufacturer, such as Walkers, on the handle. Their size (about 10 cm / 4 in), shape and toy-like quality are almost as cute as the sweets they were used to break through tiny hammering actions. So common were these tools in their heyday that other smaller hammers which resemble this tool for food are referred to as toffee hammers, such as those used in scaffolding and orthopaedics.

→ **O-Series scissors, 1967, Finland, Olof Bäckström
(Fiskars), ABS plastic, stainless steel**

These scissors are easily recognisable as a design
icon, whether by function, form or the famous orange
handles. They were developed by Norwegian engineer
Olof Bäckström for the Finnish company, Fiskars.
Fiskars was established in 1649 and were mostly known
for manufacturing knives until they diversified their
product line in the 19th century.

The original prototypes for the O-Series scissors were
carved from wood to determine the best ergonomics
for the thumb, forefinger and hand when cutting with
a clinching up-and-down motion. The famous orange
handles are the result of a happy accident – the machinist
transforming the wooden model into plastic happened
to use some leftover coloured material in the workshop;
they were intended to be black, red or green. In true
ergonomic and universal design style, a left-handed
version also exists. The scissors are dishwasher-safe and
can be used for a multitude of kitchen operations such
as snipping herbs, cutting pizza or slicing scallions
(spring onions).

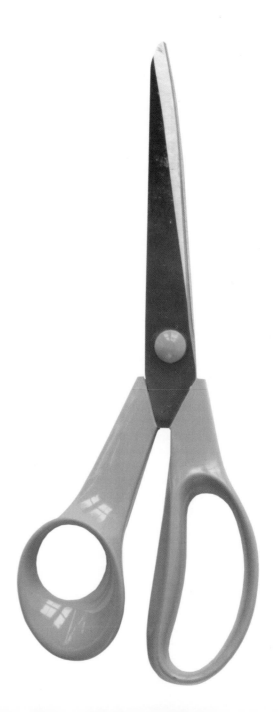

↑ **Chinese kitchen scissors, Since 1663,**
China, Zhang Xiaoquan, Steel

These kitchen scissors are as familiar in Eastern kitchens
as they are in the West, probably because they have been
around for 350 years or more. This particular iconic
style is made in both China and Japan but originates
in the former country. Perhaps there is just something
about scissor handle curves that create design icons, as
this silhouette is instantly recognisable, like the Fiskars
pair shown. The handles give ample room for gripping
and the scissors can be used for a variety of purposes
and cuts – in the kitchen for food and even for paper,
fabric or gardening. The original Zhang Xiaoquan brand
that makes these scissors is a household name in China,
and they create 120 different types with numerous
individual specifications. The company is now so large
that its scissors are made by machines in a factory;
however, smaller workshops in Japan, such as Banshu
Hamono, in Hyogo, still craft scissors like these by hand.
Many of these scissors are interchangeable for gardening
purposes, and they will last a lifetime or over many
generations when cared for properly by sharpening,
tightening the blades, and keeping them dry and
free from rust.

Known as *nigiri hasami* – *nigiri* meaning 'to fit in the hand' and *hasami* meaning 'scissors' – the intended purpose of these scissors is for sewing activities, but they are a delight for snipping herbs in the garden. They are probably one of the most satisfying tools to use of all the scissor-type objects in this chapter. Their function is entirely built into the construction of the object: the natural resistance of the bent steel provides the spring needed to cut when the scissor blades are pressed together; they are forged by hand from a single steel rod. The small size allows for easy access to herb stems that need cutting from the garden, though their function can be applied to a myriad of settings that necessitate cutting on a small-scale, bringing joy with every press of the handles. These scissors come in a few small sizes, some with curved blades used to cut threads precisely in delicate sewing projects. They will last for generations if well cared for and sharpened regularly, as is standard practice in Japan.

This object lends itself to intriguing design, its curves being reminiscent of avian forms. They somehow lend themselves to aesthetic expression, and this typology of tool is found in design collections around the world. Whether Italian, German or French, poultry shears have a sort of … *je ne sais quoi* that attracts you to their design. There must have been an original designer who sketched out such satisfyingly undulating shapes, because many shears maintain these curves in one way or another. Some shears show the spring between the handle, but others conceal it; generally, the lines of the form are clean and minimal. This particular pair was made by the German brand Rostfrei.

Poultry shears make light work of boning and separating the different cuts of birds. Instead of the difficulties that a knife might create, these scissors allow you to easily remove joints, bones and wings; most shears can be taken apart for easy cleaning. As pleasurable to look at as they are to use, they are a sturdy, useful and aesthetically pleasing implement for the kitchen.

→ **Tin (can) opener, Since 19th century,**
   USA / Europe, Various designers, Metal

Preserving food by canning came into use at the end
of the 18th century and beginning of the 19th century.
The development of this preservation method originated
in a call to find more efficient ways to provide food for
troops at war. Frenchman Nicolas Appert is credited with
winning Napoleon's award to do such a thing, with his
vacuum-sealed glass bottles. Canning in metal soon
followed and was patented in England, and thus led
to multiple industrious inventions for tools to open
these tins.

From the mid-19th century, many, many tin-opening tools
were invented and their patents registered, including
the brutal-looking, bull-head type and the lever-type
openers which were hardly efficient. They are a bone
of contention to this day – there are still so many poorly
designed tin openers that put you in danger of making
a mess of the lid, hands or fingers. The hundreds of tin-
can openers invented in the early days were clunky and
arduous to use. Rotary blades didn't appear until the early
20th century (turning 'church key' openers) and these
were not refined in design until the end of the century.
Finally, electric versions hit the market, though manual
handheld openers seem to be the easiest to operate, if
even necessary. New technology has allowed for ring-pull-
type tins that require no opener at all – a sign of the
times and man's ingenuity.

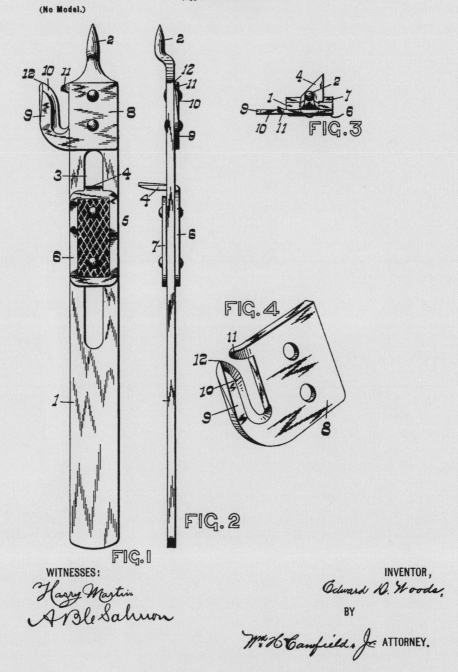

No. 684,334.

E. D. WOODS.
CAN OPENER.
(Application filed Oct. 13, 1900.)

Patented Oct. 8, 1901.

(No Model.)

FIG. 1

FIG. 2

FIG. 3

FIG. 4

WITNESSES:
Harry Martin
A Ble Salmon

INVENTOR,
Edward D. Woods,
BY
Wm H Canfield Jr ATTORNEY.

THE NORRIS PETERS CO., PHOTO-LITHO., WASHINGTON, D. C.

Grind & Grate

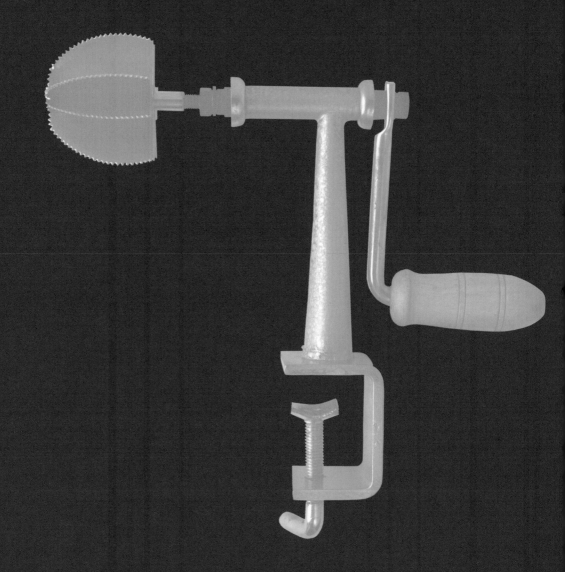

Grinding, pounding, chopping and blending are the methods that humans developed to render food edible, and then, to create new flavour combinations through amalgamations of local ingredients. Following our discovery that food could be removed from animal carcasses or chopped into smaller parts with primitive blades, grinding stones come a close second to some of the world's most ancient tools for food. Maize for tortillas, yams for fufu, beans for coffee, nuts for pesto, oils, herbs … we need to grind and grate all manner of things to enhance the flavour or nutrition of ingredients. This requires a multitude of abrasive tools made from diverse materials: from sharkskin to volcanic rock, marble, serrated bamboo, textured ceramic or punched tin.

The mortar and pestle is one of the most familiar and universal tools in the kitchen, with some of the earliest examples from the Levant (Middle East), around 20,000 years ago. Each of these archetypal devices from around the world has a unique material, texture, sound of pounding and grinding, and produces a different flavour from the act of processing foods and combining ingredients. Mortar and pestles vary greatly in scale – from the countertop-sized Japanese *suribachi* to the African human-sized versions that are pounded standing upright, the mortar sometimes embedded in the ground. Uniquely, the grinding process is done both individually and communally, such as grinding grains in East Africa or South America or pounding rice in Japan and Korea.

The archetypal forms and design icons don't stop at the mortar and pestle; whether a brass rotary coffee and spice mill, a Japanese sesame seed grinder or the violent-looking but necessarily brutal coconut grater – these are tools that are recognised as everyday necessities in individual cultures. Although electronic versions have been invented as labour-saving devices, for the most part the design of tools that grind or grate has not changed much over the centuries. From cheese, to ginger, to daikon or mooli, nutmeg, citrus zest, coconut, salt and pepper, the designers of the world have created a myriad of tools to reduce foods into smaller pieces and pastes which enhance dishes with flavours and garnishes. Round and round in the mortar, up and down on the grater, forward and back on the metate, rough textures and tiny blades aid the cooking process and centuries-old recipes. Despite the invention of various gadgets, not much can improve or change delicious morsels processed by hand with a fine set of manual tools for the job.

African mortar and pestles hold symbolic and ritualistic meaning and purposes. As in the Middle Ages of Europe, they were sometimes given as wedding gifts, perhaps because they symbolise an amalgamation of different ingredients or families into one. In Mali, a bride will traditionally bring a mortar and pestle with her into the new marital home. Though countertop mortar and pestle are common, the human-sized ones are the most impressive and memorable objects. They are used to pound millet, rice flour, cassava and palm fruit for oil. This large-scale tool has been used in a pounding technique since the Stone Age, when basalt mortars were embedded in the ground. Typically servants would be given the arduous task of pulverising grains for hours. Historically it was relatively simple to make large mortars from the trunks of trees, and their large scale made the process easier because the full force of the body could be used to pound with the pestle. In Senegal, they prefer using mango wood to impart a subtle flavour to the ground ingredients, just like the use of olivewood in southern Europe or pepperwood in Japan.

130

This illustration from a publication of 1890 depicts women processing couscous on the west coast of Africa; it is described as a 'vigorous dance' by the illustrator.

LES PILEUSES DE COUSCOUS. — L'HORRIBLE DANSE DU PILON ET DANS TOUTE SA VIGUEUR... (Composition de M. le capitaine Philippe.)

↑ **Usu and kine or Jeolgu and gongi, Since 300 BCE,
Japan / Korea, Designer unknown, Wood**

These large wooden tools are used to pound glutinous rice into Japanese *mochi* or Korean *tteok*, although they can also be made from stone or iron. The process differs from a standard mortar and pestle as this tool is used like a stamp mill, to pound rather than grind. The form and method resemble a similar tool found in Africa for pounding grain, or hominy blocks from North America that transform maize to grain; in the latter case, the pestle was attached to low tree branches, utlising the spring of the tree to push the pestle up and down to pulverize the grain.

In Japan, these tools are used in traditional ceremonies known as *mochitsuki*, which originate in 300 BCE.

The ancient method begins with whole grains of rice, which are eventually reduced to a flour after a very labour-intensive session of rhythmic pounding by two people. Water, sugar and flavourings are added and eventually *mochi* are formed into small round shapes that fit in the hand. They are unique in their springy texture and eaten at a variety of festivals all year round, especially at New Year. In Korea, they use this tool for *tteok* rice cakes, which are also eaten during ceremonial occasions, sometimes with added fruits, nuts, red beans, sesame seeds or even flowers. Less intensive, modern industrial processes are more common in creating these treats now, but the ritual and ceremony surrounding *mochi* or *tteok* pounding is certainly more entertaining.

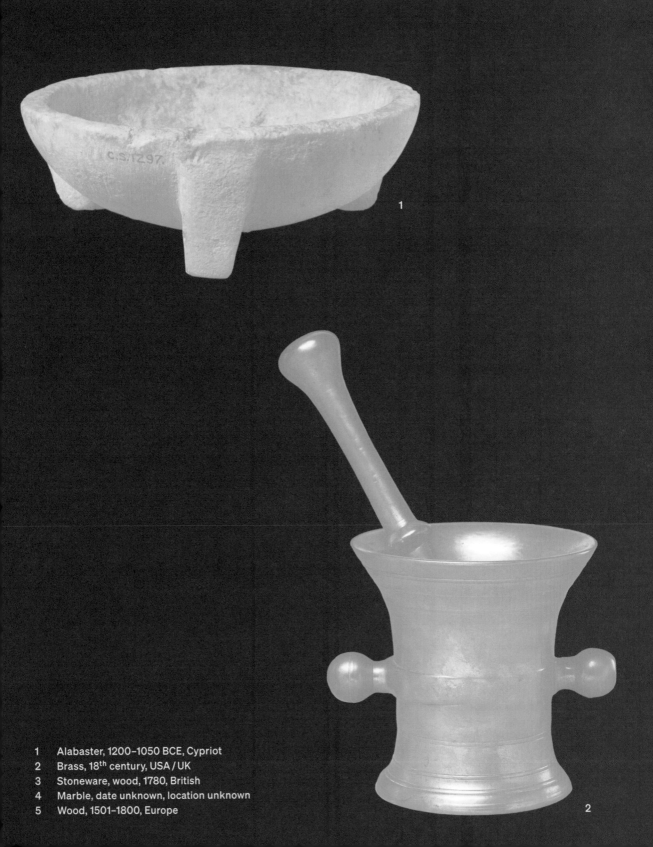

1   Alabaster, 1200–1050 BCE, Cypriot
2   Brass, 18th century, USA / UK
3   Stoneware, wood, 1780, British
4   Marble, date unknown, location unknown
5   Wood, 1501–1800, Europe

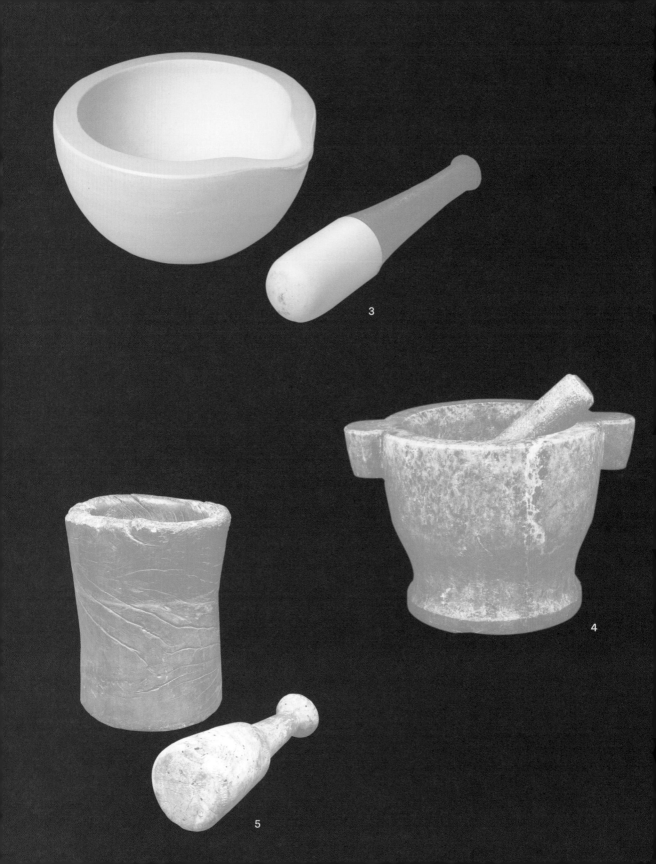

3

4

5

The word mortar comes from the Latin *mortarium*, the name for a shallow mixing bowl. The Romans did indeed use the mortar and pestle frequently, as it was common to serve food with a sauce of herbs and spices ground with tools such as these. The early Roman cookbook *Apicius*, from the 1st century CE, had a whole section of recipes dedicated to 'mortaria'. This tool set has a long and varied history, and it was often used in the context of the apothecary – this is where the archetypal symbol for the chemist derives. Its use in the kitchen goes back thousands of years, since at least 22,000 BCE. Both the mortar and pestle are made from numerous materials in different locations across the globe: marble, olivewood, apricot wood (specific to Greece), lignum vitae hardwood, volcanic rock (specific to South America and Mexico), brass, bronze and also stoneware or porcelain. Mortar and pestles come in various shapes: hexagonal, octagonal, bowl shapes, flat-bottomed, cylindrical, bell-shaped, funnel-shaped, and they sometimes feature a spout to pour out the ground concoctions. They can be set in the ground with human-sized pestles at head height or sit on kitchen countertops.

This tool is used to crush a variety of ingredients, including coffee beans, herbs, spices, salt, sugar (from loaf sugar), nuts, grains, rice flour, as well as for mashing vegetables or pounding meat. Each culture has its own preferred material for the tools. Bronze, brass and iron mortar and pestles were common in the Middle Ages, when they were given as wedding presents as part of a set of cast metal utensils for the new couple. In Spain, they are often made of wood (especially olivewood), with a separate pestle and mortar for processes including garlic. Historically in Europe, even poor households had two mortar and pestles, whereas wealthier estates had a diverse selection of materials and sizes for different purposes. From the 16th century onwards rare, decorated mortar and pestles were made from lignum vitae – one of the hardest woods that exists, originating in the West Indies. In past centuries it was common in France for mortar and pestles to be made of non-porous porcelain, marble in Italy, volcanic rock in Mexico, metal in the Middle East, and wood in many parts of Africa. In Japan, textured stoneware mortars (*suribachi*) were used with pepperwood pestles.

Suribachi translates as 'grinding stone' from Japanese, and is accompanied by its pestle, the *surikogi*. It is distinct from other mortar and pestles throughout the world due to the grooved lines within the fired clay bowl, called *kushi-no-me*, meaning 'comb'. These ridges are carved by hand and the vessel is usually glazed so that flavours do not transfer between uses. The wooden *surikogi* is used to grind ingredients against its surface and is made from a reasonably soft material that keeps the clay grooves intact. Often the *surikogi* is made of pepperwood, which is said to impart its flavour to the ground food. These tools are made throughout the country at traditional kilns in Japan, although there is a high concentration of workshops in the Gifu Prefecture. The *suribachi* pictured here is made of Bizenware in one of the Six Ancient Kilns of the country (at Bizen City); the objects made of local clay undergo a firing process of ten days.

This type of pestle and mortar was brought to Japan from southern China and is used to grind a variety of pastes and foods such as sesame, miso and daikon radish. The *suribachi* has an accompanying cleaning brush made of bamboo; its fine bristles can get into the grooves to clean the tool for its next use.

↑ **Metate, Since 1st century CE, Central America, Designer unknown, Basalt**

The *metate* is used across Central America, and the one pictured here is an ancient ritualistic example adorned with a bird's head from the 3rd to 7th centuries CE. Historically in Costa Rica highly decorated metates adorned with lizards, birds or jaguars were used for sacred meals and ceremonies, but simple everyday versions also exist for domestic preparations across Latin America. These tools are very common in Mexico, where two main grinding devices are used, both made from lava stone: the *metate* and *molcajete* or *tejolote*. The latter resembles well-known forms of mortar and pestle, while the former (pictured) has a curved flat shape, which is most useful for grinding corn into meal and flour, kneading dough for tortillas, or crushing ingredients to add to sauces. The main difference between the two tools is that a horizontal back-and-forth motion is used in the *metate*, while a vertical rotation is used in a *molcajete*. The *metate* is accompanied by a 'mano', a tool like a rolling pin that grinds foods across the abrasive lava-stone surface. This is one of the oldest primitive tools from Central America and is still used to date.

↓   **Poi pounder (pohaku ku'i poi), 18th / 19th centuries, Hawaii, Maker unknown, Stone**

The poi pounder comes in a few shapes, from stirrup-like to flared bell forms with round handles, and it is made of stone or local lava rock (basalt). The tool is used to ground boiled taro (known as *poi* or *kalo* in the native Hawaiian language) into purple-tinted mash on wooden boards called *papa ku'i'ai*. The consistency of the result varies from thick to thin, described in three stages as one finger (the thickest) down to three fingers (the runniest). Taro has been a staple in Hawaii for centuries, having been brought to the island by migrating Polynesians. Traditionally the kalo plant is highly revered by native people, admired as a life-giving force that at one time provided work in farming for a quarter of the population. Though cultivation of the plant has severely decreased since the 18th and 19th centuries, there is a renewed interest among young people in restoring their heritage by farming the nourishing *kalo*.

↓ **Bamboo grater, Date unknown, China, Designer unknown, Bamboo**

The extent of bamboo craft in Asia is vast, and this is one of many tools for food made from this versatile material. This grater differs from the 'Western' typology, as instead of holes to grate the food, the raised teeth of bamboo cut the ingredients into fine pieces. In a ladder-like formation these serrated slats held in a frame structure are used to grate ginger, radishes (daikon / mooli) and other similarly textured ingredients. Grating ginger as opposed to chopping it will give a stronger flavour and help blend it into other textures. The construction of the object is straightforward and could almost be crafted by anyone with bamboo and a knife or basic workshop tools. This tool always comes with two legs to stand on, so the last rungs can be used effectively before the ingredient hits the countertop from the downward motion. Though this tool grates wet foods, bamboo does not rot or warp despite being a natural material. These types of bamboo graters are made and used particularly in China and Japan.

→ **Graters, Since 16th century, France / USA / Worldwide, François Bouiller / J. W. Taylor, Various metals**

The first metal grater is attributed to a Frenchman called François Bouiller, who created it to get through old cheese and prevent food waste. When formerly young cheese went hard, it would be used in cooking and needed to be in small enough pieces to melt. Natural coarse surfaces such as animal skins or ceramics were used before the grater was introduced, and the first 16th-century designs involved rudimentary punched holes in curved pieces of metal. In the 18th century, graters were made of tin, known as tinware, and sometimes sold from 'floating tinshops' – salesmen selling graters, cake cutters and other useful utensils made from the versatile metal. Tin graters were punched, first by hand with a rolled edge around an iron frame, and eventually by machine with pressed seams. Tin has now been replaced by aluminium and stainless steel, as the former metal is too weak and brittle compared to other alloys.

In the late 19th century, an American J. W. Taylor evolved the grater as we know it today, with elongated sharp holes of varying sizes. They are created by punching multiple holes in sheet metal, pressing one side of the hole upwards, and sharpening the edges. The hole size and shape varies depending on the food to be grated, whether cheese, citrus zest or vegetables.

Countries around the world have their own purposes for graters, and these are usually adapted to be specialist tools. In the Caribbean, they grate more coconut than cheese; in Eastern Europe they often grate potatoes for pancake-type dishes; in Asia they can be used to grate ginger or other roots such as daikon radish.

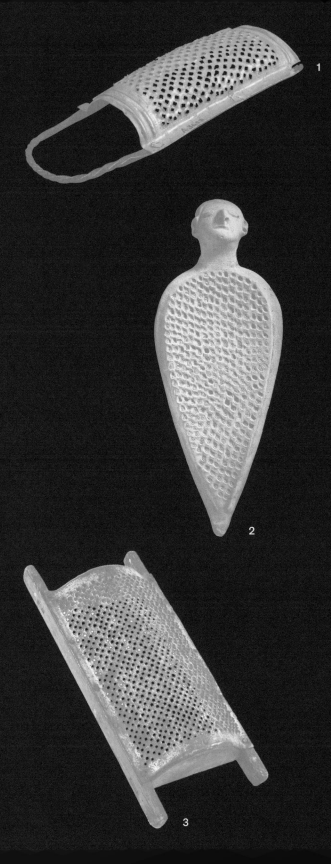
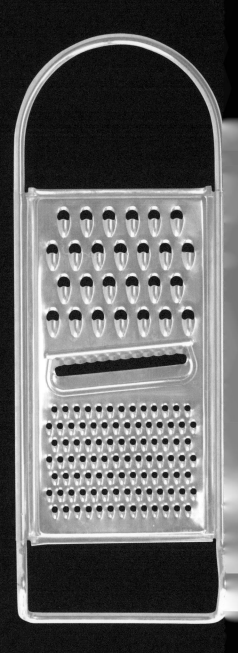

1   Brass, Sweden, 1760–1810
2   Ceramic, South America, 500 BCE–500
3   Steel, location unknown, date unknown
4   Stainless steel, France, 20th century

→ **Microplane®, 1994, Canada / USA, Lorraine Lee /
Richard Grace, Stainless steel, plastic**

The Microplane® is an expert tool for the domestic
kitchen, making the lightest work of zesting citrus fruits
or creating extra thin grates of cheese. Like the bread
rasp, it takes its cues from the workshop, and the creator
of the Microplane® describes the transition just so.
A homemaker, Lorraine Lee, cooking an orange cake,
was frustrated by the lack of razor sharpness in a
kitchen utensil that was destined for zesting, so she
picked up a woodworking tool and found it completed
the task better than anything in her drawer.

The tool Lorraine Lee originally picked up was produced
by a woodworking tool manufacturer, who had invented
a unique photo-etch production process to create
ultra-sharp blades. It took the ingenuity of Lee to see
the tool's potential, and this change of context for their
product altered the history of the company forever.
The refined design has many razor-sharp, stainless-
steel blades on a long rectangular form held by a
handle. The sales of kitchen utensils by Microplane®
now well outstrip their woodworking tools. So iconic
is the tool that its name has become a metonym
synonymous with its function and describes the object
itself, whether made by the original company or
knock-off brands.

↑ Oroshiki sharkskin grater, Since the Edo Period (1603–1868), Japan, Designer unknown, Wood, sharkskin

Made specifically for grating wasabi, daikon or ginger, the sharkskin *oroshiki* has been in use since the Edo Period in Japan. This utilitarian tool was likely discovered as a byproduct of consuming shark meat. Made with shark or ray skin (*samegawa*) and traditionally mounted on hinoki wood, these graters come in two different levels of coarseness. To grate, the ingredient is pressed over the skin in a circular motion – the slightly larger texture is for daikon or tubers, whereas the very fine-textured skin is used for more delicate ginger and wasabi. The cells of wasabi must be broken into finer parts to bring out the spice and flavour, and the enamel-like texture of the sharkskin is ideal for creating these velvety green dollops. Sharkskin graters are less common today for various practical reasons, but some chefs swear by the unique and unrivalled texture produced from these traditional tools.

↑ Oroshigane, Since 19th century, Japan, Designer unknown, Tin-plated copper

This is a modern and man-made version of the shark-skin grater, and again differs from standard Western graters as they are a specialised tool for vegetables. Rather than having punched-through holes, these metal graters have spikes hammered out of the surface to act as the abrasive surface. The finest versions of these graters are handcrafted from tin-plated copper and have a unique two-toned shine of silver and salmon-coloured buffed metal hues. As with many Japanese tools and kitchen utensils, these are tools for life, and can be taken for repair, sharpening and reconditioning. The *oroshigane* will look brand-new when repaired and is an essential utensil in the kitchen for grating daikon radish, ginger and wasabi. Like the *suribachi*, the *oroshigane* can be cleaned with delicate bamboo brushes that are designed specifically for the task.

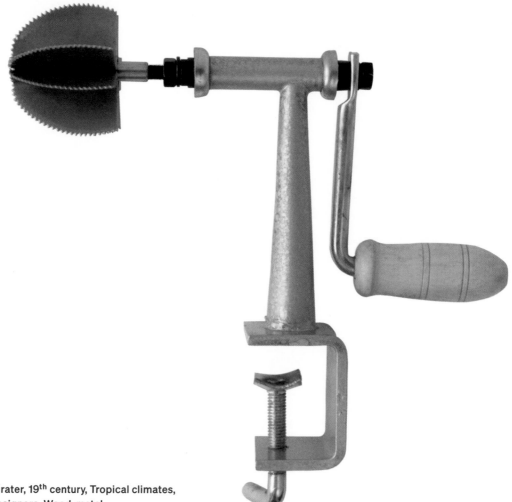

↑ **Coconut grater, 19ᵗʰ century, Tropical climates, Various designers, Wood, metal**

Coconut graters are a familiar tool and form in tropical countries where mature coconut flesh is used in local cuisines. On the west coast of India, they tend to be all metal, sometimes topping the tops of boti knives; in East Asia or the Caribbean, they are mostly a stand-alone tool. In Thailand, they are called *katai*, in Indonesia a *kukur kelapa mbuzi*, and in Zanzibar *mbuzi*, and are usually mounted on a plank of wood, with the one-dimensional grater spike at one end. These coconut graters can be as simple as one starburst form cut out of a flat piece of metal, or two to six of these forms slotted together to make a three-dimensional shredder. Contemporary versions are of this 3D kind, usually tin-plated and mounted on tabletops with a handle that spins the metal starburst form to grate coconut flesh out of its hard hairy shell. Some highly decorated, carved, wooden coconut-grating benches are crafted in Indonesia, Malaysia and Thailand, taking on the forms of animals such as rabbits or dragons.

↓   **Spice mill, Since 18th century, Greece / Turkey, Designer unknown, Brass**

These brass spice and coffee mills are familiar in Greece and Turkey, and recognisable by their distinctive tall brass form and protruding cranking handle. Legend has it that they originated from the need for Greek armies to grind coffee on the go, to make sure they were properly caffeinated for their days on the battlefield. The internal grinding cogs of this burr mill are usually made of hand-forged steel with the outer casing in brass, often ornamented with engraved patterns. The top half holds the spice or coffee, and the bottom half collects the ground ingredient; the size of the desired grind is adjustable, allowing for the very fine Turkish coffee powder for which the culture is known. The Greek company Atlas manufactures these brass mills to this day, having done so for 300 years or more.

Wooden spice mills are more common in Western Europe, and made of oak, maplewood, walnut, mahogany and more. Peugeot – the car maker – is one of the most well-known brands of peppermills, having patented their peppermill gear system and design in 1842. The case-hardened steel inside cracks the peppercorns before they are ground, allowing for a more streamlined grinding process and result.

This sesame seed grinder is a staple in kitchens and on tables of ramen restaurants. It is a design icon, instantly recognisable by its red lid, and blends into the landscape of any ramen joint. It is used to grind sesame seeds on top of noodle soup, but can also grind other small seeds such as flax. To operate, you turn the device upside down and rotate the handle round and round to grind the sesame which falls upon the bowl of noodles.

Japan is the biggest consumer of sesame, or *goma*, in the world. There are three main types of sesame: black, white and golden. They use it to make pastes for sauces, dressings and spice mixes, as a topping, to make ice cream, or use the oil to cook with, among other purposes.

Nutmeg originates from the Moluccan islands of Indonesia, which the Dutch conquered in 1667. For about 150 years the Dutch had a monopoly on this spice and many others from their 'spice islands'. In the 18th century the French introduced *Myristica fragrans* trees to Mauritius, and the East India Company propagated the tree and its spices in Penang, Malaysia.

Like many ingredients and spices that emerged as a result of colonialism (sugar, chilli, cinnamon, coffee, nutmeg, mace, pepper), various fads ensued, and once introduced to European society in the 17th century, nutmeg was seemingly grated on every food or drink. So much so that individual nutmeg graters were desirable decorative objects, destined for the pockets of wealthy, ultra-cultured society. Tools like this are fascinating when imagining the period of time where everything must have tasted of the new-fangled nutmeg and flavours introduced from the Orient. Originally these elaborate nutmeg graters were made my craftspeople and metal-workers, but eventually their popularity led to mass manufacture. By the mid-19th century mechanical nutmeg graters were on the market, along with a general burst of other mechanised implements for the kitchen. The 'coffin-type' nutmeg grater is the most common type in the kitchen today, a specialist grater for this individual ingredient.

1

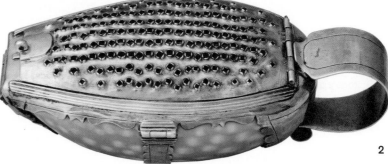

2

3

1 Fishskin, silver, Europe, date unknown
2 Silver, cowrie shell, British, 1690
3 Silver, Europe, date unknown

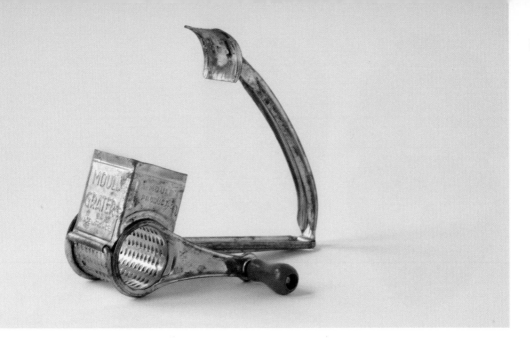

↑ **Rotary grater, 1940s, France,**
Moulinex, Aluminium

→ **Moulinex food mill, 1934, France,**
Jean Mantelet, Aluminium, wood

If there is another European country grating as much cheese as France, it may be Italy. This tool for food is often described as a Parmesan grater, though technically it is just a cheese grater, produced by Moulinex in France. The head of the company, Jean Mantelet, registered a patent for this rotary drum grater in 1947. It is a familiar utensil for compactly shredding cheese (especially Parmesan) in the kitchen or at the table. The two-part tool can be easily dismantled for cleaning, with a grating drum and handle that comes out of the main body which clamps the cheese. Though there are Italian brands that produce these utensils, by the time this was released in the early 20th century, Moulinex of France was dominating the European market with its 'Mouli grater'. Eventually the design was made in plastic, but the full metal version is the real design icon, a familiar and useful kitchen utensil for lovers of Parmigiano Reggiano.

Jean Mantelet's vegetable food mill became a bestseller in France after he registered his patent and began producing this essential French kitchen utensil. By the beginning of the 1930s he had already shifted two million of these tools, and in the 1950s his Moulinex brand – which had diversified its range – was selling 100 million units. It all started with his wife's unsatisfactory mash, with advertisements in *Paris Match* in the 1960s quoting: 'Because Mrs Mantelet's Mash Was Lumpy, Moulinex Has Become Number 1 in Europe'.

The Moulin Legumes (vegetable mill) is instantly recognisable in any French kitchen and is used to purée vegetables for soups or fruits for coulis. In the 1960s the tool was declared a liberator of women (from the kitchen), with their slogan 'Moulinex libère la femme!' Electric versions were inevitably invented, but many kitchens and chefs prefer the manual kind. There are many designs for food mills across the globe, but this is a design icon with its familiar form and distinct graphic design, pressed in relief into the handle of the tool.

It would seem that after his initial successes Jean Mantelet became slightly obsessed with grinding and grating devices; he holds about one hundred patents for designs of utensils that perform these functions, from spice and pepper mills to rotary cheese graters to coffee grinders.

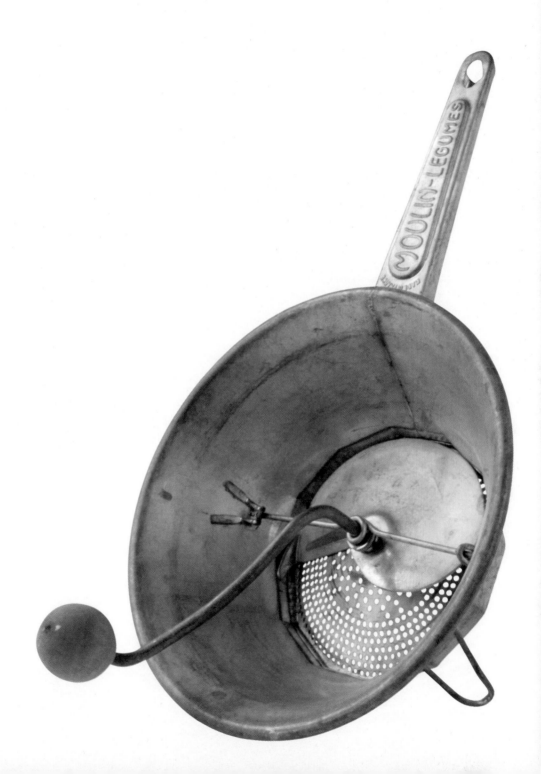

Mix & Stir

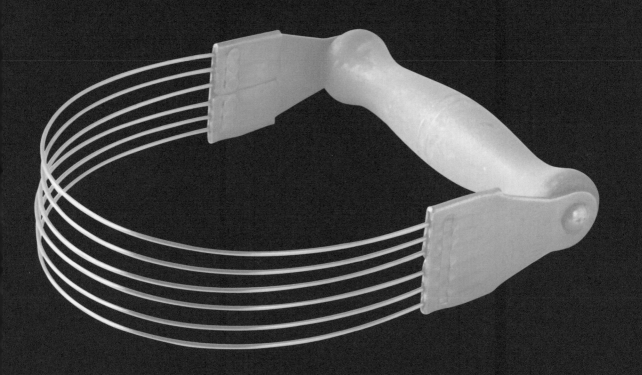

A half-mixed batter or dough is unsatisfactory – there is only so much a twig can achieve before a more refined tool is needed. Beyond our hands, we need tools for mixing, mashing, stirring, whipping, beating … thus, the wide array of wooden spoons, whisks, beaters, stampers, mashers, mixers and stirrers that have been designed over the centuries.

Some of the most technical aspects of cooking take place with these actions: whipping eggs in copper bowls for stiff white peaks, airing up cream into snowy mountains, foaming sauces for haute cuisine. This is where the magic happens, where ingredients come together, chemical reactions take place, the beginnings of cake batters, chocolate drinks and churned butter. As such, precisely shaped utensils are a necessity, matched with material suitability for ultimate performance. There is a reasonable amount of considered science behind tools such as whisks, eggbeaters and the like, and it's no wonder such a wide array of patents exist for these types of utensils.

Many of the principles of mixing and stirring are similar, but each tool has its own modifications depending on where and what in the world is being prepared. Important considerations influence the shapes, such as ergonomics and the direction in which the hand or wrist is working when performing these tasks. For instance, in North America and Western Europe potatoes are mashed, which requires hardy, open-structure implements to pulverise large tubers. Yet in Central and South America, the requirements for mashing beans in a similar fashion calls for a larger surface area of the mashing implement, with small holes to fragment the beans further into a smooth purée. Batters or sauces may require silky smooth textures, and so a slotted spoon is best to run through the mixture, while porridges require a bit more drag, so a thistle-shaped spurtle or blade-shaped mush stick is best.

One tool that takes us to the beginning of the culinary arts and will remain with us into the future is the wooden spoon. It is a truly humble yet necessary kitchen tool, omni-present in every kitchen throughout the world and will never go out of fashion. Wooden spoons don't impart flavours to food, they don't scrape pans as metal might, they can be created in any shape through the carve of a knife, lovingly crafted or mass-produced. One may think that the shape of a spoon is singularly archetypal, but there is a remarkable diversity of form in wooden kitchen spoons throughout the world. Tools that are now made of metal or plastic often started their life as a wooden or natural-fibre version, such as the twig whisk. Nevertheless, material innovations will always invoke the want and need for the new, and sometimes do, in fact, make work in the kitchen more efficient. From sycamore dairy bowls to rubber-footed melamine Margrethe mixing bowls, will our needs never cease to evolve in the kitchen?

The *holzstampfer* or 'wooden masher' is common to
Northern and Eastern Europe and is used to mash
potatoes and purées, tamp pastry into dishes and
butter into moulds, and stamp foods like sauerkraut
or other pickles into their fermenting jars. When
mashing, the bottom curved shape follows the edge
of the pan, ensuring no morsel is left un-mashed in
what effectively becomes a large pestle and mortar.
Though many mashers in use today are of the metal
variety, this traditional form can still be purchased
both brand new and antique.

These mashers are also found in North America as
a result of Northern and Eastern European emigration
to the United States, where the utensil is known as a
'beetle'. In Spain they are made of poplar wood; in Cuba
a similar tool is used for muddling limes for mojitos,
and they bear a likeness to the Middle Eastern kibbeh
pounder made of apricot wood, which is used to make
a paste of lamb and bulgur wheat. There is a vibrant
community of antique wooden masher collectors,
intrigued by the variety of seductive forms that are
unique to each craftsman who turns them on the lathe.

The wooden spoon is one of the most primitive yet
relatable and universal tools; their natural, non-abrasive
and non-heat-conducting properties means they will
always be omnipresent in the kitchen. Logically the
mixing of foods would have been done with an
improvised tree branch at first, until man began to
take care and carve these kitchen tools more precisely.
These stirrers are rarely found in archaeological digs,
as they were discarded after being well-used – after
thousands of years the organic material degrades.

In different countries, there are ever so slightly
different shapes of wooden spoons for the kitchen,
a manifestation of diverse cultures with differing forms
around the world. Each wooden spoon holds a story,
a purpose: it may be elongated, truncated, shaped for
beauty or for use – such as a hole in the spoon for
stirring sauce. They are made from particular woods
and bear their stories of use: stained with grease or
spices or burned on the edges.

Though most wooden spoons are now mass-
manufactured, there is an enthusiastic community
of spoon carvers across the globe, making a living from
this humble act. Something about this most basic
function, using a basic and readily available material,
brings an innate desire in some to carve their own.
It is a craft that consumes woodworkers and hobbyists,
connecting them to a methodical yet personal realisation
of the human touch.

'We have (though not all at once, of course) eaten the
missing part mixed up in our soup. It is continual use
that has given the spoon its new shape. This is the shape
the saucepan has made by constantly rubbing away at
the spoon until it eventually shows us what shape a spoon
for stirring soup should be.'
— Bruno Munari, *Design as Art* (1966)

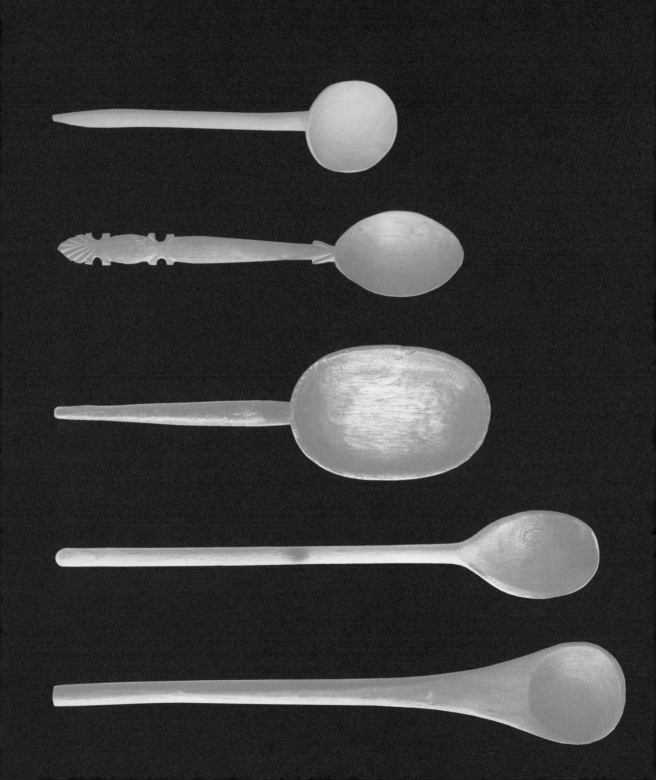

← **Spurtle, Since 15ᵗʰ century, Scotland,
Designer unknown, Wood**

The spurtle is a wooden tool traditionally made of
beech, cherry, elm or maple and is designed to stir
stews, broths and porridge. Originating in Scotland,
the form mimics the Scottish thistle plant, whose
unique shape stirs mixtures evenly without lumps or
the dragging experienced with a standard shaped
spoon. They are particularly useful for mixing porridge,
and prior to this form they had a flat, scraper-like shape
at the end, made of iron. The spurtle is also known as
a 'tweevil' and in the United States, a 'spurdle' (spelled
with a 'd'). In the 17ᵗʰ century, grain-based porridges
were a staple food for the poor; warming bowls of boiled
oats served with butter and honey were even sold by
street vendors. Porridge is known as 'crowdie' in Scotland
and 'flummery' (*llymru*) in Wales, and superstition
demands that it must be stirred in a clockwise motion
to ward off evil spirits. In the annual 'World Porridge
Making Championship' in the Cairngorms, Scotland,
winners are awarded with a golden spurtle trophy for
stirring up the best porridge made only with oats,
water and salt.

← **Molinillo, Since 17th century, Mexico,
Designer unknown, Wood, inlay**

These *molinillo* chocolate frothers were crafted and refined around the 16th and 17th centuries after the Spanish had colonised South and Central America and popularised the ingredient and drink around the world. In fact, 'chocolate houses' opened before coffee houses, with cocoa being sweetened with honey and vanilla, and sometimes coloured with annatto (achiote seed) to make the drink red. In England, in the 17th century, cocoa was mixed with egg yolks, sugar and wine, for a drink known as *chaculato*.

The ritual drinking of chocolate has been around for thousands of years – sacred cocoa (*cacahuatl* in the Nahuatl language) was revered by the Aztec Moctezuma who drank the speciality from gold cups. Centuries later, chocolate was banned for women, and only upper-class men or royalty could consume the drink. From the 17th century, hot chocolate was crafted and frothed with these elaborate tools whose name translates as 'little mill'. Larger molinillo were used to prepare the concoctions in the kitchen, while smaller, individual-sized stirrers were used at the table. Before modern processing, the fat of chocolate was not homogenised and therefore the drink had to be constantly stirred to remain mixed. The sliding rings on these molinillos ensure a good froth, as the tool is twisted back and forth in the palms in a rubbing motion. Now this tool is most widely crafted and used in Mexico, where they sweeten cocoa with flavours of cinnamon, almond and cloves, prepared and frothed with boiling water. The molinillo pictured here is from the 20th century, stained and hand-carved with Bakelite inlays.

↓ **Butter churn, 19th century, Sweden
(pictured), Maker unknown, Wood, iron**

The cream skimmed from the top of milk would have
been put in this wooden container to be vigorously
churned with its dasher – the rod that was raised up
and down to create friction in the churn. After about
twenty minutes or more the cream turns to butter, and
the buttermilk separated from the fat is the byproduct.
Butter churns took many forms and could be made
from materials such as metal, earthenware and wood.
They came in various forms such as the plunger-type
seen here that used an up-and-down motion; the
paddle churn which was rotated with an external
handle; or as is common in India and still used today,
ropes that twist the paddle within the container through
push and pulling. Surviving examples primarily exist
from countries producing and consuming butter (rather
than oil), such as Europe and the USA.

Butter was an important source of fat and nourishment,
especially for the lower classes, and a way to use the
different components of cow's milk. These tools differ
from the milk churn, which is used purely to store and
transport milk.

↑ Twig whisk, 1814, Scandinavia (pictured),
Man the Maker, Birch

Moving on from a single wooden branch for stirring,
it was discovered that smoother textures could be
achieved by integrating air into a mixture with a bundle
of several smaller sticks. In Sweden and Scandinavia,
these whisks are still used today, and are known as a
visp. Made of birch twigs, they are surprisingly robust,
mostly water-repellent, and can smooth out sauces,
though are not necessarily the best choice for whipping
up cream. They are usually about 30 cm (12 in) in length;
however, the one pictured here (top) is over 50 cm (20 in)
long, described as a 'bridal whisk' made for the occasion.
These tools are as simple as they sound: twigs bundled
together and bound at the top. The Shakers in America
used peach-tree twigs to infuse the flavour of the sap
into their mixtures. Though they may seem primitive,
these tools are actually very useful on non-stick pans
that cannot withstand metal utensils.

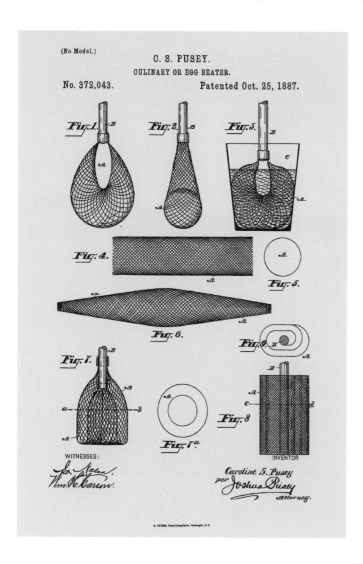

↑ **Eggbeater, 1887, USA, Caroline S. Pusey,**
Elastic wire, metal

Whisking before metal eggbeaters was done with twig whisks, or tools resembling chocolate mills (*molinillos*) whose primitive form was a wooden stick with a cog or starburst shape at one end; this task was greatly helped by the discovery of copper bowls (with chefs noting that it was quicker to whisk whites in these rather than in ceramic containers). Some chefs were even known to repeatedly squeeze egg whites through sponges to achieve the desired airy quality.

Between 1856 and 1902 no less than 692 patents for eggbeaters were registered. Here Caroline Pusey's elastic wire beater of 1887 purports 'exquisite beating with surprising rapidity and perfection.' After the *Great Exhibition* of 1851, the world was going wild for newfangled tools for new modern life. In particular, there were many designs for mechanical versions of eggbeaters in the 19th century. Beating egg whites into peaks was particularly important for baking until this time, as they were the only leavener for cakes until baking powder became available in 1843.

← **Balloon whisk, Since early 20th century, France, Various designers / Inox (pictured), Stainless steel**

Flat whisk, balloon whisk, cherry fruit whisk, magic whisk, plastic whisk … there are many tools for this action, but somehow the one pictured here seems the most familiar design classic. Its design is simple: metal loops are joined in the handle; they are flexible and provide the right amount of aeration for the utensil to function as best it can. They come in sizes as small as 10 cm (4 in) up to 50 cm (20 in) or more. Designs such as these are classified in the patent office as 'comprising mixing wires … of the closed-loop type mounted at the end of a shaft'. The first 'balloon type' such as this one was initially registered in 1896 but was refined to a more minimal design in the early 20th century. Today whisks come in many crazy shapes and sizes or with silicone-coated wires, but the original balloon form is a sturdy icon ideal for whisking tasks.

→ **Batter beater / whip, 1937, USA, Clarence Hess,
Metal, wood**

These batter beaters or whips very closely resemble
what many know as a 'fish slice' for flipping cooking fish
in frying pans. The purposes are interchangeable for
this tool, whose most similar design was registered in
the US Patent Office in 1937. The design is specified for
batter – not eggs or fish – as the fanned metal grate
breaks up lumps, integrates air, and smooths liquid
cake mixtures before baking. The larger the surface
area that comes into contact with the batter, the better,
and its shape is unique for a reason – the inscription
emblazoned on the patented beater declares that it is:
'Carved to fit the bowl'. The light and long metal spatula
also provides the delicate surface required to pick up
easily breakable fish fillets or large food in the frying
pan, which is what the tool is mostly used for today.

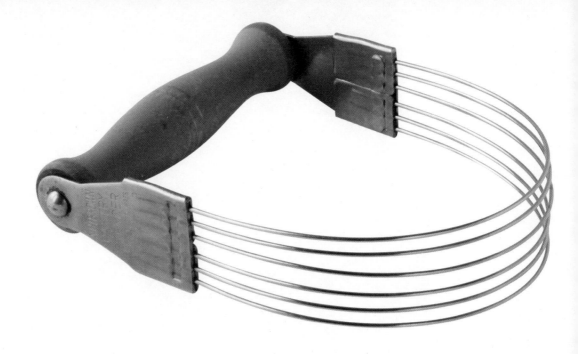

↑ **Pastry blender, 1927, USA, Elmer L. Denis,
Wood, metal**

Although our hands are the most useful and readily
available tools for kitchen processes, many utensil
designs were created to avoid getting them dirty.
Of course, pastry can be blended in the hands, but the
process does benefit from less heat (hence the use of
marble for patisserie countertops), to create biscuits,
pastry, scones and flaky baked goods.

The 'first' pastry blender was designed and patented in
1927, and was subsequently produced by Washburn Co.,
a major American manufacturer of kitchen utensils at the
time. All subsequent versions of this tool that are still
made today basically look the same – a crescent shape
for a rocking motion that fits the shape of the bowl and
parallel metal 'blades' which cut and mix the ingredients
together evenly. The design is effective at breaking
up cold butter or fat into finer and finer pieces before
liquid is added to bind mixtures together. It keeps the
pastry cold, and hands clean.

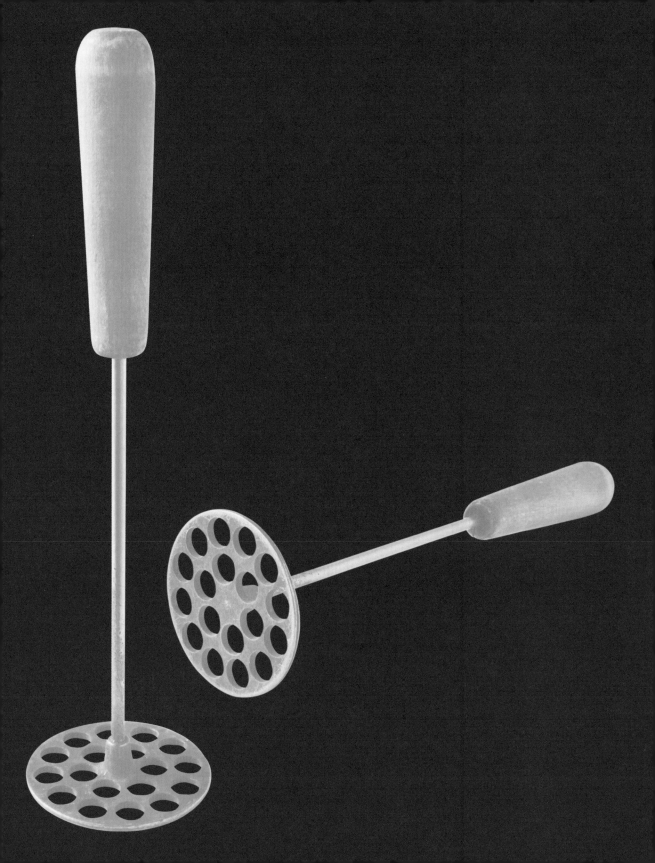

← **Potato / bean masher, Since 19th century, USA / Mexico, Various designers, Metal, wood**

A few methods and utensils are used to mash potatoes, tubers or beans (a *holzstampfer*, potato ricer or even *Moulin Legumes*), and perhaps the most familiar to contemporary kitchens is the wavy-wire metal masher. The first wire masher many recognise was patented in 1886 by a W. J. Johnson; its design is simple, effective and easy to manufacture. Metal mashers – and now plastic ones – also come in a variety of gridded patterns. Bean mashers (which can also be used for potatoes) allow the purée to be pressed through suitably sized holes, whose action breaks down the foods in the process. These bean mashers are common in Mexico for puréeing refried pinto beans and other soft ingredients. Historically bean mashers were made of wood, but now are constructed from a simple piece of stamped sheet metal attached to a handle above.

↑ **Mini-masher, 21st century, Japan, Designer unknown, Stainless steel**

These mini-mashers assist in making small quantities of purées in small containers. They solve the struggle involved when using a normal fork to mash mini amounts of food together: perhaps guacamole, baby food or avocados for toast. The mini-masher has adapted the archetype of a fork for the ergonomics of this task – the top provides a rest for the palm to exert mashing force, the bend at the bottom provides additional strength for manoeuvring, and the outer tines of the fork have been rotated 90 degrees for efficient mashing and scraping, and to prevent bits getting stuck in between. The mini-masher is a simple yet complex adaptation that fills this previously unmet need.

Dairy bowls were used to settle milk overnight so the cream could separate, to be skimmed off with a brass skimmer in the morning. Sycamore is a common wood used for dairy production tools, as it does not give any flavour to foods prepared on or within it. Usually, bowls in the kitchen were used for various preparations, but those for dairy were kept entirely separate. Any tools used to produce butter or cheese were sterilised with boiling salted water to prevent unwanted bacteria in the final product.

These antiques are classified as treenware, the name given to functional objects made of trees (wood). This particular sycamore dairy bowl is unique in that it has been patched with brass, reminiscent of a time when people respected and repaired objects for use rather than throwing them away. Some rarer versions, known as burl bowls, are made from the burls on trees, the cancerous bulbous growths seen on London planes, sycamore, ash trees and more. The wood of burls, no matter which species of tree, is extremely dense due to the pattern of growth – a writhing and twisting process. This density also makes the wood resistant to splitting, making it hardy to work with and hardy to use as a functional – or treen – object.

↑ **Margrethe bowls, Designed 1950, released 1954,
Sweden, Jacob Jensen with Acton Björn and
Sigvard Bernadotte, Melamine**

Although melamine in its early stages was first invented in the 1830s, it didn't come into its own in the domestic sphere until the 20th century. The material was, in fact, developed in response to the need to replace diminishing natural materials such as ivory or tortoise shell. As a urea-formaldehyde plastic, melamine proved to be much more robust than other plastics that had been developed in the early 20th century.

Meanwhile in Sweden, Jacob Jensen, who was working for plastics firm Rosti, and Acton Björn and Sigvard Bernadotte who had their own industrial design consultancy, were dreaming up new forms and uses for the material. Through studying the needs and functions

of mixing bowls, the trio realised that what may be useful was an unmovable base, a spout to pour out ingredients, a handle to grip while mixing, and various sizes of bowls that could be stacked to save space in the cupboard. In contrast to plastic, melamine gives the weight and sturdiness these bowls need (yet are lighter than the common earthenware bowl), as well as resistance to heat. So emerged the distinctive design of these nesting mixing bowls with non-slip rubber rings at the base. Originally, they came in just three sizes and a choice of white, pastel green, yellow or blue, but now more sizes and a variety of colours have been added to the range. The Margrethe bowls are named after the Danish princess of the time, who had recently been crowned Queen.

Compress & Form

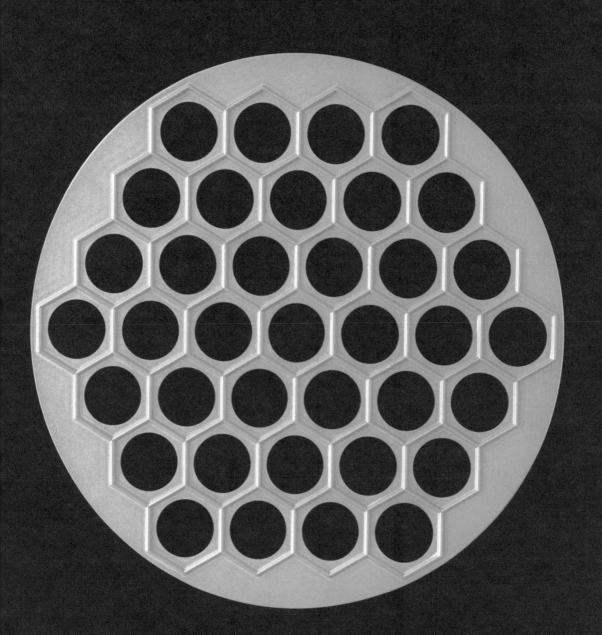

The tools in this chapter require a compression action, downward force or upward rise: squeezing with levers, compressing pulps, pounding forms, cutting cookies, or encouraging flutes in rising doughs. These tools come in all shapes and sizes, all materials, and use various mechanical means to crush shells or remove moulds safely from delicate forms. The materials speak of moments in time and industrial development; some instances show where tradition has endured, others where evolution and innovation rule with ceramic and wooden tools replaced with metal or silicone forms.

Through the quick action of squeezing, preparation time is shortened, perhaps by a garlic press (sometimes known as a garlic crusher), tortilla press or lemon squeezer. Inaccessible foods that were previously opened with stone hammers by *homo erectus* are now elegantly crushed with designer nut crackers. Lemons are tortured and their juice extracted by various methods of screwing, levered compression or boring with conical reamers. Meats that would otherwise be tough to chew (excessive chewing being a waste of valuable brain and activity time) are pounded to break down their fibres and tenderise them.

Forming devices and moulds are not a *necessary* part of cooking, but what is life without the development of arts, inventions for edible centrepieces, minds running free to sculpt and compose a dish, or an architecture of jellies? What is dining without pomp and circumstance, fluted pies, cloud-shaped brioches, moulded marzipan or ginger biscuits? For culinary and gastronomic artists, the form and presentation of food is the place to leave one's mark – as an indicator of product or master chef.

The tools that form our foods are very much *designed*, crafted as expressions of art and sculpture. The moulding and forming of foods often go hand in hand with molecular innovations, such as the discovery of gelatinous jellies or the freezing of ice cream that calls for playful shapes. As such, the tools in this chapter are some of the most intriguing, where a maker's mark or inventor's idea is clearly conveyed. For instance, a waffle iron is designed to cook batter in a particular fashion: crispy ridges and deep wells to collect butter and syrup. A butter stamp embodies indicators of the landscape, farm or household crest, or allows a producer's product to be recognised by repeat customers at farmers' markets. Formed biscuit and vegetable cutters allow us to ornament our creations with aesthetic intention, whether for children's lunchboxes or extravagant cakes. These tools integrate visual aesthetics in cuisine and tell the story of the importance of presentation in the ritual of mealtimes.

↑ Tenderiser, 20th century, Worldwide,
 Various designers, Metal, wood

Meat can be tenderised by a few methods: pounding,
piercing or treating with acidic ingredients such as
wine, vinegar or citrus. Manual meat tenderisers were
first made of wood – like a blunt instrument or weapon
– and the multifarious *holzstampfer* would have been
a predecessor. Eventually the heavier and more robust
properties of metal gave way. These tenderisers are
also known as meat mallets, pounders or clubs. Some
resemble carpenter's mallets, which is possibly where
they originated, as the endless array of tools whose use
has been transferred from the workshop.

Metal tenderisers often come with two sides, one with
pyramid-like shapes to get into the fibres of the muscle,
while the other side is flat to create a smooth surface
for beating schnitzels or other thin pieces of meat.
Some are like hammers or axes with a brutal, blade-like
side for breaking down meat fibres. Like the wooden
spoon, meat tenderisers come in all shapes and sizes,
varying by culture and location throughout the world.
Kibbeh pounders from the Middle East resemble the
holzstampfer; Scandinavian ones have an extra axe-
shaped side for breaking up bones: these tools are
especially useful when a tougher cut of meat, such as
reindeer, is used and the fibres need breaking down with
a good pounding. Today butchers run meat through
tenderising machines, though these clubs are still
a useful tool in the domestic kitchen.

↓   **Batte / Pounder, 20th century, France / Italy, Designer unknown, Metal**

In France this tool is known as a *batte* (pounder) and has a thicker middle that tapers at the edges of its rectangular form. Also called a cutlet bat, these tools can weigh about 1 kg (2 lb 4 oz), and easily flatten small morsels of food, meat or seafood such as scallops. Italian kitchens utilise a rectangular-shaped tool for flattening veal or chicken, and even crushing garlic. Other European cutlet mallets come in square or round, heavy, metal forms with offset handles that allow for pounding with a flick of the wrist. These tools differ slightly from the standard meat pounder (see page opposite) in that they are particularly used for flattening cuts of meat, rather than just tenderising.

↓ **Tortilla press (Máquina tortilladora), Since 19th century, Mexico, Various designers, Cast aluminium**

Tortillas are a staple of the Mexican diet, and the process eventually needed streamlining since they are consumed with almost every meal. Before the tortilla press, they were rolled out by hand (and some still are) with a rolling pin (*palote para tortillas*), much like chapatis in India or other flatbread doughs that require firm pressing before cooking. Often tortillas are bought fresh daily from a local torilleria, but if homemade, this labour-saving device is a necessity.

The tortilla press works with the principle of lever and compression to flatten rounds of dough (*masa*), which are commonly made of cornmeal. The force exerted between two flat rounds produces near perfect circles for this essential vehicle for taco ingredients. Typically, these presses are made of heavy cast iron, the weight of which aids the process, or cast aluminium; some of the earliest versions were made of wood. A similar tool is used to press roti breads in India. In contemporary kitchens two pieces of plastic protect the dough on both sides when pressed and clamped; originally corn husks were used. Once cooked, tortillas are kept warm in beautifully crafted baskets known as *chiquihuite*.

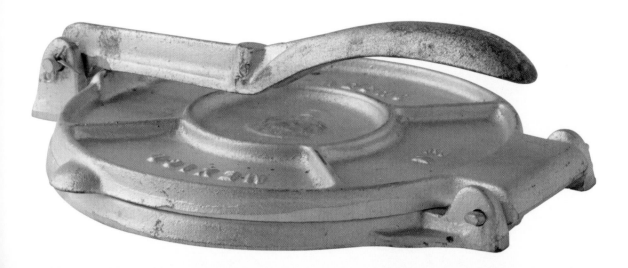

↑ **Potato ricer, Since 1887, USA, J. Fitzgerald and W. H. Silver, Stainless steel**

Potato ricers are essential for making super-smooth purées (especially for gnocchi) and are also used to squeeze excess liquid from steamed vegetables such as spinach. These tools are quicker and easier to use than drum or horsehair sieves for making purées. The potato ricer design is simple to squeeze, a utensil that forms part of the large collection of mid-20th century tools made of aluminium. By the 1950s, sleek, minimal versions were manufactured, especially by the Italian brand Cocco, though the 'first' and original design for such a device was patented in 1887. They are called potato ricers because the cooked potato is reduced to rice-like pieces that form a smooth and homogenised purée. These tools work on the same principles as orange squeezers / juicers and can, in fact, be used as such. When a potato ricer is not available, a *Moulin Legumes* will do the job as well, as will a simple masher, but not as thoroughly.

← **Lemon squeezer, Circa 1820, Europe, Designer unknown, Cherrywood, brass**

Over 200 years ago, when citrus was discovered to prevent scurvy and other diseases, juicers for these fruits began to emerge. Some of the first lemon squeezers from the 18th century can be found in Turkey, and these resemble the half-sphere-shaped juicers common today. Lemons were imported to Constantinople in the 17th and 18th centuries, as they were to many places in the world after the fruit was cultivated with intention since the 15th century. In Europe, the first designs of these tools were rudimentary and basic – such as two-hinged bits of wood with corresponding ball and bowl sides to grip the lemon being squeezed. Sometimes the concave side had straining holes where the lemon juice could flow out. The lemon squeezer pictured is a highly decorated and refined example for such a utilitarian tool. Some early designs were made of cast iron, which didn't hold out long as lemon squeezers must be made of acid-resistant materials such as glass, porcelain, robust hardwoods, or enamelled or stainless metals.

↑ **Lemon treen, Circa 1860, England, Designer unknown, Boxwood**

This urn-shaped lemon 'treen' is one of a group of more mechanical tools for food that emerged around the time of, and after, the *Great Exhibition* of 1851, yet this one is handcrafted. A treen is a small, carved wooden object, the term being an early version of the plural of tree. This particular lemon treen was carved from boxwood, which is known for its even texture, natural lustre and resistance to rot – ideal for a wooden tool used for a wet job. Inside the object is a plunger that squeezes the lemon as it is screwed into the body, with the lemon juice delicately trickling out of the spout at the bottom. This was certainly a more sophisticated and elaborate way to juice lemons than the basic clapboard squeezers. Screw-type objects such as this were common in the 19th century, like those made to crack nuts using the same principle.

→ **Reamer, 1930s, USA, Designer unknown,
Uranium glass**

The word 'ream' indicates the boring out of a hole,
which is the action driven by these conical tools.
Reamers can be made from wood, porcelain, glass,
metal (including silver), plastic, and today can be
electric. In the late 18th century, juicing devices and
reamers were produced in Europe, mostly by china
companies such as Meissen (Germany) and Limoges
(France). The USA didn't patent its first reamers until
1867, a couple of years after the end of the American
Civil War. Reamers had a noticeable boost in popularity
from 1907 onwards when a Californian co-op was
formed to promote fruit consumption, in particular
the subsequent 'Drink an Orange' campaign in 1916.

During the Depression, many kitchen items were
made of glass, as metal was reserved for the war effort;
these objects are known fondly as 'glassware of the
Depression era.' Many producers began experimenting
with the different colours of glass they could achieve
by adding things such as lead for blue and metal oxides
or uranium for green, sometimes known as 'vaseline
glass'. Uranium had been used for colouring in Europe
since the 1840s, but the proliferation of glass production
during the wars in the early 20th century made it more
prevalent. From 1947 the use of uranium became
highly regulated, and this type of glass was no longer
manufactured until restrictions were lifted in 1958.
Uranium glass made after this time was safer, as it
used depleted stock rather than the radioactive kind.
When under a black light, this glass glows neon.

↓   **Orange juicer, Circa mid-20th century, UK,
Designer unknown (Instant No 1), Aluminium, wood**

On the heels of the 'Drink an Orange' campaign, spearheaded by Sunkist (originally the Californian Fruit Growers Exchange), many juicers-as-design-objects were made to accommodate this need. Until these advertisements – which emerged in 1916 – oranges had mostly only been eaten: this was a problem for producers who had more supply than demand. The trend for consuming two or three oranges per cup of orange juice, soon caught on, and Americans – then Europeans and the world – were in need of attractive devices to perform this function. Many patents and designs of this time period were aluminium levered devices, as pictured, though some had crank-style compressors that slowly juiced the fruit. Though disruptive to a fully streamlined aesthetic, the wooden board that this juicer is mounted on doubles as a cutting surface. Inching towards the 1950s, many 'juice extractor' designs resembled futuristic automobiles; various models created across the globe were dubbed 'Atomic' juicers.

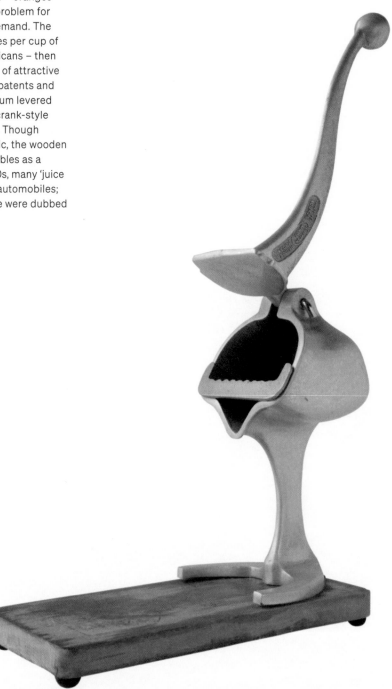

→ **Juicy Salif, 1990, Italy, Philippe Starck (for Alessi),**
Mirror-polished aluminium

Who would have thought that a juicer for lemons
could be one of the most contentious objects in design
history? The Juicy Salif says a lot about design at the
time and raised questions about form and function.
Designed by French superstar designer Philippe Starck
in 1988–1990, it epitomises design debates where the
design no longer provides a solution for a problem
(juicing lemons), but instead form overcomes function.
Its possible the object may topple over as weight and
force from above is put into extracting juice for lemonade
or margaritas. Starck himself said that this 29 cm (11½ in)
tall aluminium lemon squeezer is '… not meant to squeeze
lemons, it is meant to start conversations.' Indeed it did.

The Juicy Salif originated in a commission from Alessi
for Starck to design a tray. Yet he had a brainwave while
dining on the Amalfi Coast, in Italy, one lunchtime when
his meal was missing lemon. Something in the sea air
inspired a few squid-like sketches that eventually
became this controversial kitchen tool – or rather
kitchen conversation piece. The tray he later designed
from the original commission did not leave such
a strong impression.

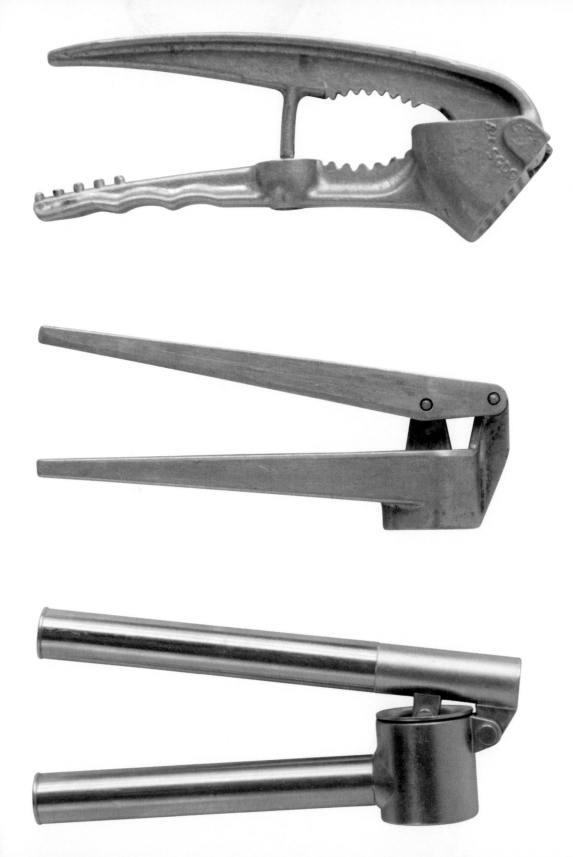

← **Garlic press, 20th century, France,
Switzerland, Sweden, Various designers**

Some well-known names from the culinary world, such as Anthony Bourdain or Elizabeth David, disdain the use of the garlic press and the resulting 'mince'. Although the jury is out, science has proven that every cut to a clove of garlic alters its flavour and pungency – slices have a milder taste, but the finer the garlic is chopped or minced, the stronger the flavour will be. The garlic press produces a much finer mince than chopping with a knife, and the peel can be left on the clove and still extract the pulp. The single purpose of a garlic press is enough to turn some off, which is perhaps why some later versions to the 'original' incorporated multiple functions.

In the mid-20th century aluminium manufacture had become economical and widespread due to the falling price of this lightweight metal. Primitive garlic presses (before aluminium ones) resembled early lemon squeezers, and though an American designer was the first to produce the garlic press in metal, many countries quickly followed with their own design such as Switzerland's Zyliss, Germany's Westmark, Tala in the United Kingdom, and various French and Italian kitchenware brands.

The French *presse-ail et dénoyauteur* (garlic press and pitter) has a charming multi-purpose design that includes a garlic press, nutcracker, cherry / olive pitter and fish scaler; similar designs go a step further with the inclusion of a bottle-opener. It is likely this style emerged after some of the first patents for garlic presses were registered, the first one being in 1954 by American Stephen O. Sarossy.

Invented after 1950, Karl Zysset's Susi garlic press for his company Zyliss has hints of Jean Prouvé's style (middle).

IKEA's own 'Koncis' stainless-steel garlic press (bottom) uses the most functional and pragmatic aspects of these designs and, with its removable barrel, is a sturdy, simple and effective tool. These garlic presses embody various aesthetics of the 20th century and leave behind their zeitgeist of form.

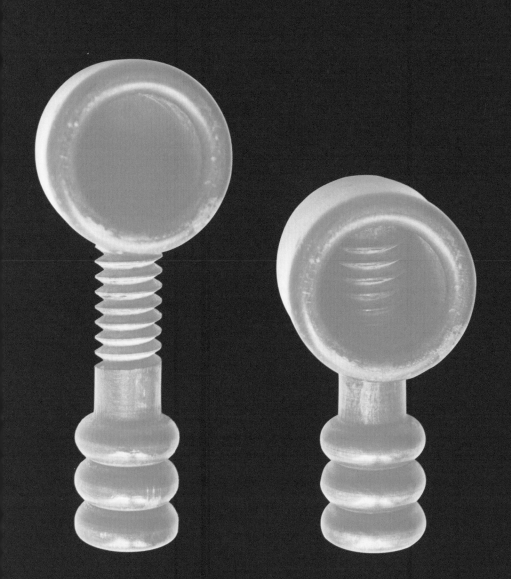

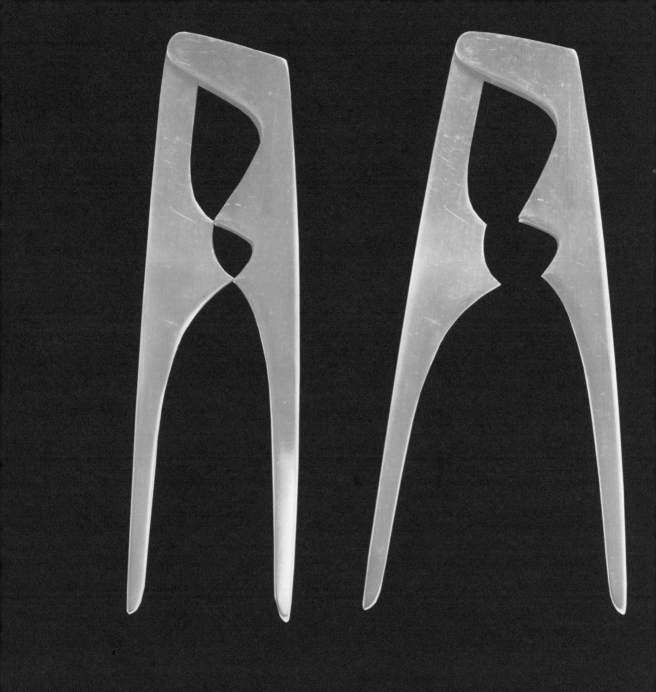

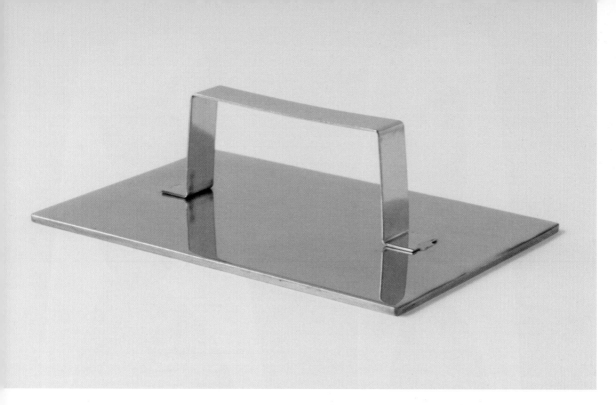

← **Nutcracker, 19ᵗʰ / 20ᵗʰ centuries, Europe / USA / Worldwide, Various designers, Wood, metal**

Nuts have always been readily available food, and we have always required a tool to open them, no matter how rudimentary or sophisticated. The type of nut consumed historically was whatever was local, but nutcrackers are more or less universal in their ability to crack open shells from hazel to Brazil-nut size. These tools are required in the kitchen and made their way to the dining table as an accessory for dessert. Early 16ᵗʰ and 17ᵗʰ-century European examples made out of boxwood were often in the form of human figures or jaw shapes.

The function has attracted a wide range of inventors, designers and aesthetes over the centuries. Nutcrackers open the hard-shelled nutrients with screw-type devices or hinged lever tools; millennia ago, stones were used to crack nuts open on hard surfaces. This utensil has inspired a myriad of elaborate and refined designs of various materials, such as those from H. M. Quackenbush in the USA or the bold forms of Robert Welch (p. 179, pictured right, 1958). It is a shame that most nuts come pre-shelled these days; though we save on labour, we miss out on using such playful and thoughtfully designed tools.

↑ **Hamburger / Grill press, Since 20ᵗʰ century, Worldwide, Designer unknown, Metal, wood**

Grill presses are weights placed on food while it cooks on hot metal surfaces. They are typically made of cast iron or stainless steel, and are also known as hamburger presses, bacon presses or steak weights. In restaurants or at home, the grill press keeps food flat while it is cooking, which in turn distributes heat evenly. In Japan the grill press is useful for a teppanyaki griddle, to press down or maintain the temperature of kobe beef during cooking; they are also familiar tools at American diners.

Food containing excess water – lower-quality meat, for example – has a tendency to shrink upwards and inwards, which makes this tool very handy in fast-food joints. Grill presses also speed the cooking process by capturing moisture and preventing heat from escaping upwards. A wooden handle is a desirable design feature so the press can be picked up easily, and some have a gridded base to add blackened lines or are in circular forms to make perfectly round burgers. This 'invention' likely derived from a clever domestic worker who found that a cast-iron iron was pretty handy in crafting a more desirable result on the stovetop.

↓   **Duck press, Since 19th century,
France, Chef Mechenet, Chrome**

The infamous duck press is attributed to a French chef Mechenet, who created the tool for the dish Caneton de Rouen à la Presse, Rouen duck in blood sauce. Its use was popularised in France and the UK in fine dining institutions, especially in the late 19th and early 20th century. To be used at the table, the duck is cooked and breasts removed before the remaining carcass is chopped and slowly pressed, with wine and brandy added to make the blood sauce. This canard pressé (pressed duck) was the signature dish at the restaurant La Tour d'Argent, and was also served at the Savoy in London. The tool gained further notoriety in the 21st century when the late Anthony Bourdain featured the item on one of his TV shows. In fact the press pictured is Bourdain's itself, which ended up going for around £24,000 ($35,000) at auction, though they are available to purchase new for £1,400 (€2,000) at the famed E. Dehillerin kitchen supply store in Paris. Though this example is chrome, typically duck presses are made of brass, cast iron or steel.

Pasta dates back to the 1st century CE, though some follow the legend that it only arrived in Italy in the 13th century from China via Marco Polo. Ever since pasta was first consumed, there have been countless innovations in how to prepare and eat it. Beyond the primitive ways in which pasta can be made, the domestic pasta maker was refined in the early 20th century. Otello Marcato was one of the early Italians to develop such a product in 1930. The most iconic tool is referred to as 'Model 150', signifying the width of pasta it extrudes in millimetres, though thicknesses are adjustable.

The pasta machine has gone through many stages since the 17th century. Before mechanical means, pasta dough was kneaded by foot, and rolling it out thinly by hand was equally as tiresome. In the early 20th century, the King of Naples had his engineer Cesare Spadaccini devise a machine for kneading pasta, fashioned out of bronze. In parallel, industrial processes for pasta extrusion using dies and pressure from steam were evolving and developing. Otello Marcato developed his domestic pasta maker to bring professional and exacting production into the domestic kitchen. The Marcato company still manufacture and distribute their sturdy pasta makers across the world today.

↑　Noodle / String hopper press, 20th century,
　　South Asia, Jamboli, Brass

These presses are used to make string hoppers
(*idiyappam*) in Sri Lanka, or various types of extracted
doughs and noodles in India. In Sri Lanka the rice flour
or finger millet (*ragi*) dough creates vermicelli that
are steamed and eaten for breakfast with different
curries. In India this tool is known as a *chakli* maker,
sev sancha or *muruku*, and is used with *ragi* or gram /
besan (chickpea) flour dough to press and turn through
the machine. Presses are used directly over hot oil to
deep-fry spiced doughs to create pieces for sweet or
savoury snacks such as Bombay Mix. The best and most
common versions are made from brass, a metal alloy
that retains sharpness and hardness, as is the case with
pasta dies and presses. Older *chakli* makers were made
of wood, with metal holes at the base.

South Asia is not necessarily known for noodle or pasta
consumption, as most meals are served with rice or
bread. However, due to the proximity to China or simply
as a result of homegrown ingenuity, noodles eventually
made their way to these countries almost 4,000 years
ago where they are created and consumed in ways
unique from Eastern Asia and Italy.

↑ **Falafel maker, 20ᵗʰ century, Israel,
Pesach Bash (Pal-Ed), Aluminium**

Falafel are made and consumed across the Middle East; it is difficult to ascertain their exact place of origin between Lebanon, Palestine, Israel, Egypt and surrounding countries. Falafel is a popular food of spiced chickpeas, which need to be formed into small balls or patties before deep-frying. They were especially popular in Israel in the late 1940s, when austerity was introduced to cope with the influx of postwar immigrants – falafel were cheap to make and delicious to eat.

These falafel makers by Pal-Ed speed up the process, especially for restaurants and street-food vendors; the double-headed scoop produces them even more quickly. This tool works through a lever / spring action that ejects forms with diameters of 3 cm (1¼ in), 4 cm (1½ in) or 5 cm (2 in) straight into hot oil.

Pal-Ed is one of the original producers of the falafel maker, founded by Pesach Bash. Bash came to Israel in the 1940s, and after working in steel factories he struck out on his own in 1953 with the ambition of making his own line of kitchen utensils. He invented this falafel-making device, hoping to 'ensure that every household in Israel could make falafel.' In Syria, falafel makers tend to have a brass finish, and their final product has a dimple in the patty to allow them to cook more evenly.

↓ **Sushi mat / Makisu, Since circa 3rd century CE and earlier, Japan, Designer unknown, Bamboo, cotton**

It is difficult to determine when objects such as these were first created and used, due to their material qualities and temporal life. Although bamboo is long-lasting and robust, when mats such as these come to the end of their usefulness, they are discarded. Evidence of sushi consumption dates back at least 2,000 years, so it is possible the *makisu* has been used since then, for many hundreds, if not thousands, of years. This tool is constructed of bamboo slats woven together with cotton twine. There are two different sizes: the thicker mats have slats with a pyramid-like shape and the smaller version has round or flat bamboo pieces joined together. The *makisu* is used in both domestic and professional kitchens to roll out sushi (*makizushi*), to squeeze liquid out of foods such as spinach, or for shaping Japanese omelettes.

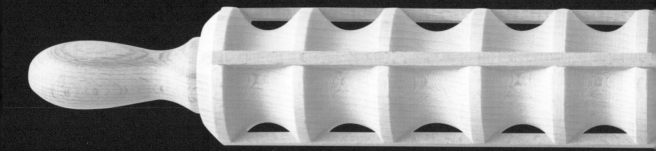

1   Chapatti pin
2   Standard handle-less
3   Ravioli pin
4   Standard pin

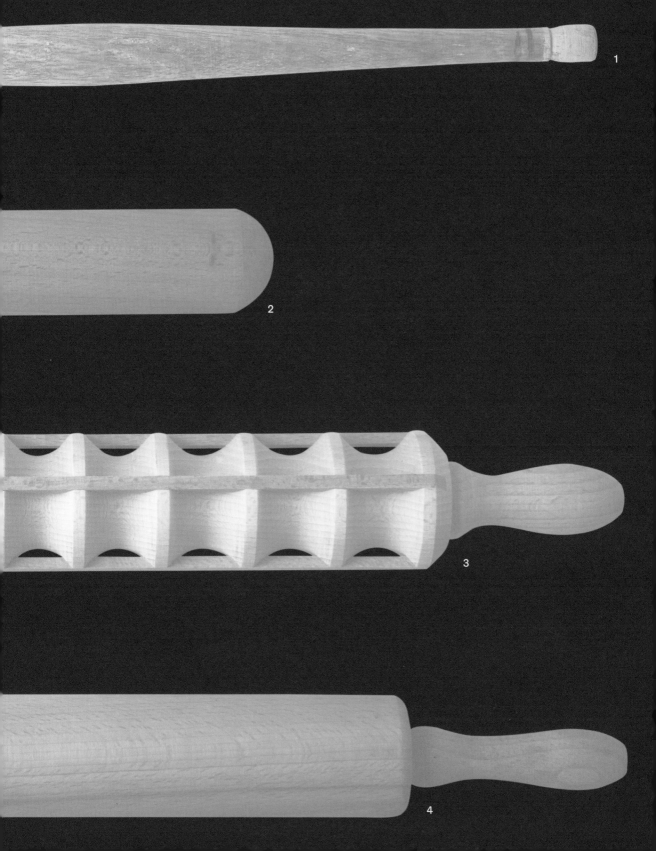

← Rolling pins, Since 8th century BCE, Worldwide, Various makers / designers, Various materials

Compressing doughs made of different ingredients across the world exemplifies the use of vernacular materials and how culturally specific forms are created. This tool has been used for at least 3,000 years, as far back as the Etruscan civilization in the 8th century BCE. The simple action of rolling has been adapted beyond the process of flattening to include textured pins that can cut noodles, prick pastry, and form raviolis, sweets (candy) or biscuits. Convex pins help to keep piecrusts thicker around the edges, while fluted pins in France aid the process of rolling butter through puff pastry. Materials and forms are dictated by necessity: a cold roller (made of marble) to keep pastry extra cool, or carved wooden cylinders to form dumplings, biscuits or textures. Rolling pins are made of wood, porcelain, marble, glass or makeshift items such as a wine bottle from around the kitchen when no pin is to hand. It is a manual way of speeding up and perfecting cooking processes, the handheld version of a factory production line.

↓ Chapati pin and board (velan and chakla), 19th/ 20th centuries, India, Designer unknown, Wood

Chapati or roti, commonly eaten in South Asia, are similar to Mexican tortillas in that they are unleavened flat-breads. They are made of atta flour (wholewheat), oil and water. Like the tortilla, they need flattening before being cooked on a griddle, and this is done with a special wooden board and small rolling pin. In Hindi, *chapat* means 'slap flat', an onomatopoeic description of the bread-making and cooking process. These roti breads can be crafted through a slapping action with the hands, but rolling them is a quick and effective method to achieve a flat disc. After dipping a ball of dough in flour, chapati are rolled out on the *chakla* (board) with the *velan*/ *belan* (pin), until roughly 15 cm (6 in) in diameter. The pin can be a straightforward long cylinder shape (about 40 cm / 16 in long), or wider in the middle with two narrower handles at the side. The circular board gives guidance as to how large and perfectly round your bread will be. These tools are often made of hard Sheesham wood (Indian rosewood), a deciduous tropical tree cultivated in the Punjab area and known for its unique grain and durability.

↑ **Nailsea rolling pin, 1840, Bristol,
England, UK, Nailsea Glassworks, Glass**

These intricate glass rolling pins from the Nailsea
Glassworks in Bristol were originally made for the
galley kitchens of sailing ships, but their unique
appearance led to a rich surrounding culture. Nailsea
first manufactured the pins from bottle glass that was
taxed lower than other types such as flint glass, making
them cost-efficient to produce. Early examples were
made of green bottle glass, occasionally decorated
with swirls and splashes of white. Often, they had a
hollow centre that could be filled with salt, which kept
the precious commodity dry over long sea journeys.
When salt taxes were high between 1694 and 1845,
a glass pin filled with this mineral was a very generous
gift. The centre could also be filled with water to keep
pastry cool, while adding to the weight of the pin to
roll pastry more effectively.

From 1810 more colours were added to this style, (royal
blue known as typical Nailsea design) and techniques
such as festooning, mottling and flecking (the glass is
rolled in enamel chips, reheated and blown) gave the
pins an attractive and mesmerising style. As such
beautifully crafted desirable objects, eventually these
tools transformed into souvenirs and mementos rather
than utensils to be used in the kitchen. Some rolling
pins were used as love tokens which sailors gave to
their betrothed, with slogans such as 'wait for me'
inscribed in the glass. Though the company closed
in 1873, the term 'Nailsea' is often used to describe
objects made with swirled glass, whether produced
at their factory or not.

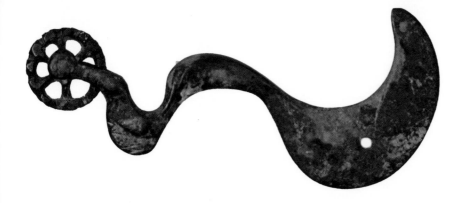

↑   **Pastry cutter / jagger, 16ᵗʰ century,
    Italy, Maker unknown, Brass**

Pastry cutters have hardly changed for hundreds of
years. Even some of the oldest models operate with the
same design of a wheel that cuts as it rotates across
a dough surface, either with a straight or crimped edge.
This example from The British Museum in London is
estimated to be from the 16ᵗʰ century; this type of tool
also appears in Bartolomeo Scappi's cook's handbook
of 1570, *Opera … The Art and Craft of a Master Cook*
(1570). Made of brass, the unique shape almost looks
ergonomic, if gripped with the palm in the back and the
forefinger in the groove at the front. These tools are
also known as pie crimps, pie rimmers or jaggers, for
making jagged edges; 'scrimshaw' jaggers were made
of whale bone and carved by sailors at sea. Otherwise,
these pasta- or pastry-cutting wheels can be made of
wrought iron, wood, steel, and in the past century, in
plastic. Brass is favoured, especially in Italy, as a material
for this utensil even today, because this metal alloy
retains its sharpness over time. Some cutters come
with tweezer-like crimpers on the handle side, or simply
a striated or carved shape to press two pieces of dough
together. Extravagant jaggers for cutting in bulk have
multiple expandable wheels that can cut six or more
strips of various sizes at a time.

↓   **Cookie cutter, 1953, USA, Foley Manufacturing
Company, Aluminium, plastic**

This rotary cookie cutter could cut a whole sheet of
dough into shapes in no time. This mid-20th-century
aluminium utensil was made by the Foley Manufacturing
Company of Minnesota, USA, and is formed of six
different cutting shapes; it is quite small in size, at 10 cm
(4 in) in diameter, so creates tiny, sweet, one-inch morsels.
Early rotary cutters were simply shapes mounted on
rolling pins, but in the 1930s these lightweight wheel
cutters demonstrated an improvement on the technique.
There are a few patents registered for similar devices
such as this, rotary wheels that cut croissant shapes,
biscuits, hearts, spades, stars and more. This particular
cutter is pleasing to the eye and sits in the Museum of
Modern Art's design collection in New York.

↓ **Dumpling maker, 20th century,
China, Designer unknown, Plastic**

Dumplings are almost universal: gyoza in Japan, ravioli in Italy, pierogi in Poland, *jiaozi* in China. Some dumplings work with straightforward joining techniques – a simple pressing of two sides together. However, for certain types of dumpling in China and some other Asian countries, a more particular fold is traditional, requiring a fold and press to make a pleated joined edge on one side. This dumpling maker allows you to make these filled parcels through a single fold and press action, creating uniformity and a comparable look to handmade versions, though not quite. The dumpling press saves stress in the kitchen from imperfect folding techniques. Some similar manual tools were patented in the 1950s, but this design – particular to Asian-style dumplings – was developed more recently; its use is not limited to one singular cuisine, but any dumpling from around the world that needs to press a filling between a thin sheet of dough.

→ **Pelmeni maker, 20th century, Eurasia,
Designer unknown, Cast aluminium**

Like the Italian *orecchiette* nomenclature, Russian *pelmeni* get their name from their ear-like shape; when boiled, they shrivel slightly to resemble our acoustic organs. However, *pelmeni* are a type of dumpling (not pasta) filled with different meats, fish or mushrooms, and are a staple of Russian and Siberian cuisine. Originally, they would have been made by hand, but eventually this tool allowed many to be constructed at once. Like the honeycomb of a beehive, the *pelmeni* maker is comprised of multiple hexagons in a cast metal frame. To make *pelmeni*, a thin sheet of dumpling dough is placed over the cast aluminium mould, filling is placed in each depression, covered with another sheet of dough, then flipped and pressed on the counter-top to form multiple dumplings.

Pelmeni are notably smaller than some types of dumpling, being more akin to Italian tortellini than larger Tibetan *momo*. *Pelmeni* can be purchased readymade in the freezer section of Eastern European supermarkets; amazingly, this is not far from their origin – Siberian hunters used to carry frozen dumplings with them as they travelled as a preserved food, which they cooked as and when needed.

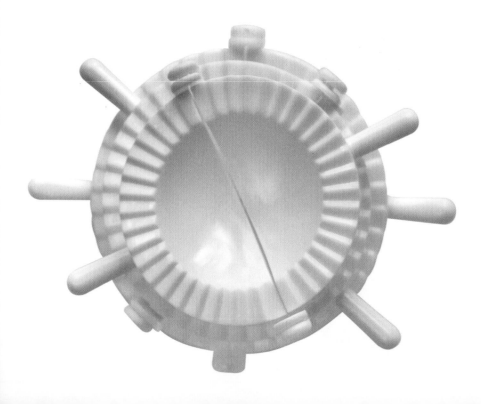

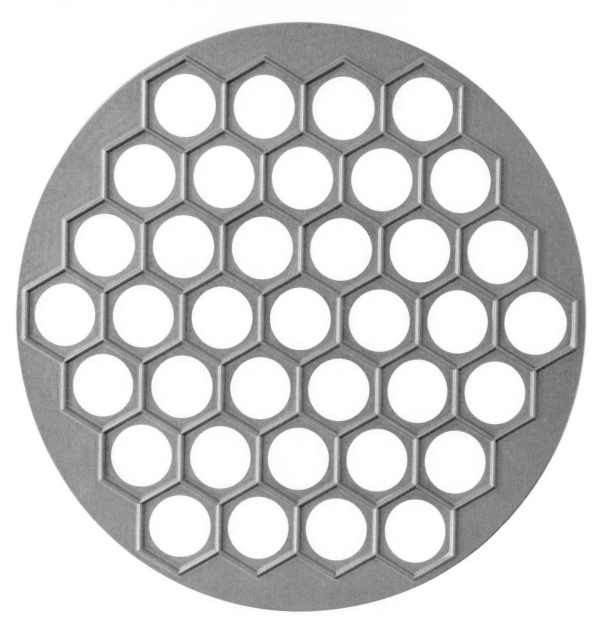

N. WATERMAN.

Egg Pan and Cake Baker.

No. 23,517.   Patented April 5, 1859.

Fig.1

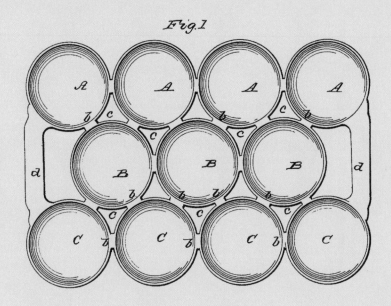

Fig.2

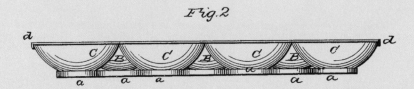

WITNESSES
Lawrence Lyons
Arthur Neill

INVENTOR
Nath'l Waterman

←   **Muffin pan, 19th / 20th centuries, USA, Nathaniel Waterman, Cast iron**

These muffin pans predate familiar cupcake or Yorkshire pudding tins. Although sometimes known as muffin 'tins' (as in the UK), the original moulds were not made from tin but cast iron, and so were called muffin pans or gem pans. The form and shape are clearly influenced by the production process: in order to use the least amount of material the moulds are joined by small channels rather than a sheet of metal. There is no excess material to form a tray where bubbling over batter can be caught. Eventually these muffin moulds were made of cheaper tinware, produced by the stamping manufacturing process rather than cast such as the one pictured here. One of the first designs was registered by Nathaniel Waterman in 1859, who established his own kitchen and homewares brand in 1825. Made primarily by American foundries, these pans came in various baking shapes – circles, rosettes, rectangles, corncobs – and were used to make muffins, bread rolls, cornbread, popovers and more.

↑   **Cupcake liner, 1935, USA, Stuart Kimberley, Paper, foil**

Cupcake liners are a discreet and extraordinarily useful kitchen tool. Their carefully considered design helped solve a key problem: that of extracting intact, single-portion baked cakes from muffin tins. They are made from affordable materials that can be disposed of after one use, have a clever concertina design whose folds allow the eater to easily peel off the casing, and are simple to use at the front and back end of the process. The original patent states: 'A further object of our invention is to produce a cooking utensil at a minimum of expense, enabling its use but once, to which a pie for example will have no tendency to adhere, without the necessity of greasing, and one which may be utilized not only for the baking operation but also for delivery and storage of the product.' Originally the foil layer was needed for extra structure and non-stick qualities, but newly developed paper materials meant that the extra layer was eventually no longer necessary.

↑   **Garnish cutters, 20th century,
Japan, Designer unknown, Steel**

These vegetable garnish cutters are used to create
small shapes (about an inch on average) that contribute
to a range of aesthetically pleasing meals in Japan.
The art of carving fruits and vegetables into shapes and
sculptures is known as *mukimono* and is traditionally
done with a knife. These cutters are easier and quicker
for those less skilled at *mukimono*, and in autumn they
cut orange-leaf shapes from carrots, flowers in spring,
fishes or simple star shapes to garnish dishes.

Japanese cuisine is known for the care and attention
spent on presentation, all the way from *kaiseki* meals
to the everyday lunchbox. In recent decades, infamous
kawaii (cute) lunchboxes for school children have gained
attention for their elaborate creations: either housewives
in competition with each other or to bring pure joy to
children. This practice does have origins in the traditional
makunouchi bento, which is a lunchbox divided into
four quadrants influenced by the seasons, landscape,
nutrition and Zen practices. The designer of the
Kikkoman soy sauce bottle, Kenji Ekuan, suggests in
his book *The Aesthetics of the Japanese Lunchbox*
(2000) that Japanese design, aesthetics and culture
can be understood through the *makunouchi* lunchbox.
These vegetable garnish cutters form part of this story.

↑ **Biscuit / cookie cutters; baking moulds, Since circa 15th century, Europe / USA, Various designers, Various materials**

Before baking moulds, most dessert foods were cooked in the pan (pan cakes), fried as fritters, baked in wood or metal hoops, or made with flaky pastry that did not require baking in a container. Biscuit or cookie cutters evolved from rudimentary devices (and are still improvised today), to wooden moulds, ceramic cutters, and finally metal, tin, and now plastic.

The Egyptians moulded 'cooked dough', but the primary purpose of baking early on was focused on bread rather than cakes. Sugar only began to circulate in Europe in the 12th to 15th centuries, before becoming widely available and affordable thereafter. Around this time, cake and biscuit baking was developed and refined. In the 15th century, French bakers who specialised in patisserie formed a corporation, and dedicated tools soon followed. After cast-iron and steel moulds, tinware

was developed for optimum heat distribution and sharp edges in cakes and pastries. Whitesmiths (as opposed to iron-forging blacksmiths) crafted fluted and straight tins or cut patterns from sheet metal that were hammered on anvils and soldered together. In America, tin cake-cutters were known fondly as 'hearts, rounds and diamonds' by tinsmiths. When demand for tin kitchenware increased in the 19th century, the price of these moulds went up, but eventually 20th-century manufacturing innovations and falling aluminium prices made them affordable for the masses. Today most baking tins are not made from tin at all, but aluminium with non-stick coatings, or even moulded heat-resistant silicone. Cookie cutters do create uniformity in the production process, yet in English the term 'cookie cutter' is a derogatory phrase equated with objects or people that lack originality.

The mould pictured is from 1868, used to create raised pies in the UK. It has the same hinged feature as eye-shaped moulds in France used for pâté en croute so that the supporting mould can be dismantled from the creation once the shape has set in the oven. Eye-shaped ovals of tinned steel, with fluted sides and a three-piece hinged construction, were used for the most prized meat pies or *pâté en croute*, topped with pastry shapes of leaves or other flora. This unique form, which looks as if it has a cinched waist, allowed for the filling in the centre to be well cooked. British food historian Ivan Day notes that decorative moulds proliferated in the 19th century, though fluted and teardrop forms (pictured) were most common. Though elaborate pie-making had been around for a few hundred years before then, these new hinged moulds and improved metal production techniques allowed for a wider variety of moulded decoration. These forms create sharp golden edges of pastry that would have glistened in elaborate banquets hundreds of years ago, and still do today.

Pâté en croute has a pâté or meat filling covered with a layer of aspic and pastry on the top; it has been eaten since the Middle Ages and was initially created as a way to preserve meat. These types of hinged, dismantle-able moulds are also used for French terrines, though mostly made in long rectangular shapes with herring-bone patterns on the side; this long shape is easy to portion slices in a restaurant, at the butchers, or at home.

↑ Kugelhopf mould, Since 16th century, France, Germany, Switzerland, Austria, Designer unknown, Metal

The *kugelhopf* holds a special place in the hearts of Alsatian French, Germans, Swiss and Austrians. It is a yeast-risen sweet bread made with raisins and almonds, eaten both at rituals such as weddings or on informal occasions in the morning, afternoon or night; it can be taken with tea, coffee, beer or wine. The *kugelhopf* has a distinct, tall, fluted shape with a hole in the middle. Traditional moulds are made of terracotta, glazed on the inside, not the out, and sometimes decorated; eventually metal *kugelhopf* baking tins became more common for their durability and cost-effectiveness. Some say the shape resembles a turban, to celebrate the defeat of the Turkish by the Hapsburg Empire in Vienna. This enriched bread is also known as *gugelhupf* and various other spellings and dialects from the area in which it originates. A comparable mould is used to make bundt cakes, an Americanised baked confection created by an émigré in the mid-20th century, whose only resemblance to *kugelhopf* is in form, not style.

→ **Copper moulds, Since 18th century,
Europe / UK, Various designers, Copper**

Copper moulds are distinctive items that hold pride of place in a kitchen with their exquisite forms and shiny colour; they are as beautiful to display as they are to use for blancmange, flummery or jellied creations. Wedgewood of England had initially popularised earthenware moulds for jelly-making, but eventually the durability, malleability and availability of copper took hold. Harrods of London featured various copper shapes in their catalogues for moulded jellies, which were originally the reserve of the wealthy. These moulds were made through the stamping manufacturing process, the edges on the bottom rolled for stability; tin was used as a cheaper alternative, and some brands – such as Jell-O in the USA – gave them away with their products. From the 18th century copper moulds were lined with tin, after it was discovered that the copper seeped into jelly or was otherwise making consumers ill. The moulds come in various sizes: for large jellies, individual jellies, puddings and savoury fish moulds, or to shape cooked rice timbales and puréed vegetables.

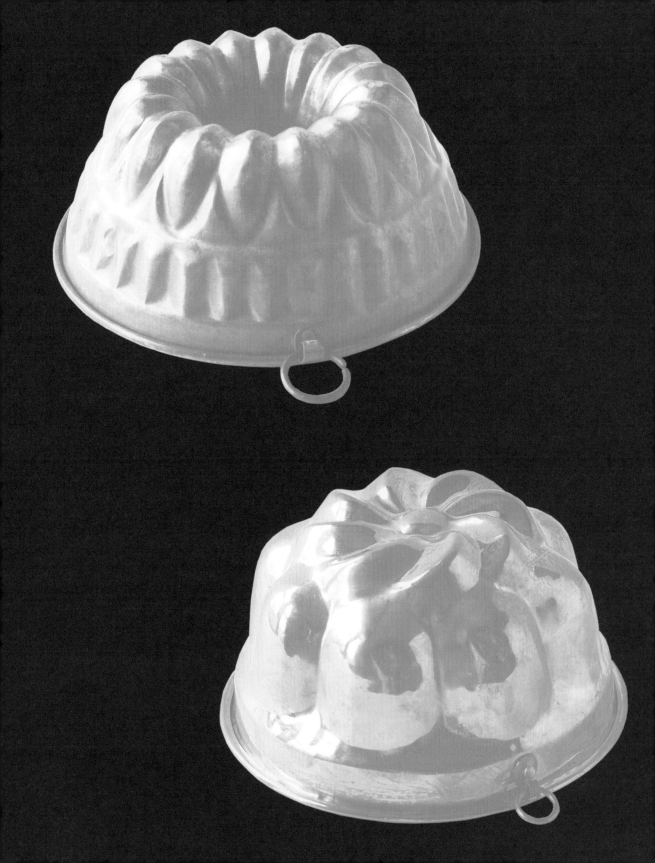

← Butter mould / Stamp, 18th century, Sweden / Europe, Maker unknown, Wood

At the market, a moulded form of 'print butter' would fetch a more handsome price than a standard block of 'tub butter' simply formed straight out of the churn. These butter stamps were typically made of sycamore – a fast-growing wood that does not impart any flavour to delicate dairy – but could also be made of boxwood, which is equally robust and suitable for working with moist food products. Some of these stamps were crafted in bell shapes that could mould a pound of butter. The carved motif was either pure pattern, as was the case with many examples made in Sweden (pictured) or reflected the farm or household they came from. A swan might indicate that the farm was near a river, a sheep would reflect a homestead in the hills and a thistle could point to a Scottish dairy. Hobbyist craftsmen and carpenters made them for their own domestic production, though eventually stamps were machine-made. American butter moulds typically featured tulips, wheat sheaves or hearts; inevitably advertising crept in and slogans such as 'Good Butter – Taste It' were carved into these stamps.

↑ Bread stamp, Date unknown, Greece, Maker unknown, Wood

The Greeks were the first true bakers who developed bread from grain and flours that were previously only eaten as porridge or pan cakes. These bread stamps are made by Orthodox Christians in Greece, but also further afield where this sect of Christianity is common such as Serbia, Russia and elsewhere. These moulds are used to stamp wafers for Christian events or ceremonies and for Prosphora, a two-tiered bread made with two slabs of dough. The inscriptions on these bread stamps contain affirmations such as 'Jesus Christ Victorious'. In Britain, monks stamped the bread baked in the abbott's kitchen with crosses to prevent evil spirits from stopping the bread rising.

Beyond Orthodox bread stamps, similar tools were used to help identify loaves baked in communal ovens, especially in France, Italy and Greece. Where bread was consumed, communal ovens were standard across the world for a few thousand years; personal ovens were expensive to build and run, and a shared resource solved the problem. Often run by the state, daily bread was baked in the 'fast' hot oven, and pots of stew slowly cooked as the oven cooled over the day. These public ovens were even used by master bakers; therefore, tools such as these were necessary to identify and retrieve loaves, and also to distinguish their products for loyal customers. The bread stamps of Matera, in Italy – known as *timbro del pane* – have particularly elaborate handles carved in the form of a figure or animal; they are still handcrafted there today.

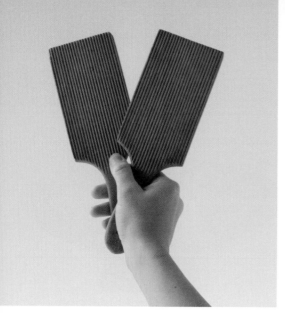

↑ **Butter pats, 18ᵗʰ/19ᵗʰ centuries,
Europe, Designer unknown, Wood**

Butter pats are also known as Scotch hands, butter
paddles, beaters, clappers or spades. They are used
in the final part of the butter-making process, to remove
the remaining buttermilk and to integrate salt – both
tactics that prevent butter from going rancid. The ridges
provide channels for watery buttermilk to flow away, and
they are often made from sycamore wood. Prior to
these wooden paddles, butter was kneaded by hand
in bowls once it came out of the churn, until about the
19ᵗʰ century. These paddles evolved from other wooden
butter tools such as long flat sticks or shallow scooping
ladles used to remove butter from the churn for kneading.
Butter pats can also be used to press butter into moulds,
or to shape balls of butter for individual portions. A 'pat'
is also the term for a lump of butter. In formal dining
settings in America, guests were given their own butter
pat plate to present these small nuggets of dairy for
bread. In Italy, a paddle with these grooves can also be
used to form ridges on potato gnocchi, or garganelli
and cavatelli pasta when used with a small rolling pin.

↑ **Mooncake mould, Since 13ᵗʰ century, China, Various designers, Wood**

Mooncakes are traditionally eaten in China to celebrate the Mid-Autumn Festival during the first full moon of the season; this is the eighth full moon of the Chinese lunar year, eight being a lucky number in the country. These mooncakes are filled with either lotus seed paste, red bean paste, or jujube paste; sometimes the centre contains a salted egg yolk to resemble a full moon. The filling is contained within a rich pastry with a distinctive and elaborate pattern on the top, varying from lotuses to chrysanthemum, fish or butterflies. The tradition to celebrate mid-autumn goes back thousands of years, and folklore tells a tale of secret messages communicated in mooncake patterns. Hidden messages could be divulged from packs of four mooncakes by cutting them into quarters and reassembling them. Precison and clarity of pattern were essential for these moulds. They were traditionally made of carved wood, though now they are found in mass-produced plastic for domestic or commercial kitchens. As ovens are not that common-place in individual Chinese homes, mooncakes are mostly produced commercially, providing an occasion for a trip to the bakery and a special treat.

Other wooden moulds originating in East Asia come in simple shapes, for moulding rice for Japanese *onigiri* or cute lunchbox accessories.

→ **Springerle board, Since 15ᵗʰ century, Germany / Netherlands, Various makers, Wood**

Springerle translates from a south German dialect to 'jumper', believed to be a reference to the charging horse often carved in these wooden moulds. These elaborately carved intaglio forms, often featuring people and scenes of everyday life, were used to make biscuits to celebrate the New Year. The original springerle biscuits were made of water marzipan, a cheaper version of almond marzipan consisting of eggs, fine sugar and flour, with an anise or cardamom flavouring that was spread directly on the board. This hardy dough is pressed into the mould and left to dry for a day before baking, to ensure the detailed forms keep their shape in the oven; after baking they are hardened further for a few weeks to create a characteristic crunch. Traditionally, the moulds were hand-carved and some come in rolling pin forms; they were also known as springerle cards and made of various woods such as beech, walnut, pearwood or boxwood. Some were made of cast iron or pewter directly moulded from the carved wood, but eventually tin replaced traditional wooden moulds, as metal did with many advancements in the manufacturing of kitchen tools. Springerle boards resemble the moulds used for spicy gingerbread (made since the 13ᵗʰ century) and Dutch *speculaas* (made sincethe 17ᵗʰ century).

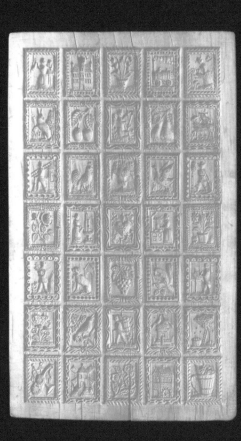

1   Crafters mould, location
     unknown, 18th century
2   Property of a Franconian
     (Central German) bakery, 1800
3   Stuttgart, late 1700s
4   Stuttgart, Biedermeier period,
     carved 1814–1836

2

3

↓   Curd mould, circa 1780, England,
    Maker unknown, Creamware

Evidence of draining curds from whey goes back to at least the 1st century CE, with rush baskets used by the Gauls, and ceramic curd drainers by the Romans and lake-dwellers of Neuchatel, now modern-day Switzerland. These processes were the beginning of the development of the complex and varied world of cheese, which, apart from most of Asia, is eaten throughout the world and made from different animal milks in various shapes, sizes and ages. As the centuries went on, curd was refined into complex cheeses, but was also served fresh, sometimes moulded in multi-tiered forms such as this. This mould is made from creamware, a glazed earthenware developed by

Josiah Wedgwood, noted for its resemblance to cream. After rush baskets or woven straw, terracotta was a common material for draining and shaping curd (used by the Romans), and eventually glazed ceramic was used. These moulds were perforated with straight holes, but sometimes had decorative cutouts to let the whey drain from the soft cheese. In Britain, the tier-shaped curd was often served decorated with fruit and is the origin of what became syllabub dessert. In France, they have a heart-shaped mould for *couer à la crème*, a sweetened soft cheese served with red fruits or *fraise de bois*.

↑ Bombe mould, 19th/20th centuries,
France / Europe, Designer unknown, Tin plate

Ice cream moulds were *de rigueur* with the advent of freezing capabilities and the rising popularity of frozen treats in the 19th century. Indeed, a Mrs. Marshall in Victorian England wrote various cookbooks with recipes to fill elaborate moulds to make 'fancy ices' (published in a book also called *Fancy Ices* in 1894). Mrs. Marshall aside, by the late 19th and early 20th centuries, novelty ice cream shapes became tiresome, and moulds were simplified. The 'bombe' mould was ideal for making frozen desserts for dinner parties or special occasions, and was popular in France, Italy and the UK. The mould takes its name from the similarity of its shape to archetypal bombs, and it comes in two main forms: either a perfect sphere or an elongated dome form. The mould was often made from copper with a handled lid, though tin versions (pictured) were less expensive. In France, the mould is used to make *bombe glacée*, a dessert favoured and distinguished by the well-known chef Escoffier; he invented a protective outer custard layer that improved the overall structure and flavour of 'bombes'. In Italy, this tool is used to make the famous spumoni treat, consisting of three layers of cherry, pistachio and chocolate gelato. The term bombe is now more or less interchangeable with any moulded frozen dessert, and today is used to form the American frozen and cooked Baked Alaska.

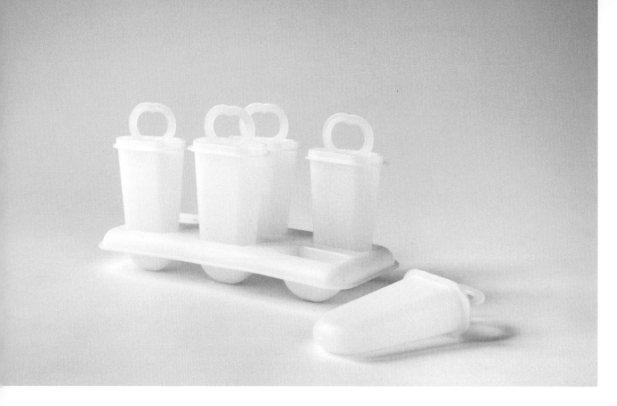

↑　**Ice popsicle maker, 1955, USA,
Earl S. Tupper, Polyethylene**

The Tupperware company, founded in the late 1940s, always kept on top of food trends and new innovations. Their product range did not stop at storage containers, but also included other objects and tools that benefit from the versatility and durability of plastic. Domestic refrigeration only materialised in the early 20th century, with domestic freezing available from the 1940s. The 1950s was the true beginning of the company's success, with the growing popularity of Tupperware parties, spearheaded by the pioneering finesse of their Vice President of Marketing, Brownie Wise. By 1955, these ice popsicle makers were precisely the next fun thing a housewife needed to utilise the freezer to its best advantage, keeping young children – and therefore the family – happy. Before these moulds, popsicles would have only been available shopbought as opposed to homemade. Earl S. Tupper's contribution to the world of design is somewhat understated – his inventions and innovations with plastic are probably the most everlasting of our everyday objects, especially in the kitchen.

↓ **Candy modellers, 19th/20th centuries,
Europe/USA, Designer unknown**

These tools are another direct descendent from the
workshop: similar utensils are used for sculpting and
shaping ceramics in the artist's studio. As with clay
modelling tools, they were originally made of wood
(especially boxwood), but they are now found in robust
plastic. Indeed, working with marzipan, royal icing and
sweets (candy) is similar to working with clay, and it
makes perfect sense that their use was transferred from
one discipline to the other. Often sweets, chocolate
and icing are moulded or extruded from piping bags,
but there are occasions when it is sculpted on site for
large confections and elaborate cakes made by expert
patisseries. Turning food into sculptures and extravagant
shapes is the ultimate expression of our unique ability
to transform nature into culture.

↑ **Plating tweezers, 1990s,**
Worldwide, Stainless steel

→ **Piping bag and forms, 1949, Germany,**
Christian Fleck, Cottong, stainless steel

Plating tweezers are on the extreme side of the gastro-nomic spectrum, but they say a lot about where we have come from and where are now in turning 'nature into culture' through cooking (as pointed out by Claude Lévi-Strauss in *The Raw and the Cooked*, 1964). These plating tweezers are used in Michelin star or fine dining restaurants, to put final delicate touches of garnishes on dishes ready for service. Tongs would have been used originally, until dishes became smaller, more detailed and nuanced. The tweezers resemble surgeon's tools, and in some cases the placing of foods on plates requires a similar precision to the one needed in an operating theatre, unachievable by large shaking hands. These tools differ from standard tweezer designs in that they have much longer handles. Tweezer food is sometimes described as 'international rich people food', and it emerged in the boom of molecular gastronomy in the 1990s. These specialist tools – repurposed from the operating table – are currently here to stay, though there has been a recent rise in popularity of more relaxed dining that doesn't require the finickity detail of using tweezers.

A German patent exists from the 1940s for a pastry bag with nozzles that are 'grooved or fluted', and, in fact, the German company Schneider is one of the main manufacturers of piping (pastry) bags today. Their design encompasses wholly reusable materials: a coated cotton bag and metal nozzles that create various shapes of piped dough or icing. Simple piping can be recreated at home by cutting a corner off a plastic bag, but for true professionals and perfectionists only piping bags will do for detailed final touches.

Heat & Transform

Beyond tools for food preparation, inside clay pots and iron cauldrons is where the history of cooking really begins. The skewer, grill or pot over the fire not only creates flavour and kills bacteria, but also transforms enzymes to make food easier to digest. Michael Pollan wrote of the pot being akin to an external mouth, which softens food for those without teeth such as infants and the elderly. Once hearths were common, even the simplest dwellings would have a fire, hook and a cauldron. Ancient households typically had three pots – one for water, one for cooking, and one for laundry. Family life centred around the fire, as is still the case in contemporary life when friends and guests gravitate and gather in the kitchen, the heart of the home.

For thousands of years, fire could not be taken for granted – before safety matches were invented in 1840, making fire was tricky and laborious, and keeping it going was important work. Every night a *couvre feu* (fire cover), or curfew as it was known, was placed upon the embers of the hearth to keep them alight for the next day. Once fire was harnessed, we found multiple ways to exploit it: grilling, roasting, boiling, braising, steaming, baking, smoking … slow, quick, delicate or fierce heat – each technique transforming raw food into exquisite dishes. Yet the kitchen hearth was a dangerous place to work, especially for women, and 'hearth death' – caused mostly by skirts catching on fire – was the second highest cause of death in women after child-birth up until the 17th century. By the end of the 1700s, stovetop ranges with flat hotplates were developed, followed by gas cookers in the 1820s (though these were not widely used until the 1880s), electric in the 1930s, and time-saving microwaves in the 1960s.

Heating and cooking food is a true science: across the world, tools come in a variety of materials and shapes that facilitate heat surrounding and cooking food in particular ways. In 4000 BCE Britain, before metallurgy, clay pots were used for cooking as evidenced by bonfire marks on pottery vessels. To boil liquids, stones were heated until hot and then placed in water-filled ceramic or other lined vessels. Cooking in glazed or unglazed earthenware is still a method used today, from Georgian bean pots to Japanese *donabe*, Indian *handi*, North African tagines, and contemporary 'chicken bricks'. In 16th-century India, vessels of particular metals were used for their believed medicinal values – gold to ward off poison or tin to cool the body – and these symbolic influences persist to this day, such as using sacred copper pans (now lined) to cook thalis.

Heat and ovens are precious resources, and sometimes used communally, as in Greece or Morocco. A lack of personal oven ownership led to innovations such as the tagine, which slow-cooks food after the daily bread is baked; the 'Dutch oven' pot (*doufeu*) also solved this problem, creating an oven environment on flames or the stovetop. For centuries chefs have used heat with specific tools to give extra-special touches: bruléed cream using salamanders, sesame seeds toasted in a *goma iri*, or succulent clay-pot cooking. Although tools have slight differences across cultures, they often use similar materials, shapes and techniques, but to cook distinctive regional dishes throughout the world.

↑   **Skewer, 18th century, Sweden (pictured) /
Worldwide, Maker unknown, Wrought iron**

Threading meat or other foods onto a stick to cook
over fire is evidenced from over 300,000 years ago.
Wooden skewers could have been made of hard beech
or bamboo before metallurgy. The Turkish are particularly
known for this tool, and this cooking technique is said
to originate in the Ottoman Empire, when armies would
pierce meat with their swords to cook over the fire.
Historically, more refined and intentionally charcoal-
grilled food has been found in India, the Caucasus, on
into Russia, Georgia, Armenia and Azerbaijan. It's possible
both the tool and technique made their way to the
West via the Silk Road. Skewers were typically made
of hand-forged wrought iron or steel, always designed
with a loop at the end to be stored nicely on their rack.

← **Toasting fork, 17th century,
Spain, Maker unknown, Iron**

The most primitive way to cook anything is to pierce
it with a tool and place it over a fire – beginning with
sticks and skewers, then evolving into a specialised
tool. After the skewer comes the toasting fork,
particularly for cooking meat and days-old bread,
important staples of the diet in the Western world.
In the 17th century these tools were cast in two halves
and were generally two-pronged until the 18th century
when advances in forging and metalwork allowed for
more tines. On the contrary, the very advanced Romans
had three-barbed flesh hooks for cooking meat, the
design of which somehow got lost between the
centuries. Developments into staggered prongs were
especially useful for holding together crumbling old
bread which was being transformed into toast. Once
production techniques were mastered, toasting forks
became decorative items, along with the racks that hold
them. Long-handled, two-pronged toasting forks were
advertised in the Harrods catalogue as late as 1895,
when it was still common to toast bread over an open
fire or hearth.

→ **Marshmallow roaster, Since 1930s,**
  USA, Various makers, Steel

The Egyptians created marshmallows in about
2000 BCE when they discovered the sweet sap of
the marshmallow plant, which actually grows in
marshes. The French refined a recipe in the 1800s
with egg whites and more sugar, until an American
perfected an extrusion system for the confection in
1948. Prior to the American refinement, a 1920s girl
scout handbook mentions the practice of roasting
marshmallows for s'mores. S'mores consist of roasted
marshmallow and chocolate sandwiched between
two graham crackers (which closely resemble digestive
bisuits), and stands for 'some more' (so good, you
want s'more).

In 1936, improvements were made to the wire
coat hanger, with the addition of a cardboard tube
on the central support to prevent clothes wrinkling.
Ingenuity quickly took over in finding other purposes
for these versatile clothes hangers. Among their
many tangential uses, the coat hanger marshmallow
roaster may be the most sentimental and nostalgic.
Clever makers can create a two-pronged skewer,
though it runs the risk of one mallow falling off into
the fire before the other is equally toasted. An easy,
off-the-cuff and cheap way to roast marshmallows
over a fire, this coat hanger provides a sanitary and
fireproof alternative to a stick out of the woods.

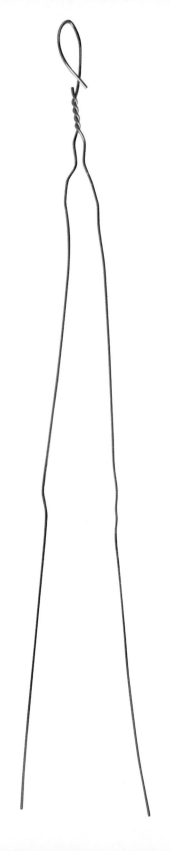

↓   **Salamander, 18th century, Europe,
Designer unknown, Iron**

Salamanders, as we know them today, are their own device: a special one-purpose oven used to brown the tops of foods and used in restaurant and catering settings in particular. Historically they were a simple tool, a cast or forged wrought-iron disc that was heated in the fire until it was red-hot, then put on the top of food to make it brown.

Salamanders get their name from a legend that amphibians lived on fire for nourishment, but their shape also has an anthropomorphic quality. Some salamanders had feet on the long handle so they could rest in the fire to heat up, rather than having to be held. These tools were still used by professional bakers up until the 20th century, mostly for browning the tops of buns that didn't attain enough of a golden colour while in the oven. Domestically we now have grills (or broilers) in our ovens that perform this task, or even blow torches for specifically directed heat for *crème brûlée* (literally 'burnt cream').

This particular cauldron was recovered from the shipwreck of the Witte Leeuw (a Dutch East India Company vessel) and is dated before 1613.

← **Cauldron, Bronze Age to 19th century, Worldwide, Designer unknown, Iron**

Following earthenware pots and developments in the Bronze Age (from around 3000 BCE), the archetypal cauldron was created. Cauldron cooking then became the dominant method of cooking for centuries to come. They were used to heat water (for cooking or otherwise), boil meat, stews and even bake bread; some foods were steamed inside them over wooden shelves, while grains or beans in linen bags would be hung inside to cook in the pot. Accompanying tools included a flesh fork to fish out pieces of meat and a scummer to remove the scum from boiling stocks and stews.

In the 16th century cooking in cauldrons was still common in England, though by this time most of Europe had moved towards developments in roasting, baking and pan cooking as well. The earliest cauldrons were made of bronze, then hammered iron or copper, and eventually cast iron. The ridges that you see on many cauldrons are from the sand-casting process, where two halves were cast over a clay core mould. These hardy pots were repaired within an inch of their lives, before being melted down again when they could no longer be used.

Cauldrons have either round or flat bases, with or without legs: without legs, they were hung over the fire by their handle; with legs, they sat directly over it. These legs often degraded or were worn off from being pushed and pulled from the fire after many uses. Flat-based cauldrons were created in Britain when coal was used instead of wood (after this had been used up to build ships), as the curved edge was no longer necessary to receive licks of flames. Confusingly, these pots were also referred to and known as kettles, though today the nomenclature is associated with the water boiler for tea and coffee. Cauldron cooking was the original one-pot meal; today this cuisine is made with plug-in Crock-pots.

↑ **Chimney crane, 18th century, England, Maker unknown, Wrought iron**

When cooking was done over an open fire, a chimney crane installed at the back or side of the hearth made it easier to move pots across the fire. The limited temperature control that a chef had during these time periods could be managed more easily with this tool. Chimney cranes appeared in the 17th century and were a step up from pot hooks, a much simpler ratcheted device for holding pots over the fire. There were three types of cranes: single, double, or treble, referring to the number of axes (eg x, y, z in three-dimensional space) in which the tool could move. The chimney crane pictured could swing side to side on its mount, be raised and lowered, and also move pots forward and backward. When closed range cookers were developed in the 19th century, chimney cranes and pot hooks ceased to be produced, though they were still used in rural locations until the 20th century. Interestingly, these chimney cranes bear a resemblance to the now popular 'pasta arm', a craze taking America by storm whereby a swinging tap (faucet) can fill pots with water directly on the stove.

The manual rotating of meat became too much for kitchen workers, manpower and even dog power in the hot heat of the hearth. Spit jacks or mechanical turn spits were developed to rotate meat independently through clockwork, steam or smoke. Georgian clockwork versions were powered through spiral torsion from winding up, as with the mechanics of a clock. The 'bottle jack' style of brass or japanned metal from the 19th century was so named because of its shape. It also functioned by winding and clockwork, and it could hold a few pieces of roasting meats from hooks on its circular rotating wheel. During this time, these tools were more or less universal in Britain, and some old fireplaces still have holes where the legs of the jack were originally screwed. These machines marked the beginning of mechanised work in the kitchen, the beginning of a long, labour-saving history of cooking.

↑   **Dog spit, Designer unknown, 15th–18th centuries, England, Designer unknown**

During the medieval period, roasting spits or turn spits were time-consuming methods of cooking that required constant tending. In Tudor times, dog spits were developed and installed in kitchens to hand this laborious task over to tread-wheeling animals. Known as turnspit dogs, they typically had long bodies and short legs in order to run the wheels most efficiently; they were bred specially for this purpose. The spit wheel, measuring 1 m (3 ft) in diameter, was made of wood or iron, and recessed in the wall directly above or adjacent to the hearth, or installed in a separate room. Usually there were two dogs in relay to slowly turn the meat as it cooked, which could last three to four hours. These dog spits were used in coaching inns, homes in the town and country, and farmhouses, for about two to three hundred years from the 15th century. Eventually this method was replaced by mechanical spits powered by clockwork, steam or smoke, although dog spits were still common in the West Country and Wales even after mechanical versions came along.

Dog spits made their way to America and were used particularly in large hotel kitchens. It is said this practice contributed to the founding of the American Society for the Prevention of Cruelty to Animals in 1866, on the heels of the already established British RSPCA (Royal Society for the Prevention of Cruelty to Animals, 1824).

← **Kettle, Date unknown, Worldwide, Various designers, Copper / Various materials**

The kettle was originally interchangeable with the cauldron, as it was also used to cook food and sometimes to keep a stock or glaze bubbling away in the hearth. Early examples of kettles are rare, as when they came to the end of their useful life their valuable metal would be melted down and recast. Though we are now most familiar with the word as a vessel used in the tea-making process, kettle nomenclature still applies to cooking food, as is the case with the fish kettle. Eventually the kettle's purpose was solely for boiling water, for the kitchen and other household needs.

Typically, these vessels were made of iron, copper or brass. They did not have a handle or spout, as we know them today, but a round bottom, and they were hung in the hearth or set directly on the fire. Kettles evolved to a sort of cistern with a tap, which made boiling water safer and easier to access. Boiling water for tea was non-existent until after 1660 when the leaves were exported across the world, and they took on the familiar spouted form we know today around the 18th and 19th centuries. Finally, the vessel made its way from the kitchen to the salon and dining room, crafted in fine porcelain and silver. Its now archetypal form has been drawn and redrawn by design icons and well-known brands, or otherwise blends into the background of our kitchen counters, plugged into the wall for ultrafast boiling.

↑ **Hot Bertaa, 1989, Italy, Philippe Starck (for Alessi), Aluminium, resin**

In *starck* contrast to the previous kettle, this water boiler was designed by French designer Philippe Starck for Alessi in the late 1980s. It shows how far design can stray from its origin, on the other end of the spectrum for synthesizing form and function. Hot Bertaa's Postmodern design resembles a pared-back, futuristic train locomotive, propelling forward with steam. The large stick protruding out of the back at the top is the handle, as well as the receiving end for the water that goes inside the un-openable container. Similar to the design debates initiated by his Juicy Salif, with Hot Bertaa Starck again challenges form-over-function in product design. When pouring water at a 90-degree angle, the steam rises up to the hand holding the kettle. Alessi commented that Hot Bertaa was their 'most beautiful fiasco'. The company withdrew the product after less than ten years on the market, though it sits in a few design museum collections. As Alberto Alessi said, 'A true design work must move people, convey emotions, bring back memories, surprise, and go against common thinking.'

→ **Ale warmer, Circa 1880, England, H. Bradley, Copper**

Food isn't the only thing that needs to be warmed over
or in a fire, and in Britain ale was warmed in the winter
in copper containers such as these. A conical, funnel-
type shape was more common, but this shoe-shaped
ale warmer allowed the drinker to continuously warm
and then drink or pour from it as they liked by digging
the tip into the coals. At 44 cm (17 in) long, this ale
warmer holds 1.7 litres (3 pints), so could be shared
among friends. Funnel-shaped, tinned copper warmers
would likewise be lodged into the coals of a fire, though
slightly more precariously. The ale was warmed not only
for heat and to kill bacteria, but also to mingle added
spices such as nutmeg, for an extra-rich intensity of
flavour. In instances when ale warmers were not available,
sometimes hot pokers would be heated and then sizzled
in customers' tankards until the liquid was warmed.

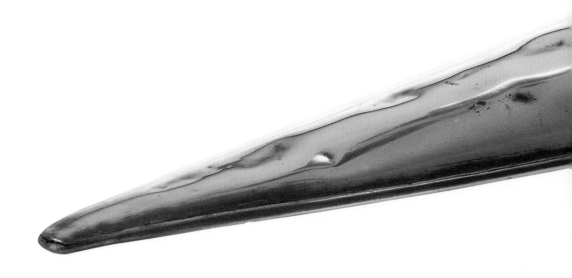

↑   **Clay stove, Date unknown, Worldwide / Asia,
Designer unknown, Ceramic**

Before metallurgy, food was cooked in clay pots,
although due to their fragility ancient examples are
rare. Beyond placing the vessel directly on the fire, it
was soon discovered that both pot and flame benefited
from the circulation of air. Though clay-pot cooking
is practised across the world, the stove pictured is
the most common in Asia and South Asia, where the
method is still very much part of everyday life and
cuisine. The coal or wood fire, as well as the clay the
food is cooked in, imparts unique flavours to the dishes
cooked in them all over Thailand, Vietnam, China, India
and Sri Lanka. In Mexico, they use a similar *braseros
de barro*. Besides clay-pots, other types of vessels and
pans can be placed on top of the stove, to fry flatbreads
or to boil or steam rice.

↓ **Mongolian fire pot, Since 12th century,**
   Mongolia / Asia, Designer unknown, Brass, wood

The Mongolian fire pot and Chinese hot pot are a step up from clay stoves, although they have a similar form. In contrast, these pots are used directly where the dining is taking place, with guests cooking and eating their food from the pot rather than it being brought from the kitchen. This form and style are well-known in Mongolia and China for 'hot pot' cooking and cuisine. It's no surprise the practice and form originated in Mongolia from nomads of the Asian steppes, as the warming broth in which meat and vegetables are cooked throughout the meal is especially suited to winter months and cold climates. Legend has it that Mongolian warriors invented the cooking method through necessity when they turned their helmets over to use as pots to cook in when nothing else was available.

Bronze cauldrons were already being produced from the 7th century; the use of brass followed shortly after and became the chosen material for this uniquely shaped pot. Traditional 'fire pots' have a central chimney that allows steam and smoke to escape from the coals beneath, heating the broth in the process. Contemporary Chinese hot pots have two compartments, one for spicy broth, one for standard; each region of the country has its own versions of hot pot recipes. Similar hot pot-style dishes are eaten throughout Asia, with individual design variations on the cooking utensil, recipes and style of eating.

The tagine is another kitchen vessel used in slow communal ovens and is still common in Morocco today. The tagine (tajine, marqa or maraq) goes back over one thousand years, and its use was even described in the famous 9th-century tale of *One Thousand and One Nights*. The name translates as a shallow pot made of earthenware, of which the bottom is comprised, topped with a cone- or tent-shaped lid; the word tagine is a metonym, meaning that it is interchangeable when describing the dish cooked inside. The lid's unique shape remains cooler than the base while cooking, resulting in condensation that gathers and falls back down to the bottom, continually basting ingredients and resulting in tender meat and flavourful stews. The top of the conical lid sometimes has a hole for adding water or letting steam escape and is shaped as a handle for lifting the lid to theatrically reveal the steaming results of a slow-cooked meal. These tools are used throughout North Africa and the Middle East, with each country and region creating their own specific recipes, often with meat, vegetables, and sometimes fruit and nuts. Originally tagines could have been cooked directly on charcoal, though the versatility of earthenware means they can also cook for many hours in the oven, as opposed to direct heat.

↑ **Chinese clay pot, Date unknown, China,
Designer unknown, Earthenware, metal**

These clay pots are distinctive, with their wire reinforce-
ments that help to dissipate heat evenly and historically
provided additional structural support. Like many
earthenware cooking pots, this one is glazed on the
inside but not on the out, so that heat can penetrate
the porous outer surface. Taking this into account,
the pots are usually soaked in water before cooking to
prevent cracking when the heat increases. The handle
is hollow, so it is cooler for handling, and the lid has
a hole to release steam. These pots can be used to
make soups, braise, or cook clay-pot dishes such as
chicken or pork belly in which ingredients are layered
to steam over the rice. Similar pots without wire are
used throughout Asia, such as the Japanese *donabe*,
Korean *ttukbaegi* or Vietnamese *nồi đất*. These
attractive pots can be used to cook and serve from
directly at the table.

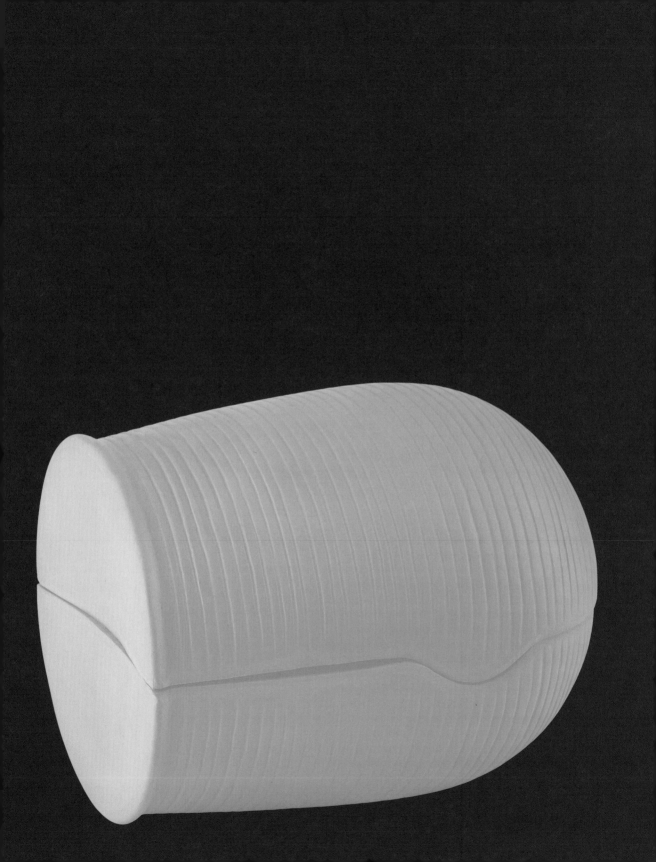

← **Chicken Brick, 1968, UK, David Queensberry (for Habitat), Terracotta**

Based on ancient techniques and tools for cooking, this unglazed terracotta 'chicken brick' works in the same way as clay pots have for thousands of years – sealing in heat and moisture and creating succulent meat as a result. Released four years after the British Habitat brand launched in 1964, the Chicken Brick was one of their best-selling items at the time. Their original chicken brick was designed by David Queensberry who realised that rather than making the object on a thrown pottery wheel, they could make both halves in press moulds – a quicker and more economical method.

The original British manufacturer of the Habitat Chicken Brick no longer exists, and they are now made in Portugal – a major hub of ceramic and terracotta production. Later versions of the chicken brick by designers such as David Mellor include a handle-like nose on the front of the object, which gives more control when lifting the lid. Germany has their own modern clay pot cooker made by Römertopf (*Römertopf* means 'Roman pot'), featuring traditional relief patterns on the exterior. Römertopf released their first pots in 1967, one year before Habitat put a more contemporary and minimal version on the market. Cooks must take care of the flavours cooked inside, as the porous nature of the material can easily absorb fishy flavours or washing-up liquid.

↑ **Doufeu, 20th century, France, Staub, Cast iron**

The doufeu pot has a unique shape that aids its particular cooking process, taking its name from *doux feu* meaning 'slow fire'. The lid was designed to fill with hot coals, so that the food inside was completely surrounded by heat, creating the effect of an oven, when most people did not have this luxury (the pot is also known as a Dutch oven in America). Now the lid is filled with water or ice cubes instead, causing condensation and a constant basting of the ingredients inside; as steam rises, the cool top causes it to quickly condense back into liquid so it cannot escape the pan. No additional moisture needs to be added when cooking in a doufeu.

Though its use goes back at least a couple of hundred years, this current design was refined in the 20th century. The doufeu originates in France, and this particular one was made by Staub, who are known for their cast ironware. The Japanese company King created a similar pan in 1953, though out of thick cast aluminium, made in Hiroshima. This *musui nabe* is described as an 'anhydrous pot' which does not require added liquid, so maintaining vitamins within the foods. This pot is used for 'dry' baking, frying, poaching, steaming and more; the lid can be used like a pan, giving the object a dual purpose.

Le Creuset probably produce the most well-known enamelled cast-iron pots and pans in the world. They have been making these out of their factory in Fresnoy-le-Grand in northern France since 1925. Cast iron has been around since at least the 7th century, but the vitreous enamel coating of molten glass was only invented in the 18th century and then refined in the 19th century. Older enamelling processes were quite toxic – involving lead and arsenic to name just a couple of nasty ingredients, with a tendency to flake off during cooking. Eventually a British patent of 1799 provided a less poisonous baked-on enamelling process, and lead-free coatings were used from 1840 onwards.

Original Le Creuset products were hand-cast in sand moulds, with each mould destroyed after one pouring; needless to say, the production process has since been streamlined, although they are still hand-finished by craftspeople today. The double layer of porcelain enamel used by Le Creuset is fired at 800°C (1,470°F), and their famous fiery gradiated orange mimics the molten lead used to cast them. The cast-iron and enamel coating means heat spreads evenly through their pots and pans, and they can easily transition from stovetop to oven.

From acquiring the 400-year-old cast iron company Cousances in 1957, to collaborations with designers such as Raymond Loewy and Enzo Mari, to new colour releases, the brand has evolved with the times over the last century, though with a clear and consistent identity. They make hard-wearing lifetime products, which can be passed down through generations, just like cauldrons were back in the day.

↑   **Sarpaneva pot, 1959, Finland, Timo Sarpaneva,
Enamelled cast iron, teak**

The 'Sarpaneva' pot, named after the designer, follows the same principle as Le Creuset: using a cast-iron pot with an enamelled interior. This pot goes a step further with its unique modern design, incorporating a wooden handle that can be used to lift the entire pot or just the lid to peak inside. Finland has abundant forests, and Timo's design is said to be inspired by traditional cooking over the fire in Finnish folklore; hence the evocative cauldron form and wooden handle accent. In the mid-20th century this design was part of a new wave of multi-functional 'oven to tableware' that was more practical for modern living, accommodating the desire for less pomp and circumstance, blurring distinctions between the kitchen and dining space. The pot is much loved as

a design classic and icon in Finland, and it featured on Finnish postage stamps in 1998.

Timo Sarpaneva was a well-known Finnish designer and sculptor, primarily working in glass, though he also dabbled in other materials such as textiles, metal and porcelain. His work in industrial design brought a unique artistry and aesthetic to everyday kitchen tools and domestic objects. His original pot in this design was red, made for the now defunct Rosenlew company in 1959. Eventually the pot was manufactured in black, and is now produced by Iitala (Finland), who are known for meaningful designer collaborations in the products they develop.

The *molcajete* is interchangeable as a grinding tool like a mortar, but also a cooking vessel. It has been used for thousands of years by the Mayans and Aztecs and by modern-day Mexicans. They are made from granite or volcanic rock, which is not only abrasive for grinding, but can also withstand high temperatures when cooking inside the bowl. Before its first use, a *molcajete* is cured by grinding rice flour or salt into the stone to 'seal' and smooth the inside. Typically, it stands on three feet, and the food cooked or ground in the bowl takes on flavours from the stone's minerals; equally what is prepared leaves behind aromatics for future meals. Salsas, guacamole or mole sauces can be ground in the *molcajete*, and when the stone is heated it melds flavours for serving hot dishes, often bubbling at the table long after it is removed from the heat.

↑ **Posnet, 1850s, Europe / Sweden,
Designer unknown, Iron**

Posnets are as close to the saucepan that we know today; they were used around medieval times in Europe and eventually in North America. They are recognisable by their three short feet, were made in various metals, and sometimes had covers just like modern-day saucepans. As an accompaniment to cauldrons, posnets cooked skillet- or sauce-based dishes which required a smaller pot for more focused flavours and textures. In the hearth, a small pile of coals would have been separated from the main fire to put under this small pot and on top of the lid if it had one.

The name posnet derives from the Welsh *posned*, meaning a porringer or small dish. Pots with short legs and long handles such as these are also known as spiders. Eventually the short legs were removed once stovetop cooking was developed, to sit directly on the hob. Many of these pots were made of cast 'bell metal', so named because it was the bell founders who had experience in casting with alloys of copper and tin, and thus the task was left to them. This bronze or brass-like metal alloy was also fit for purpose: as a poor conductor of heat the contents inside could boil away while the handle was kept moderately cool for handling.

↑ **Griddle, Date unknown, Europe / Worldwide, Designer unknown, Iron**

The Scots described spreading out a batter on a 'riddle' board, using a spatula called a 'thible', and then transferring this to be cooked with a 'spittle' on a griddle. They would use these flat, pan-like griddles and tools to cook oatcakes, oatbreads and any sort of 'pancake'. The first griddles were made of stone or sandstone, as used by the Romans, and were known as bakestones; in Scotland they were called bannock stones.

Upon metallurgy and developments in cooking besides the cauldron, these metal sheets of iron or brass were primarily used for breads or baking. Early griddles or baking irons were designed for hanging over the hearth; sometimes the structure was separate from the flat baking iron itself, so the sheet could be removed for easy serving or cleaning. In Mexico cast-iron griddles such as these are known as comal and used for tortillas, while in America the term is familiar as the hot surface for grilling hamburgers in diners. Contemporary griddles are made of aluminium or steel, and they are a popular method of cooking in Japan for teppanyaki cuisine (*teppan* means 'metal plate'; *yaki* means 'grilled'), or for Korean barbecue. Teppanyaki cuisine and restaurants were made especially popular in the late 20th century, and they are still enjoyed across the world today.

↓   **Paella pan, 8th century / 19th century,
     Spain, Designer unknown, Various metals**

Paella pans originate from and are used in Spain, and
are made from iron, steel or tinned copper. Though
non-Spanish speakers know the name *paella* as
referring to a particular cooked dish, the word actually
translates as 'frying pan' in the Valencian dialect, where
the cuisine originates. Traditionally this dish of rice and
meats varied widely, as it was a combination of
whatever was available to put in the pan on any
particular day: snails, chicken, vegetables, eels or other
seafood. As with many well-known and loved dishes of
the world, paella was a peasant food, made by farmers
or labourers. Paella as a dish emerged after the Moors
brought rice to the country in the 8th century; the pan
as we know it was designed in 19th century.

These pans are big and shallow (30–80 cm / 12–31½
in diameter), designed to provide the maximum surface
area for heat to cook the rice and other ingredients,
and for sharing food between many people at once.
The bottom of the pan sometimes has a hammered
texture, to keep the structure robust from heating such
a large area. Paella is still cooked outdoors, as it was
traditionally, where large flames can accommodate
large pans for feeding big groups and gatherings. Diners
used to eat directly from the pan with their own spoons,
though this is not as common anymore.

↓   **Saucepans, 1920s, USA,**
     Daleware, Aluminium, melamine

The first saucepans were made from iron and copper,
then from tin, enamel and aluminium, then steel. These
square pots were part of this evolution, made as space-
savers for electric hobs. They came in decreasing sizes
that nest inside one another, with discreet pouring lips
at one corner for drip-free decanting. These aluminium
pans with melamine handles were produced by Daleware;
another company called Siddons Ltd. produced an
enamelware version in the 1930s. Various companies
at the time also produced square frying pans.

↑   **Wok, Since 1ˢᵗ century CE, China / Asia, Designer unknown, Iron / Steel**

Wok cooking originates from a scarcity of fuel, goes hand in hand with chopping food into small pieces, and eating with chopsticks. The wide and deep bowl allows food to be cooked quickly on the surrounding surfaces with continuous movement of the pan or by 'stir-frying' with large *saibashi* (the Japanese term for cooking chopsticks). The sloping sides of the pan cause food to fall back to the very hot centre, cooking ingredients quickly as they constantly move around. The shape of the pan is also designed to fit easily on what were common brazier stoves.

The best woks are made of iron, which conducts heat well, though they are also made of carbon or stainless steel. It is essential to season the pans before and after use, by rubbing them with an oil-soaked towel and drying them over the flame for a few seconds. Woks are used throughout Asia, in China (*chūkanabe* is a Chinese pot), Japan, Indonesia (*kuali / wadjan*) and even India (*karahi*). Woks typically have long handles to keep the hand far from the flame, or two handles on both sides; they also have accessories such as metal grill trays for steaming and generally the pan can be used for multiple purposes. Some woks require ring stands to function in Western kitchens where gas burners aren't designed for the wide, round pot bottom.

↑ **Fish kettle / Poissonière, Since 17th century, France, Designer unknown, Aluminium**

→ **Bain-marie, Since 1st century CE, Worldwide, Mary the Jewess, Various materials**

This fish kettle or *poissonière* is one of two main types of pots for cooking *poisson* (fish). They are both shaped more or less for the fish that go inside them, the other pot being a *turbotière*, in a diamond shape to fit a turbot lying flat. These pans are uniquely extravagant (this one is about 50 cm / 20 in long), and loved for this reason, albeit they are quite useful for cooking various fish. The tray inside allows for perfect poaching and gentle lifting of the fish, as it is otherwise a messy ordeal prising it out with spatulas and not enough hands.

Food-specific fish cooking pans are also common in Norway, where the diet consists of a high proportion of seafood. The finest of these pans are made from copper, in true French style, though many are made of aluminium or steel. Fish kettles are not to be confused with a 'kettle of fish': this term refers to a cauldron-type vessel (known as a kettle), which historically was brought to picnics by the riverside in Britain or Scotland and filled with fish for cooking for guests. 'Kettle of fish' is also an idiom with various meanings in Britain, though it is unclear how this was construed from a pot full of riverside picnic food.

A bain-marie was traditionally used to keep food warm, especially when punctual attendance at the dining table was haphazard across the centuries, for various reasons. The French term is a translation from Medieval Latin of *balneum Mariae*, 'Mary's bath', attributed to Mary the Jewess who 'invented' the technique for alchemy in the first instance, about the 1st or 2nd centuries CE. The technique was mentioned in the ancient collection of Roman recipes *Apicius*, from the 1st century CE, and is evidenced in Ancient Greece and Rome in double vases called authepsa, which were used to keep water hot (they have been likened to samovars).

Today the tool is also known as a double boiler or water bath. Some historic houses and kitchens have large bain-marie vats which were used to keep many pots warm at one time. This method is still used to keep food warm (in buffets, for example), but also to cook food gently, such as melting chocolate to be incorporated into whipped egg whites, creating special sauces such as hollandaise, or to bake cakes of a delicate constitution in the oven.

These specialised two-tier pots usually consist of a copper container beneath, which is filled with water and gently heats the contents above, often in a glazed porcelain or earthenware container with a lid. They are also made in enamelware or tin, and stainless steel in catering environments. The method can be easily replicated or improvised without fancy tools, by placing a heatproof bowl over a pan of simmering water.

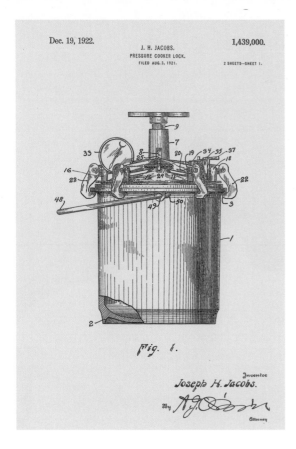

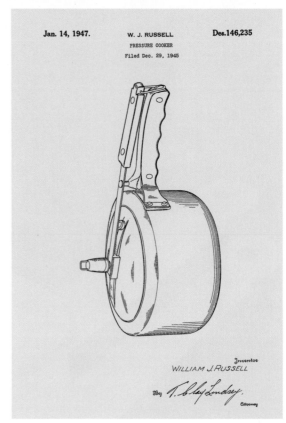

↑   **Pressure cooker, Since 1680, France /
Worldwide, Denis Papin, Metal**

Pressure cookers were originally called 'digesters' and their invention in 1680 is comparable to the invention of microwaves in the 20th century. Denis Papin's original design for the steam digester created a pressure of 35–50 lb per square inch and was capable of softening bones. By trapping 100 per cent of the steam inside during cooking, pressure builds which in turn raises the temperature at which water boils, so reducing the cooking time. Early designs of the Papin cooking pot are quite serious-looking machines with ridged sides and screw-top lids. The French influence certainly persisted, as this kitchen tool was and still is commonly used in the country; the use of pressure cookers is also customary in Mexico and Eastern Europe.

By the 20th century, design merged with function in countertop-worthy, less intense-looking 'digesters', such as the one pictured above. Saucepan-style pressure cookers were first released in 1939 at the World's Fair in New York – this form was much more recognisable to domestic cooks. Frédéric Lescure and brothers branded the *Cocotte Minute* (instant casserole pot) in 1953, described as a time-saver that retained intensity of flavour in the cooking process; to date the company has produced over 50 million of these pressure cookers. These tools must be used with care, as if the pressure gets too high and cannot escape through a faulty release valve, there is the possibility they will explode. This is rare, and the pots have been carefully designed to avoid this. With the advent of the countertop microwave in the 1960s the use of pressure cookers declined, though the result of what they cook is not comparable to the former method.

↓ **CorningWare, 1958, USA,**
  S. Donald Stookey, Pyroceram®

CorningWare is distinctive because of its original blue and white cornflower pattern on the side, which by the 1970s had evolved into full-colour illustrations of fruits and vegetables. Though the first designs bear cornflowers that mirror its name, the company was a spinoff of Corning Glass Works, named after its factory location in Corning, New York. Their products are a classic of the American kitchen, made of a particular type of heat-resistant glassware invented in the 1950s by S. Donald Stookey. Stookey was an in-house engineer at Corning and filed around 60 patents in his lifetime relating to developments in glass. This glass-ceramic hybrid is known as Pyroceram® and was developed for space rockets as a material that could withstand extreme temperature fluctuations. The space race eventually made its way into the kitchen, with CorningWare producing various 'triple-duty' casseroles that could go 'directly from the freezer to the oven to the table'. These cooking vessels were also designed with accompanying lids, which allowed them to transition from the table to the refrigerator for storing leftovers.

Though we associate most grilling actions with metal,
in Portugal these terracotta chouriço grillers, the *assador
de chouriço*, are used to cook the southern European
sausage. Chouriço is similar to what many know as
chorizo from Spain, though morcelas, linguiça, and
other types of sausage can be cooked in this portable
tool just as well. Instead of heat from hot metal, the
meat is cooked by alcohol (such as brandy) that is
poured into the bottom of this receptacle and set alight.
The grills of the ceramic simply hold the sausages away
from the flame rather than help to cook them.

↑ **Gridiron / Whirling broiler, 19th century,
Sweden / Europe, Maker unknown, Cast iron**

Though in contemporary life we associate these tools
with grilling steaks, their original purpose was varied.
Roman gridirons were used to warm food in vessels on
top of ovens, which closely resemble modern stovetop
ranges. Typically, gridirons had short legs, with a handle
to adjust their position over hot ashes. They could be used
to hold vessels on top, but eventually their use as a grill
for meat was discovered – if meat wasn't being roasted
on a spit or boiled in a cauldron, it could be grilled on
the gridiron; the tool was also used for bread and toast.

By the 16th or 17th centuries some gridirons were
designed with grooves in the irons to allow fat to run
off into dripping pans; blacksmiths even created ornate
designs with patterns of hearts and swirls. Most surviving
examples of this tool are from the 18th century onwards,
and from the 19th century there were revolving versions
known as 'whirling broilers', as pictured here. Indeed,
the ability to rotate the food over hot coals or ashes was
quite useful, especially when controlling temperature
was tricky with rudimentary tools and no thermostats.
The use of gridirons was still noted in *Mrs. Beeton's Book
of Household Management* (1861), and the grilling of
steaks on such a utensil was also described in *Practical
Housekeeping* of 1884.

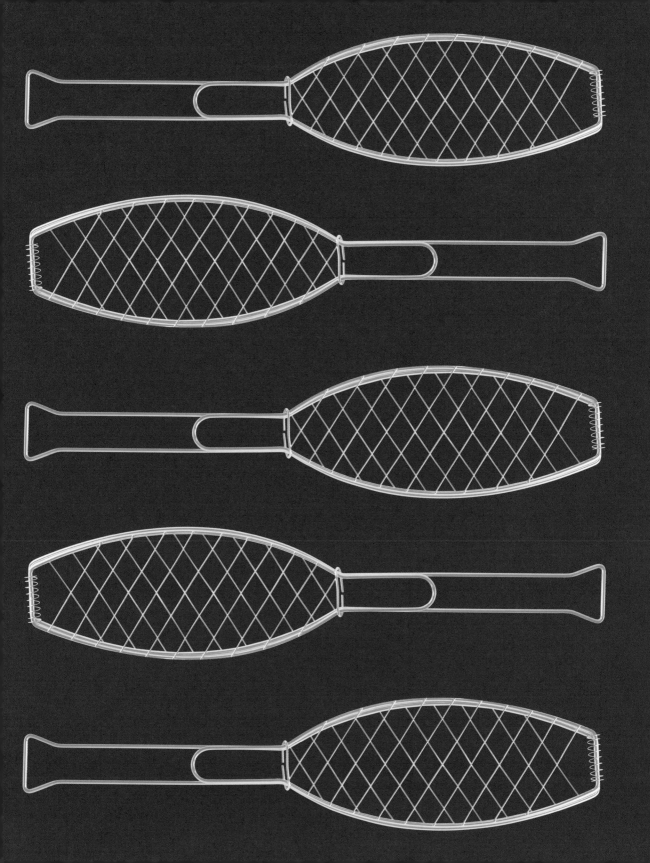

← **Fish grill, 20th century, USA,
Designer unknown, Stainless steel**

The concept of enclosing fish in an open structure
and placing it over a fire is not new. However, the tool
has been developed to meet this need perfectly in
what is known as a fish grill. These utensils can be as
straightforward as long, square and oval, hinged, open-
structure grills, or as detailed as multiple individual
sardine-shaped units arranged in a circular starburst
pattern. Some come with legs to be set directly over
a fire, while others are designed to sit on top of modern-
day grills. The handle is long so that you do not burn
your hand when flipping the fish for even cooking on
each side. Historically, a myriad of tools has been
designed for cooking and eating fish, and these all help
to facilitate that lovely charred flavour, while keeping
the delicate flesh safe from falling apart, as it would
otherwise without the support of this utensil.

↑ **Waffle iron, Since 14th century, Northern
Europe, Designer unknown, Cast iron**

We know waffle irons as plug-in devices for the countertop, but like the fish grill, these tools were originally held
over the fire to bake batter in moulded forms. Waffle or
wafer irons were used across Europe, especially in their
14th-century places of origin: in Belgium for their famous
deep-welled version; in the Netherlands for small, wafer-
like *stroopwafels*; and in France for *gaufres*. The word
'waffle' is, in fact, an American bastardisation of *gaufres*,
and perhaps a riff on the word wafer. In Victorian England
and also Scandinavia, waffle irons moulded several
heart-shaped pieces at once; the émigré Pennsylvania
Dutch in America made various patterned designs, and
the tool was given as a love token, especially by bride-
grooms to brides for good luck. These days waffle irons
are still made of cast iron (hence the name) and are
no longer held over the fire, being plugged into the
wall instead.

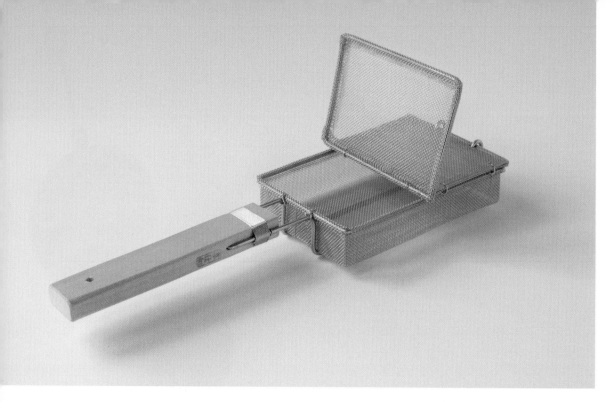

↑   **Goma iri, 20th century, Japan, Wasaburo Tsuji,
Stainless steel, cypress**

Sesame is an important ingredient across Asia, Africa
and the Middle East, both as a seed and an oil; its use
in various forms can be found across the world, whether
topping an American burger bun or ground as tahini in
hummus. Sesame is particularly prevalent in Japan,
where black or white seeds are used as part of garnishes
such as *gomashio, furikake* and *shichimi togarashi*, which
can be sprinkled on ramen or rice; it can be ground in
a *suribachi* mortar to make sauces for tofu or turned
into oil for frying and salad dressings.

The *goma iri* is a fine wire-mesh tool for roasting golden
sesame seeds on top of a flame, which gives them extra
flavour. The tool can also be used to roast gingko nuts
or coffee. This particular *goma iri* is made by Tsujiwa
Kanaami who have been crafting wire-mesh products
in Japan for over 50 years. Traditionally the handle is
made of cypress wood, although it can also be made
from bamboo. Wire-mesh craft has been practised in
Japan since the Heian Period (between the 8th and 12th
centuries CE) for tools such as wire storage baskets,
tea strainers, and more.

↓   **Chestnut pan, 19th century,
Europe, Designer unknown, Steel**

'Chestnuts roasting on an open fire' is a familiar tune in the Western, English-speaking world, though it is a practice that has died out somewhat due to the laborious nature of preparing them. Chestnuts have been eaten for thousands of years, as a readily available food that doesn't need close agricultural management. They were consumed in large quantities in Europe before corn and other grains or starches were brought from the New World, and they have been eaten in East Asia for thousands of years. These pans were – and sometimes still are – used across Europe in France, Italy and Spain for roasting the meaty carbohydrates over open fire or heat. At first glance to the uninitiated, the tool looks like a joke, but its design is, in fact, superbly practical for roasting this specific type of food; other ingredients or tree nuts might fall through the gaps or disperse nut peelings on the stovetop. Though the original 'designer' is unknown, they probably had a good sense of humour, but were also clever enough to meet the requirements for cooking the food to perfection over hearth or stove fire and heat.

This handcrafted bamboo *shikizaru* is as delicate in its construction as it is in its use. Woven by hand into a traditional and precise hexagonal pattern, the *shikizaru* only lasts about twenty uses. This netted construction is used to wash delicate foods or gently steam fish, avoiding small tears or breaks in the flesh when cooking. It is particularly suited for cooking sea bream or conger eel (*anago*), which is a popular dish in Japan. The care taken in preparing such foods is common in *ryōtei* restaurants for kaiseki meals comprised of multiple courses of carefully thought-out forms and the flavours of seasonal ingredients.

The use of this material and form in cooking was likely introduced by a bamboo weaver, who noticed their scrap piece of woven material could be very useful for this particular task. Bamboo weaving dates back to the Neolithic Period in China (around 10,000 BCE).

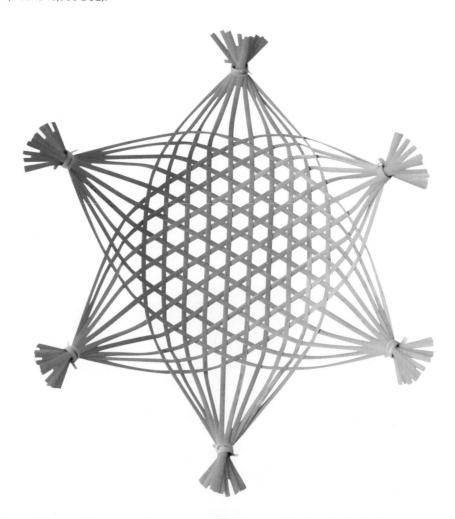

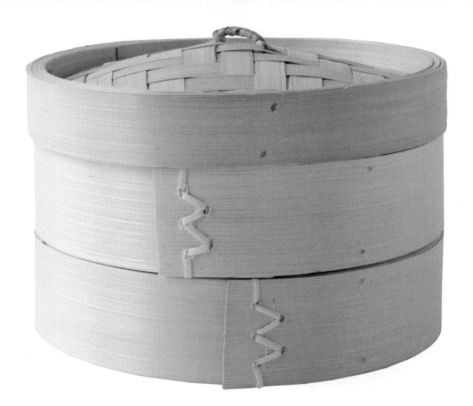

↑   **Steamer, Since 3000 BCE, East Asia,
Designer unknown, Bamboo**

Bamboo steamers are versatile in that they can fit on top of or inside various vessels such as pots or woks, for cooking dim sum, vegetables and dumplings, and come in a variety of sizes. The cooking technique and utensil has been used in China since at least 3,000 BCE, though the form it takes has varied over the centuries. The steamer pictured here is the most iconic, which can be simple and inexpensive to produce, though highly crafted versions are still made by hand in China and Japan.

Bamboo is robust and won't crack or warp when subjected to the heat of steam. These steamers are often made with stackable layers, allowing for different foods to be cooked at the same time; over a lifetime's use, they take on a proud amber colour. From the 1950s onwards, when dim sum teahouses were popularised in places like Hong Kong and Chinatowns around the world, the production and export of these steamers from East Asia increased. The bamboo steamer is an essential staple of the *batterie de cuisine* in Asian and global kitchens.

↑ **Rice kettle, Since 8ᵗʰ century BCE, Japan / Asia, Hagama (pictured), Cast iron / cypress**

In Japan, the original rice cookers were cast-iron pots with lids made of cypress wood; now they are electric devices plugged into the wall that cook the grains with minimal effort. They can also be made from earthenware. The metal version is known as an okama pot, named after the crater lake of the Okama volcano, which is geothermic and therefore akin to a bubbling cooking pot. The large ridge in the middle of the pot would have sat comfortably on top of a traditional Japanese kamado cooking range, lower than hip height with fires beneath and two holes for placing pots on top of the heat. In Indonesia a different method is used, where the rice is steamed in a conical *kukusan* bamboo container placed above a pot of boiling water, after the rice has been parboiled. The *kukusan* is used to shape a tumpeng rice form, reminiscent of volcanoes in Indonesia and symbolising the fertility and richness of the soil that surrounds the bases of these volatile mountains.

↓   **Otoshibuta, Date unknown, Japan,
    Designer unknown, Wood**

The *otoshibuta* 'drop' lid sits inside a pot during cooking, rather than on top of it. This allows for even heat distribution, and gentle simmering that subsequently requires little or no stirring. The direct covering on top of the food prevents liquid from evaporating and creates smaller boiling bubbles, thus protecting the structure of ingredients from breaking apart. Made of untreated wood, the *otoshibuta* must be soaked in water before use and washed and dried directly after. Its construction is simple: a wooden circle with a dovetail-jointed handle that slides directly into the lid when assembled. Some *otoshibuta* are made from perforated metal or as single layers of silicone, though wood is the most traditional and recognisable type in almost every Japanese kitchen. In a tight situation, an *otoshibuta* can be improvised by making a disc of aluminium foil pierced with a few large holes in the top, set directly above simmering food.

Jan. 26, 1954

E. M. MILLARD ET AL

2,667,117

ADJUSTABLE COLANDER FOR COOKING AND
SERVING VEGETABLES AND THE LIKE

Filed June 2, 1950

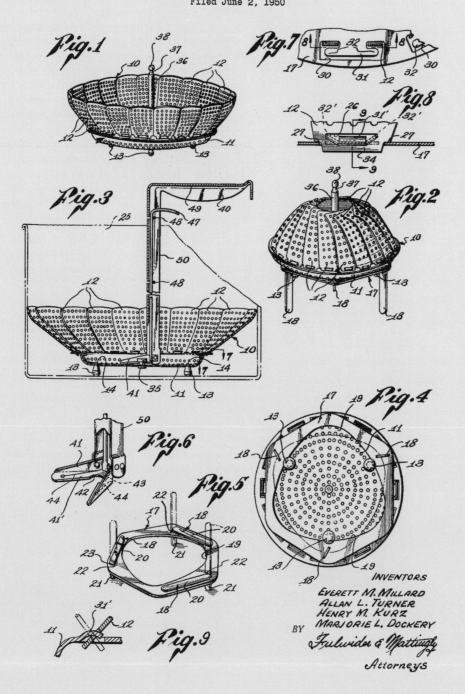

INVENTORS

EVERETT M. MILLARD
ALLAN L. TURNER
HENRY M. KURZ
MARJORIE L. DOCKERY

BY Fulwider & Mattingly

Attorneys

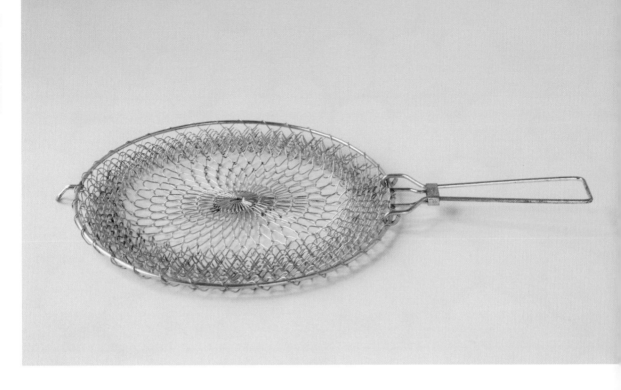

← **Metal steamer, 1944–1950, USA,
E. M. Millard et al, Steel**

Bamboo is certainly robust, but in the USA where
bamboo is less common (as is the steaming process)
this metal steamer insert was invented in the 1950s
to simplify the method for Americans. This 'adjustable
colander for cooking and serving vegetables and the
like' fits into pans where water is boiling underneath so
the contents can be steamed, which is then easily lifted
by the central pole. The metal steamer expands and
contracts like a blooming flower, so fits various pan
sizes, or allows a cloche to be placed over the cooking
ingredients; the function also saves space in the
cupboard. Sometimes the leaves dismantle from the
main body, making it a cumbersome gadget at times.
Metal steamers conduct heat so food cooks at a higher
temperature than in the bamboo type; bamboo also
absorbs some of the moisture when steaming whereas
in the metal version condensation drips back onto the
food. Bamboo steamers or *shikizaru* are a safer bet
for more delicate foods or dumplings.

↑ **Frying basket, 20th century, France / Worldwide,
Various designers, Steel mesh**

Wire-mesh weaving has been around since the Egyptians
used the technique for jewellery. It was later used by the
Vikings, and from the 5th century in chain-mail armour.
Taking cues from looms and textiles, by the 19th century
wire weaving by machine had advanced, and it wasn't
long before innovative kitchen products were making
best use of the production process and potential
applications of metal mesh structures. The strong open
construction of a metal weave is ideal for a number of
purposes: draining, steaming and deep-frying. In the
early 20th century, inventors and designers came up
with various safety versions of frying baskets, collapsible
iterations, and versatile multi-function wire-mesh baskets.
These tools are designed to sit in pots of hot frying oil,
with the ability to remove fried contents safely and easily,
rather than picking individual items out of hot oil with
tongs. Similar tools to these, but narrower and deeper,
are used in Asia to scoop noodles out of boiling water
for a multitude of dishes such as ramen or stir-fries.

← Baking beads, 19th century, Europe / USA,
  Designer unknown, Ceramic

Ceramic beads were usually used in industrial
processes, until it clicked that their properties could
also be applied in the kitchen. Culturally ceramic and
glass beads have been made for thousands of years for
decorative jewellery; in industry, beads such as these
are used to grind metals or minerals in rotating drums.

Before ceramic baking beads, grains like rice or beans
were used to weigh down pastry during the 'blind baking'
process, which precooks pastry before a filling is added.
Subsequently, these ceramic versions were also known
as baking beans. Pie dishes and ceramic dishes lined
with pastry are covered with baking paper, with the
baking beads on top to prebake the shell. This avoids
rising, bubbles, 'soggy bottoms' or undercooked pastry
in the finished pie or tart. Ceramic is more efficient than
natural grains, as it distributes heat evenly and provides
weight that prevents the pastry bottom puffing up or
the sides collapsing. In contrast to actual beans, these
beads are endlessly reusable for this purpose.

↑ Pie vent, 19th century, England / Europe,
  Designer unknown, Ceramic

The pie vent / funnel / chimney / whistle allows steam to
escape from pies when cooking, to avert the risk of small
explosions in the oven, leaking pies and split pastry tops.
This tool was particularly useful in rudimentary ovens
with variable temperature control. At first the shape was
utilitarian – a conical, upside-down funnel shape with
arches on the bottom for steam to enter – though the
Victorians created bird-shaped versions, known as 'pie
birds'. With a pie bird, no slashes in pie tops are required,
though slashes are more common than pie birds these
days. When placed in the middle of meat or fruit pies,
the pie bird helps keep the pie structure from collapsing.

This tool resembles a similar ceramic device known
as a milk boiler, which is placed in a pan of milk being
heated to prevent it boiling over. The milk boiler creates
a continuous fountain-like action of milk flowing through
it; without this piece of ceramic, milk sticks to the bottom
when heated. Pie vents and milk boilers are hardly used
today, but they are appreciated as a collector's item in
the kitchen.

↓ **Straw pot mat, 20th century,**
   Japan, Various makers, Rice straw

This traditional straw mat was woven by craftspeople on Sado Island, part of the northern archipelago of islands of the Niigata Prefecture, Japan. They are made from dried rice straw and used to protect surfaces from large *donabe* pots, or smaller cast-iron teapots with round or flat-bottomed surfaces. These trivets are woven across a few regions of Japan, and they are crafted from coconut fibres, rice straw or rush stalks. These sensitively handmade trivets are a unique example of rural craftsmanship, and the eyelet at the top allows you to hang the straw circle neatly in the kitchen.

Though trivets are often made of metal, similar natural-fibre pot stands are found across the world in different cultures from many time periods: Africa, the Middle East, the Americas and across Asia (besides Japan). Though incredibly simple objects, their creation and use mark a significant moment in human advancement, placing importance on craftsmanship, the decorative arts and ritual. By crafting an ornate object that prevents the heat of a pot from marring a well-made table surface beneath, we understand that we are no longer eating in dwellings with dirt floors, but elevating mealtimes to a moment of social celebration.

↑ **Universal Tool, 1881, USA, W. H. Thayer, Cast iron**

It almost looks like a knuckle duster, and in some ways,
it is, as this Universal Tool can tenderise meat with the
four outer spikes. Patented by William Henry Thayer in
1881, this cast-iron, multi-purpose tool could be used
as a trivet, potholder, lid lifter, pie crimper and bottle-
opener. The patent states: 'By providing the implement
with finger-holes, the user is enabled to hold it in any
position desired without danger of slipping or turning
in the hand ... a simple, cheap, and efficient implement
for kitchen use.' This tool is an exemplar of the boom
in new inventions and trinkets for the kitchen and home,
which came into their own at the end of the 19th century
and beyond.

Hold & Scoop

In previous chapters, we saw that chopping, grinding and mixing are standard processes which, in some cases, require little innovation of a tool beyond minimal alterations to sticks, stones and blades. In this section, the tools define more sophisticated cooking and eating patterns: utensils performing refined tasks such as flipping flatbreads and cakes (cake turners and spatulas), retrieving foods from hot oil (spider strainers), or ladling portions of batter into specifically shaped pans (*takoyaki* ladles). These actions go beyond stirring stews in cauldrons with sticks or grinding pastes with stones. Tools used for gripping, scooping or flipping food require a new dexterity, accompanied by the invention of highly specific and erudite cuisine.

As the American poet Alfred Billings Street quoted, 'Nature is man's teacher. She unfolds her treasures to his search, unseals his eye, illumes his mind ... an influence breathes from all the sights and sounds of her existence.' And thus, as we see throughout the book, many tools are a *natural* evolution from what exists already in nature: bunches of twigs for whisks, volcanic rock as abrasive graters, feathers for egg washing, seashells to skim, gourds for scoops. The shapes and textures of these objects logically lend themselves to their respective uses in the 'kitchen', and remind us of holistic, sustainable and circular approaches to the use and reuse of materials. Beyond these intuitive pairings, we progressed from materials and forms to elongated boards to push and retrieve breads from ovens (peels), paired two long sticks to act as cooking chopsticks (*saibashi*), carefully shaped implement edges to match their bowl, and turned rubber from trees into highly specialised scraping tools.

The objects in this section trace and confirm the fact that each utensil used for cooking holds within it a history of evolution, the imagination and the creativity of humanity. No cuisine could have evolved without its tools, nor its tools without its ingredients. The diversity of our cultures again shines through when we observe how different regions of the world create unique purposes for ladles, or actions for skimmers, flipping a myriad of foods with a variety of spatulas in specific materials and endless decorative or minimalist forms. As these holding and scooping objects progress, the next step is serving: the notion of sharing with others, breaking bread with our families and extended tribes. These tools send us on our way to the table, with scooping turning into offerings to others and the formalities and rituals that ensue during mealtimes, once we have left the kitchen for our moment of celebration.

Though these tools were first mostly used to retrieve water, their story is an important one as an early signifier of man's innovation with materials at hand. These ladles are a hardly altered scoop-shaped form of kalabash gourds with a naturally grown handle. Examples of cultivating and crafting gourds come from across the world – Africa, South America, Asia, the Americas, Europe, the South Pacific – transformed into useful objects in the kitchen, rattling instruments, drinking containers, colanders, and much more. Sometimes these gourds were even grown into elaborate moulds. After civilisations developed new materials to replace these natural tools, such as ceramics, the form of the gourd was still replicated in decorative vases and vessels, especially in China. The cultivation and use of gourds go back centuries, and they are still used today, dried as is or ornately decorated. Without a ladle cutout, they are used as water vessels or to store other liquids, and the plant itself is known as a 'bottle gourd'.

↑   Ladle, 20th century, Europe,
    Maker unknown, Steel, wood

In places where coconuts and gourds do not grow,
ladles were first crafted from wood (as with wooden
spoons), earthenware, then finally metal, and now
melamine and plastic. Though initially food was
sometimes shared directly from the pot, eventually
we needed to dish out individual portions with these
bowl-shaped utensils, servings that a standard wooden
spoon cannot accommodate. Ladles are used for a
variety of purposes: scooping butter from churns, basting,
pouring batter into *takoyaki* pans or serving soups and
sauces. They require different materials, shapes and
ergonomic handles, and refined designs include a
spout for drip-free pouring.

↑   Takoyaki ladle, 20th century, Japan,
    Designer unknown, Metal, plastic

These small ladles are used in street-food stalls in Japan,
particularly Osaka where the *takoyaki* octopus cake
snack originates. This unique dish actually requires
a few dedicated tools, such as a specially shaped pan
and a couple of small sticks to rotate the batter quickly
as it cooks to make perfect round shapes. The bowl
of the ladle is small, about 7.6 × 6.4 cm (3 × 2½ in), with
a pouring spout to portion batter into the spherical
depressions of the pan.

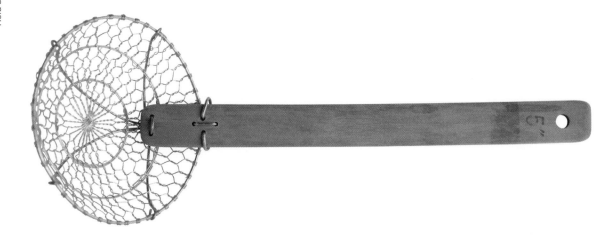

← **Skimmer, 19th century, England,**
   Designer unknown, Brass

Skimmers were used to separate the cream from the milk, the fat which naturally rises to the top; the result below is 'skimmed' milk. Historically skimmed milk was used to fatten pigs, which is ironic since today it is consumed by those watching their weight. The leftover cream at the top can be found in bottles of unhomogenised milk. The cream skimmed off the milk can be turned into butter or sour cream or whipped into peaks.

Historically brass (an alloy of copper and zinc) or bronze (mostly made of copper) was the best metal for this process in dairy production. These materials do not impart flavour to milk, and in tandem the milk is less likely to corrode these metals, meaning no rust in the product and fewer replacements or less financial loss. Though this form is quite simple, some skimmers have elaborate handles or specially formed and patterned scoops. By 1840 when enamelling metal became more economically viable, many skimmers were made of this material. Eventually centrifugal machines replaced the method of skimming by hand. Although they look the same, skimmers are not to be confused with scummers, which serve a similar yet different purpose in another form: for scooping the scum off the top of bubbling broths of meat, beans or jam. In India, skimmers like this are used to retrieve fried food from oil, and to make small boondi dumplings of chickpea flour, pushed through the holes, much like spaetzle in Germany.

↑ **Spider strainer, Date unknown, East Asia,**
   Designer unknown, Brass, bamboo

The spider strainer gets its name from the web-like shape of the body of the bowl of this open-structure, basket-type ladle. It originates in East Asia, but has found its way into kitchens across the globe. This tool has a wire-mesh structure that is seen elsewhere in the kitchen and can be handcrafted or machine-made. Traditionally, the basket is made of brass, although they are also found in stainless steel. The spider strainer is indispensable for a multitude of functions, such as skimming scum, taking objects out of boiling liquid, removing food from hot frying oil, or even – it has been known – as a television aerial. The scooping shape is a reasonably flat and shallow concave form, ideal for collecting floating items: its typology sits somewhere between a sieve and a spoon. The handle is made of bamboo or wood (not metal), which protects the chef from excess heat. It is a staple in both the Western and Eastern *batterie de cuisine*, equally as useful for scooping up fried wontons or pasta.

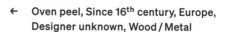

← Oven peel, Since 16th century, Europe,
Designer unknown, Wood / Metal

Given that ovens were large and long before they were
small and domestic, the oven peel has been a necessity
for a good few hundred years. Bartolomeo Scappi
recorded a few long-handled tools for ovens in his
cookbook *Opera … The Art and Craft of a Master Cook*
(1570), including an oven scraper and oven sweeper
that accompanied the peel. These shovel- or oar-shaped
tools help to place and retrieve various breads, pastries
and pizzas when baking is complete. The long handle
allows items to be pushed back into the hottest part of
the oven, and prevents the baker's hand from burning
when using, though oven gloves are usually used in
tandem. Like shovels, they originally had wooden handles
and metal spades; they evolved to be made completely
of wood but are sometimes metal. Before using they are
covered with flour or meal to prevent the raw or cooked
item from sticking. Of course, the French used them in
early boulangeries and patisseries, and this is said to be
where the name comes from, *pelle* translating to 'shovel'
and 'spade' in English.

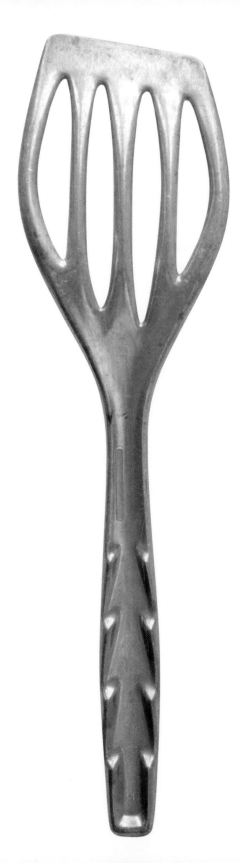

← Spatula / Cake turner, Mid-20th century, Germany, Westmark, Aluminium

The word *spatula* derives from Latin, meaning a split piece of wood. Fastforward to metallurgy and this spatula made of aluminium. This German *pfannenwender* was made by Westmark, but a few intricate examples exist from the same time period in Europe. The notches on the back of the handle prevent the turner from slipping when balanced on a pan. This ornate food turner bears within it a marker of history and political indicators. As well as the Westmark *Kuchenfreunden Orig* (original kitchen friend) branding, this tool has a 'W. Germany Pat' mark, indicating that the patent for the utensil was valid in West Germany. Similar prewar spatulas bear the mark 'D.R.G.M' (*Deutsches Reichsgebrauchsmuster*), indicating that the design was officially registered inside all German states of the Reich as a 'utility model'. After the Second World War, when the Allied occupation ended in 1949, and because registration was valid for three years, from October 1952 all registrations were then marked with D.B.G.M. (*Deutsches Bundesgebrauchsmuster*) or simply *Gebrauchsmuster / Gebrauchsmusterschutz*. This translates as being a registered federal design, rather than a Reich one. This same Westmark *pfannenwender* is still made today, as a spatula and in tong form that is manufactured in plastic.

↓ **Crepe spatula / Spreader, 19th century, France, Designer unknown, Wood**

The pancake is more or less universal across the globe, though in slightly different forms. In France, they have the crepe, which is eaten both savoury and sweet. The crepe spatula (spanell) comes with an accompanying spreader (the rozell). The simple rozell tool of perpendicular pieces of wood joined in a 'T'-shape is essential for spreading crepe batter evenly on a large griddle (the bilig), usually around 30–55 cm (12–22 in) in diameter, which is made specifically for crepes. The spatula could initially have been a single stick or dowel, but it evolved into an elongated flat surface that is required to flip, roll and fold large and long French crepes; the edges are bevelled to prise under the thin surface of the pancake. These tools are completely cuisine-specific: the liquid-y crepe batter and the large diameter it cooks into require special utensils beyond standard spatulas, where a twirl of the pan to spread the batter isn't sufficient.

Crepes originate from Brittany in northwest France, as legend has it due to an incident of thin porridge accidentally pouring onto a hot surface in the 13th century. The word crepe comes from the Latin *crispus*, which means 'curly' or 'crisp', and a written recipe for 'crespus' was recorded in the 14th century. *Le Jour des Crêpes* (Crepe Day) is celebrated in France on 2nd February each year.

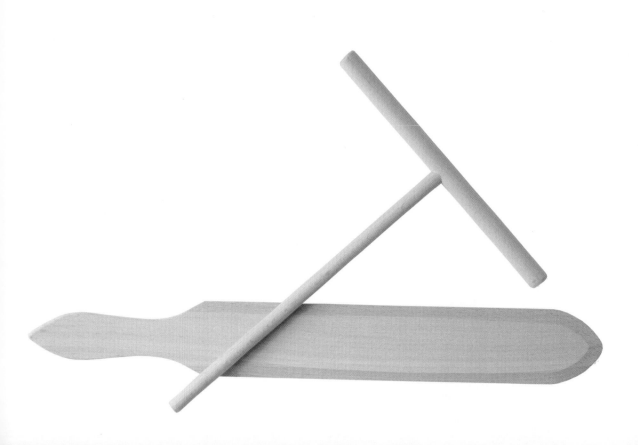

→ **Rubber scraper, 1996, USA,**
Frank J. Sullivan, Rubber, wood

Scrapers have been around in the kitchen for a while, though they were initially used for cleaning. Originally scrapers were made of wood or metal, before plastic and rubber forms appeared. Our contemporary versions for cooking and mixing have one straight side, with the other curved and flexible so it can scrape final mixtures from bowls or help to fold egg whites into batters. Early 20th-century patents had various shapes for different kitchen purposes, often still described as 'dish scrapers'. Mid-20th-century patents described a scraper that could 'adapt itself to curved or irregular surfaces of containers, bowls, etc. to remove food or other particles therefrom' (US Patent 290176662). Frank J. Sullivan finally met our needs in 1996 with his heat-resistant, flexible blade that 'resists melting, burning, cracking, discolouring, or permanently bending, even under vigorous cooking situations' (US Patent 5491869). Since then, these silicone scrapers have been made by various brands across the world.

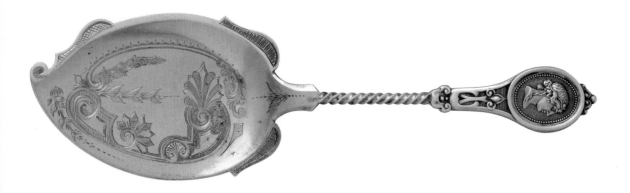

↑ **Ice cream slicer / hatchet, 1863, USA,
Kidney, Cann & Johnson (attributed), Silver**

These tools look nothing like what we use to prise sweet
frozen cream balls into cones today; however, they have
a slight resemblance to the flatter scoops used for gelato.
European records of ice cream eating go back to about
the 17th century, though most ice cream slicers and
'hatchets' were crafted in the 18th and 19th centuries,
once the delicacy was readily available and affordable.
The frozen concoctions were slightly harder than the
ice cream of today, thus requiring blunt and forceful
tools in hatchet shapes, though the pictured example
is more akin to a shallow shovel. Ice cream served with
this tool would have been in wedges, slices and shards,
as opposed to perfect spheres.

The concept of refrigeration and freezing was a true
spectacle and demanded ceremonial objects to serve
ice cream; early versions were made of silver and later
in steel. This server's slight shovel shape has ornate
border decorations and engravings in the blade, which
has been gilded. The production of this object was in
line with the expansion of the silver industry in America
at the time, and the increased demand for luxury items.
It is attributed to a silversmith in New York City, and
came with a set of ten matching spoons to eat the new
novelty dessert of the 19th century.

→ **Ice cream scoop, 1939, USA,
Sherman L. Kelly, Aluminium**

This ice cream scoop and design classic was created
by Sherman L. Kelly in 1939, after he refined a few of his
designs from 1933. There are several variations on this
well-known form, and many preceded this typology
following the eating of frozen-type desserts in the 3rd
century BCE in East Asia. After hatchets and slices, the
next scoopers were conical; this shape was inefficient,
however, and the form was replaced by spherical tools.

As it is difficult to scoop liquids that are almost frozen
solid, Kelly took into account particular angles of the
scoop, warming the device to aid the process, ease of
cleaning, as well as the idea of creating standardised
portions. In fact, the patent lists the design as a 'service
portion gatherer' as opposed to an ice cream scoop.
Many 20th-century scoops are made of aluminium due
to its heat-conducting properties; however, production
ceased during the Second World War between 1939–
1945, when metal manufacturing was diverted to the
war effort. The thick hollow chamber of the Zeroll
handle provides a good grip (better than a spoon, for
instance), and is filled with antifreeze which conducts
body heat and helps to warm the object for prising out
standard portions. The Zeroll company still manufactures
Kelly's design to this day.

Aug. 6, 1940.   S. L. KELLY   2,210,623

SERVICE PORTION GATHERER

Filed April 28, 1939   2 Sheets—Sheet 1

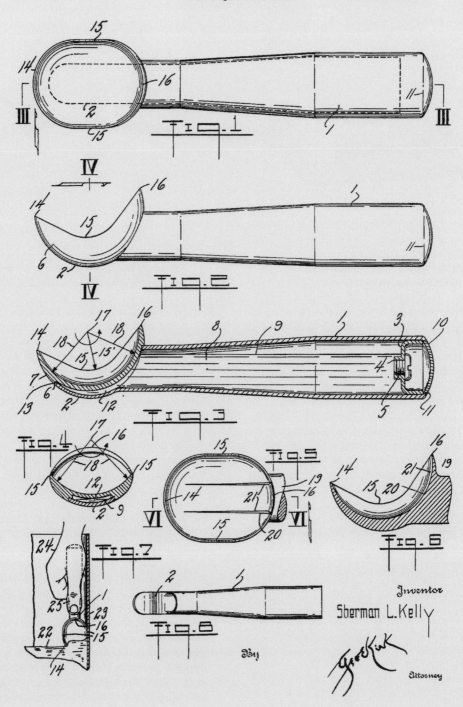

Inventor

Sherman L. Kelly

Attorney

↑ Stilton scoop, 18th–20th centuries, England, Various makers, Silver

When Stilton was established as a cheese variety in the 18th century, a specialised tool for scooping it soon followed. This tool probably took its cues from the cheese tester but was used to serve directly from the wheel in Victorian England. This unique version is a bit later in the life of Stilton scoops, from 1930, and features a small mouse ready to pounce at the extracted morsel.

Scooping Stilton joins the long list of cutting, serving and cheese-eating etiquette across Europe. The 18 cm (7 in) diameter wheels were kept in dedicated cheese 'bells', large covered ceramic dishes that housed the Stilton for serving with specialist scoops. The utensil was particularly useful for Stilton that was potted in a purpose-built crock. Some Stilton scoops had an ejector slide that could dispense the cheese onto the plate, though most resemble a small plain shovel with a long handle.

→ Cheese tester, Since 19th century, Europe / Italy, Various designers / Giulio Gianola, Stainless steel

Instinctively you may think that cheese ripeness and suitability is checked by taste, whereas in the case of Parmesan cheese at least, it is checked primarily by sound. The purveyors of Parmesan, in their deep and lengthy caves, are equipped with tools that have a hammer at one end and a sharp corer at the other. The cheese maker taps the wheel of cheese in various places, and through years of experience will know by listening if the cheese is ready, or if something is amiss. This particular cheese tester was made by the Bharbjt company in northern Italy, who began make knives, scissors and blades in the 1960s; when the company's founder Giulio Gianola began receiving requests for cheese testers, he found the gap in the market and they still manufacture them today.

In English these tools are known as 'cheese irons' or cheese testers, and are indispensible, whether for making, inspecting or trading in aged dairy. Most cheeses are indeed tested by smell, taste or texture, which makes the sharp scoop element of this tool essential. The cheese tester extracts a plug sample from large wheels of aging cheese, inspects it and then returns the cylinder of cheese to its place. These tools are generally made of stainless steel, though antiques exist in silver, some with bull's-horn handles, some with rubber hammer-handles, which are useful for checking cheese reflexes and ripeness.

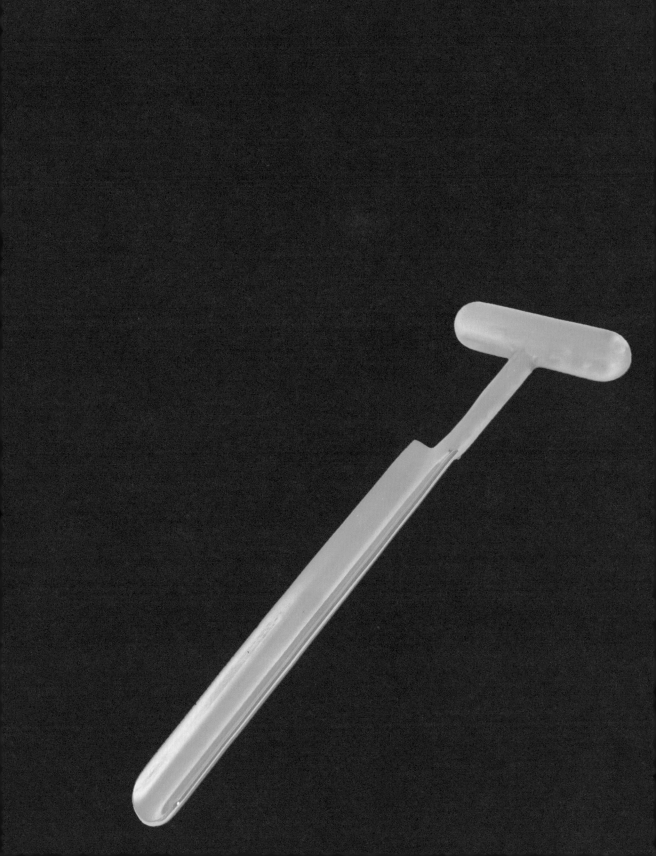

↑ Sleek Spoon, 1962, Italy, Achille Castiglioni
and Pier Giacomo Castiglioni, Plastic

The one design fault of preserving jars is that it is
difficult to excavate the last bit of material from them
when the contents come to an end. Another tool is
required, the Sleek Spoon. Achille Castiglioni couldn't
stand not being able to extract the last morsels of
gianduja (the Italian equivalent of Nutella) from jars,
and so made this purpose-built tool, in characteristic
1960s bright, pop design colours. Achille and his brother
Pier Giacomo were champions of Italian Neo-modernism,
bringing their own aesthetic to this functional tool
while using state-of-the-art production processes
and materials. The utensil was initially released as a
promotion for Kraft products, to scrape out the last bit
of mayonnaise, jam or peanut butter. The spoon can
scrape with its curved or straight side and the thumb
rests on the handle for a comfortable grip; it is made
of a hard-wearing, flexible and hygienic plastic known
as PMMA (Polymethlmetacrylate). Since 1996, Alessi
has produced the design icon in a number of colours.

↓   **Rice paddle (shamoji), Since circa 18th century, Japan / East Asia, Designer unknown, Bamboo / Plastic**

The *shamoji* rice paddle is as universal in the Japanese kitchen as the electric rice cooker. The original tool was made of wood or bamboo, though these days many are made of plastic. The utensil is used to mix vinegar into rice and give a final stir before serving; they are said to have talismanic or magical properties that bring good luck.

The *shamoji* has been carefully designed so that it does not break the polished and steamed rice grains when serving, or the traditional cypress *hangiri* or *ohitsu* rice tub it is scooped from in Japan. Rice paddles are not made of metal, as this would damage the integrity of the rice; rare versions are made of lacquerware. *Shamoji* made of natural materials are dipped in water before use to avoid sticking; however, the contemporary plastic style is more or less non-stick, sometimes with ridges to avoid this. As the *shamoji* was traditionally used by the 'housewife' to portion out rice to the family, it has important symbolism in Japanese culture; when responsibility for household management was transferred from the matriarch to a daughter or daughter-in-law, it was referred to as 'passing the *shamoji*'. This symbolic and physical tool is therefore passed down through generations.

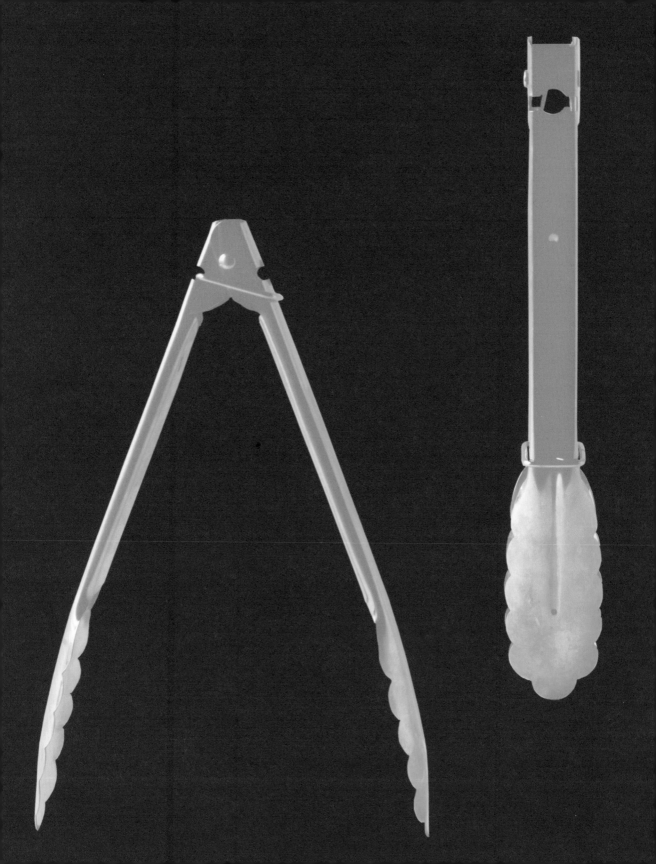

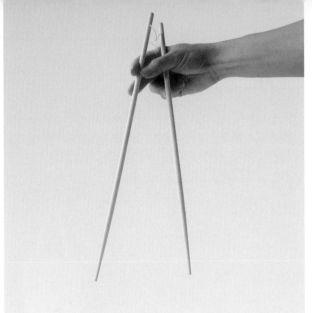

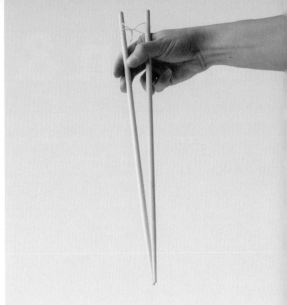

← **Tongs, Date unknown, Worldwide, Various designers, Various materials**

Tongs are used across the world, in one form or another – the need to grab, bite, hold and flip things with tongs in the kitchen is universal. Their design is a natural evolution from *saibashi*, or two long elements connected at one end that can be gripped to grab food in a pot or pan. There are many variations on the theme: Indian *chimta* used to turn flatbreads, toaster tongs to remove cooked bread from electric machines, even cabbage tongs to take sauerkraut and pickles out of fermentation crocks. In contrast to *saibashi*, tongs are connected at one end, usually using the natural spring of wood, bamboo or metal to provide a biting grip. The etymology of the word comes from various Northern European languages including töng, tång, tange, tang, or German *Zange* whose original meaning is 'that which bites'. They're versatile and quick when a spatula is too cumbersome and inefficient.

↑ **Cooking chopsticks (saibashi), Since circa 3000 BCE, East Asia, Designer unknown, Wood**

The first chopsticks were used for cooking rather than eating and evolved from using two twigs to move food about in the process. Called *saibashi* in Japan, they are at least 30 cm (12 in) or longer, thicker than the eating version, and often tied together at one end for easy handling and hanging in the kitchen. The logic behind them has been the same for centuries: length in the tool handle to keep the arms and hands safe from burning. In Vietnam, the chopsticks they use for cooking or serving rice are called 'grand chopsticks' or đũa cả. Typically, cooking chopsticks are made from bamboo, but for frying they are metal on the oil end and bamboo on the handle, since metal stands up to heat more efficiently. For preparing fish, metal *manabashi* are used in Japan, so that the cook's hand does not touch the food being sliced; for plating the final dish, another type of chopsticks is used called *moritsukebashi*, particularly for placing sashimi and sushi on plates and boards.

Clean & Scrub

It's no secret that cleanliness in the kitchen is essential for health, but it is also important for the head chef to have a well-organised kitchen, safely stored food, a properly functioning work area, and all the tools required to keep it so. Cleanliness in the kitchen is fundamental: it can mean life or death, but it is as important a process as the others that precede this final chapter of *Tools for Food*.

It may sound silly to refer to these items as 'tools for food', but they are, in that they are indispensable kitchen items which are necessary to keep kitchens hygienic. In cookbooks and guides throughout the centuries, it is a point that is reiterated time and time again, that work areas must be kept clean: if they are not, then vermin, pests, and parasites may take over. Mrs. Beeton's words of wisdom in her *Book of Household Management* (1861) wrote: 'A dirty kitchen is a disgrace to all concerned. Good cookery is impossible without absolute cleanliness. This is specially so with regard to the hands.' Her useful instructions also included: 'Clear as you go' and 'Never waste or throw away anything that can be turned to account.' Many of these tenets form the basis of catering education and awards of food safety certificates that permit trading in the culinary arts.

Cleanliness is a process in the kitchen that happens before, during and after cooking. It not only involves wiping surfaces and washing up, but also keeping out pests, both small and large. Food must be stored and kept away from vermin, and if present we must eliminate them – from the smallest fly to the largest rat. Surfaces must be continuously wiped, vegetable peelings cleared away, and we must 'clean as we go'. Hands must be washed of personal bodily fluids, germs from daily life (unpleasant yet true), and hair should not make its way into Christmas puddings or bridal cakes. Clothing and undergarments are kept clean by wearing aprons, smocks and pinafores. Over time, natural materials have served us well: elder hung in dairies to dispel flies, sand as an abrasive to scrub pots, coconut fibres turned to scrubbing brushes, twigs and grasses gathered into brooms. Eventually progression ensued: scullery maids using chain mail to scour pots clean, metal shovel-like objects to scrape dried dough from the countertop, and blue-light fly zappers.

Our kitchens are arranged – and even painted certain colours – to aid clean practices while preparing meals. When it was discovered that insects are less attracted by blue because this colour appears dull to them in the UV spectrum, kitchens were sometimes painted these shades to deter bugs and flies. In the end it was discovered that the wavelength of blue light has the ability to kill in itself, hence electric insect zappers. These days airtight containers and well-sealed homes and kitchens mitigate most associated risks of pests and disease; however, care must still be taken to keep food away from prying eyes or they will find their way in. Take note: 'A clean chef is a good chef.'

Beauty meets necessity in this Victorian glass flycatcher.
These hand-blown vessels trapped fruit flies in the
kitchen by luring pests with beer, vinegar or a sweet
liquid in the base. They are filled by tilting the vessel
by 90 degrees and carefully pouring liquid bait into the
spout, which drips down the side of the bottle into the
depression at the bottom. The vessel sits on three glass
feet, which allow flies to enter underneath. Once flies
come for the bait, they drown or otherwise find themselves too confused to escape via the route by which
they came. Fine examples of glass flycatchers have a
glass closure, while others were sealed at the top with
a cork. These Victorian vessels were used in kitchens
as well as sickrooms and at outdoor barbecues, and
were the original fly zapper.

↑   **Food cover, 19th century, USA / Europe,
Designer unknown, Steel**

It is difficult to trace the origin of the mesh fruit fly
dome and food cover, but it emerged some time after
innovations in wire mesh manufacturing in the 19th
century. In the latter half of the 1800s, wire mesh products
such as screen windows and doors were developed,
and naturally in tandem smaller objects utilising the
material also appeared. Food covers are made in hot
countries or those with scorching summers. In one form
or another they have been around for centuries, though
at first made with natural materials. In Ancient Egypt they
used to cover wine glasses with lotus leaves to protect

the contents from insects, and woven basket-type food
cloches are still made and used across the world. Rather
than entrapping and exterminating, these structures
keep out flies, which can harbour and breed dangerous
diseases on food. Food cloches would have been
essential tools for keeping food to be served clean
and proper, whether this was delicate fruits, cheeses
or cooked dishes. With the advent of modern refrigeration
these domes are now less common, except in places
where serving fruit and vegetables at room temperature
for maximum flavour is of paramount importance.

← **Brooms, Ancient World, Worldwide,
Various designers, Various materials**

Brooms are a necessity across the world and are made from vernacular materials in every place they are crafted. Bamboo in Asia, birch in Scandinavia, sorghum in North America, they are made of palm fibres, horsehair, pine needles, and more. In Britain they were made from broom (Genisteae plants), where the English term originates. Whatever the natural fibre, this is bundled together to create sweeping devices that remove crumbs, leaves, dirt and insects from the kitchen, or clean hearths, ovens and kettles (the cauldron type). In order to sweep effectively, the bristles must be closely bundled. Hand-crafted brooms demonstrate their artistry where this bundle is joined: ornate patterns of coloured twine woven into dynamic lines and graphics, sophisticated in form and function. Sometimes the brush is a continuation of the wooden or bamboo handle, splintered into very thin pieces that become soft and pliable for sweeping. The simplicity of function and material has inspired precise broom-making crafts across the globe: dedicated craftspeople make extra-ordinarily striking objects of reasonably banal utensils. Brooms also have superstitious magical qualities, from being used in bridal ceremonies in North America to witches riding them in the sky. Sadly, these items – like many others today – are often made of plastic or mass-produced in factories, and they are nowhere near the beautifully crafted objects of yesteryear.

→ **Bamboo brushes, Date unknown, Japan /
East Asia, Designer unknown, Bamboo**

The bamboo wok brush, cleaning whisk or sasara brush (sasara is bamboo grass), as it is known in Japan, is an essential part of taking care of kitchen utensils. In fact, the task of looking after tools for food is part of the entire cooking process – it is importat to respect and love your implements through proper maintenance if you are to enjoy the best functioning utensils. This practice is outlined in the book *How to Care for Japanese Kitchen Utensils* by Akiko Hano (2017) in particular. Woks are made of iron or steel and must be properly cleaned and seasoned after use, so they do not rust. This non-abrasive bundle of split bamboo scrubs off food effectively, while not damaging the surface. Another version of brushes for this function is a bundle of palm fibres, held tightly together by a series of steel bands. This tool is not exclusive to cleaning woks and can be used on cast iron and other pots and pans.

The small brush is also made of bamboo, cut at the end to make small bristles for cleaning the grooves of the *suribachi* mortar, *oroshigane* graters, or other tools with small-scale ridges and indentations. A marriage of simplicity, beauty, attention and care.

↓ Dough scraper, 1800–1830, Pennsylvania, USA, Maker unknown, Iron

Dough scrapers were used to clean tough dried bits from the bread-making process and originally objects like flat stones or shells were used for the task. Dough scrapers were often made of wrought iron but polished by a whitesmith to look like steel. The maker of these particular tools is unknown, the pair bear the initials of M. K. on one and G. K. on the other – possibly two bread-making lovers who worked in the same kitchen. Serving classes who worked in kitchens did have a reputation for 'unbridled sensuality', due to their constant contact with food and the heat of the environment in which they worked.

Although the older 19th-century forms take up more space, they seem slightly more ergonomic as they don't require a bending of the wrist. These days modern scrapers tend to be a flexible piece of steel with a wooden handle, used to cut dough and clean work surfaces, including *teppanyaki* griddles and bread-making stations. Tupperware, plastic and silicone versions also exist, which can be used for surfaces or scraping pots and pans.

→ Pot chain / Scrubber, Early 20th century, USA, Designer unknown, Metal

Some pot chains had handles, though most came without a handle, which is more practical considering loose links need the direct force of a hand and elbow grease behind them. Chain-mail pot scrubbers exist from the 19th century and probably from medieval times when scullery maids cleaning cast-iron pots might have been given scraps of spare armour to use. Originally the lowliest servants completed the arduous task of pot cleaning, and they used brick dust, sand and horsetail plants (known as scouring rush) to clean off muck. Herbs such as thyme were also used, as they were hardy but also have antiseptic and fungicidal qualities. Also known as a 'kettle scraper', the chain-mail pot scrubber was a fit-for-purpose tool that could really get through tough cooked-on food. It's possible that chain-mail pot scrubbers inspired steel wool, which was mass-produced during the Second World War to clean aluminium cookware.

↓ Tawashi brush, 1907, Japan,
Shozaemon Nishio, Palm fibre, metal

These brushes are made across Japan by a number of companies, keeping the form of this scrubber alive using natural materials and traditional techniques. The Kamenoko Tawashi company in Tokyo claims the invention by their founder Shozaemon Nishio in 1907. About the size of the palm of a hand and the shape of a turtle (*kamenoko* means 'turtle'), they are made of a bundle (*tawashi*, meaning 'bundle') of coconut palm fibres (known as coir) and metal. The fibres are tough enough to scrub food from pots, yet delicate enough to keep surfaces intact. A few companies make their brushes from palms grown in Japan, though many import fibres from Sri Lanka, one of the world's biggest producers of coconut. In Japan, the *tawashi* brush is a metonym, a term interchangeable with other forms of brushes used for cleaning. Brushes using these palm fibres are also made by craftspeople into brooms, pot mats and body scrubbers. The *tawashi* dish brush form is replicated around the world as the product and choice of materials function so well.

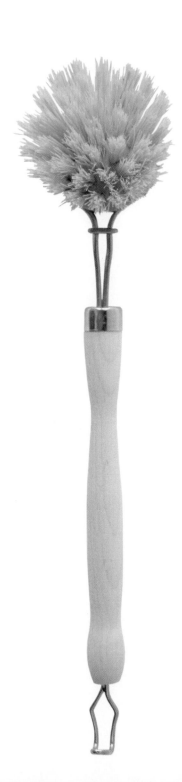

→ **Lola brush, Since 1936, Germany,**
Paul Schmidt, Wood, metal, tampico

The Lola brush is a classic in German kitchens, a
sustainable option with its replaceable brush head.
It emerged from Paul Schmidt's brush-making factory
in 1936. 'Lola' was short for the original name of the
storage warehouse, Lockstedter Lager in Northern
Germany. The company produces the brush using
sustainable wood and hardy natural fibres from tampico
plants of Mexico (such as agave or yucca). The brush
features a hook for storing it above the sink. Lola brushes
– official and non-official versions – can be found in
DIY shops and street markets throughout Germany.
The Lola brush is noted as an object of 'democratic
design' – good design that is attractive, useful, functions
well, and is easily accessible both economically and
through distribution networks.

Across the world, different cultures have their own protective coverings, varying in style and design for domestic and professional kitchens. The Japanese have *kappōgi* cooking smocks, maekake work aprons (pictured), there are standard tieback aprons in the West, and pinafore types that tie around the waist. Historically designs evolved to cover particular clothing, to denote roles and functions in the kitchen, or were even a stylish addition to the domestic environment. What and how aprons are made of are indicators of time, place and social structures – originally, they would have been improvised from scraps of textile: in times of hardship or scarcity they may be made from old sacks, yet at the height of domesticity in the 1950s they were almost fashion accessories. What originally may have been a simple loincloth has evolved into a language of semiotics.

The loose and easy-to-put-on Japanese smock emerged in the early 20th century to protect women's kimonos and its design functions well: large enough to fit over the garments, no ties to crease the kimono, and easy to put on in one movement. The first *kappōgi*-type designs are claimed by Yoshimatsu Akahori, the founder of the well-known Akahori cooking school in Japan. The maekake apron is worn both in workshops and kitchens, a familiar sight in ramen bars across Japan. In Mexico, a smock akin to a sleeveless top is common, colourful and sometimes decorated with embroidered patterns. Bib aprons are the traditional forms in the Western world, which slip over the neck and are tied at the back. Blue and white striped aprons are well-known and loved, though they were originally used solely by butchers and symbolised their profession. In fact, from medieval times apron colours across vocations denoted a purpose: cobblers wore black, barbers wore chequered, stonemasons and chefs wore white. Curiously, aprons became items of fashion beyond domestic purposes, with Elizabethan long coverings, embroidered Swiss versions, or frilly and patterned half-aprons to cover the lap. In the 1950s aprons were made in decorative matching sets, with accompanying oven gloves (mitts) and dish towels. With the women's liberation movement and the apron as a clear signifier of domestic work and labour, the garment fell out of fashion in the late 20th century. Eventually the apron re-emerged and has regained some popularity with the growing collective interest in home cooking and foodie culture.

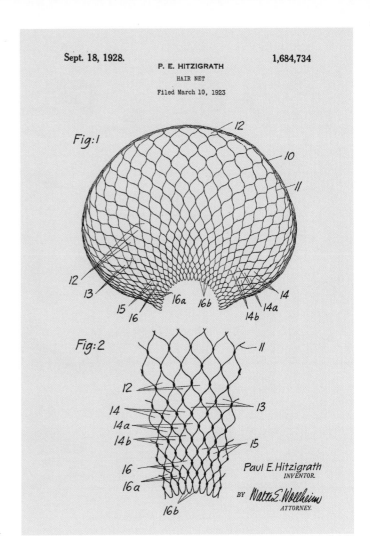

Sept. 18, 1928.

P. E. HITZIGRATH

HAIR NET

Filed March 10, 1923

1,684,734

Fig:1

Fig:2

Paul E. Hitzigrath
INVENTOR.

BY *Walter E. Wollheim*
ATTORNEY.

↑ **Hairnet, 20th century, USA,
Various designers, Nylon**

Historically hairnets and snoods were used to keep hair in place, not in the kitchen, but for fashion. Their use in catering environments was introduced in the 20th century, and now beard nets accompany those for the head. Nobody wants to find a stray hair in their food, and this bodily remnant can indeed carry bacteria and disease. These delicate nets are made from nylon or thin pieces of elastic, although hundreds of years ago they were made from thin pieces of silk. Though many of the hairnet patents registered in the 19th and 20th centuries were for holding hairstyles in place, the patterns of their weaves and construction are mesmerisingly beautiful. One of the largest disposable hairnet manufacturers in the world writes that 'it can take an entire day to thread a hairnet machine … for some nets, the operator must thread 2800 holes before the knitting process can begin.' It is complex work to make and keep these hair containers from tangling together in a thousand knots.

FIG. 1759. — Pièges à rats.

1. Souricière ; 2. Ratière assommoir ; 3 à 9. Pièges à ressort ; 10. Assommoir en grillage ;
11. Ratière dite *anglaise* ; 12. Ratière assommoir dite *pyramide* ; 13 Souricière et ratière à
deux entrées ; 14. Ratière automatique ; 15. Assommoir dit *quatre de chiffre* ; 16. Nasse ;
17. Assommoir.

↑   Mouse and rat traps, 20ᵗʰ century, France /
Worldwide, Various designers, Various materials

These mouse and rat traps come from Larousse's
Ménager Illustré (Illustrated Household Guide, 1926),
and show the myriad ways you can catch and kill
vermin that are a nuisance in the kitchen. The guide
first suggests you start with a cat or dog which might
discourage the pests; it goes on to say that you should
pass a flame over a trap after each use, to remove
suspicious odours of man or dead rat, and that essence
of anise can be used to attract them. Despite the most
determined efforts, these rodents always seem to find
a way in, but any number of these pictured devices
could help keep the kitchen pest-free: stunners, hatches,
automatic traps, some with chemical poisons or virus
pathogens that are only dangerous to rodents. Many
of the first registered patent designs are from the end
of the 19ᵗʰ century, though improvised devices would
have been used well before then; mousetraps have been
referenced across a few household records in the 16ᵗʰ
century. Now more humane methods exist and though
not a pleasant task, these are essential for a clean and
hygienic kitchen.

About the Author

Corinne Mynatt is a Nashville-born, London-based writer, curator and producer. Her work spans across design, food, architecture, art and the places where these disciplines meet. Corinne studied Fine Art and Design in New York, London and Eindhoven before developing a focus of the intersection between food and design. She has been an avid cook since her teenage years, and almost never cooks the same thing twice. When not writing, she is scouring markets across the world to discover new and unknown tools and their subsequent cuisines. Follow the journey on @tools_for_food.

Acknowledgements

Thank you to friends and family who supported the writing of this book in France, and my dearest sister Nicole during the final stages written in Nashville. I am indebted to Clara Kraft Isono for her help with the photo shoot, likewise to Daniel Chaytor. Thanks to those who lent their tools, including Clara, Ryoko, Elisa, Steph, Eve, Helen & Jamie, and those who wish to remain anonymous. I'm grateful to the antiques houses across the UK and USA who enthusiastically provided some of the images. The author would like to thank Eve Marleau for taking the leap of faith with this project. Thank you to all of the designers at A Practice for Everyday Life for the brilliant work and unique mind-reading abilities.

Bibliography

Acton, Elizabeth, *Modern Cookery*, London: Longmans & Co, 1845

Alexander, Brian, *Spiffy Kitchen Collectibles*, Iola: Krause Publications, 2003

Barlow, Ronald S., Ed, *Victorian Houseware, Hardware, and Kitchenware*, New York: Dover, 1992

Barton, Stuart, *Kitchenalia: Buyer's Price Guide*, Kent: MJM Publications, 1982

Beard, James, Milton Glaser and Burton Wolf, Eds, International Cooks Catalogue, New York: Random House, 1977

Bishop, Christina, *Miller's Collecting Kitchenware*, London: Miller's, 1995

Coatts, Margot and Elizabeth Ogborn, Eds, *Alternative Kitchens*, Southampton: Southampton Art Gallery, 1980

Curtis, Tony, *Kitchen Equipment*, Galashiels: Lyle Publications, 1977

De Haan, David, *Antique Household Gadgets and Appliances, c.1860 to 1930*, Dorset: Blandford Press, 1977

Deeley, Robert, *The Cauldron, The Spit & The Fire: Over Five Hundred Years of Downhearth & Bargrate Cooking*, Great Yarmouth: Gold Cockerel Books, 2011

Dunne, Patrick, *The Epicurean Collector*, London: Little, Brown and Co, 2002

Eveleigh, David J., *Old Cooking Utensils*, Princes Risborough: Shire, 1994

Ettlinger, Steve, *The Kitchenware Book*, New York: Macmillan, 1992

Feild, Rachel, *Irons in the Fire: A History of Cooking Equipment*, Marlborough: The Crowood Press, 1984

Florence, Gene, *Kitchen Glassware of the Depression Years*, Lexington: Collector Books, 1987

Franklin, Linda Campbell, *300 Years of Kitchen Collectibles*, Fifth Edition, Iola: Krause, 2003

Gould, Mary Earle, *Early American Wooden Ware & Other Kitchen Utensils*, Springfield: Pond-Ekberg, 1942

Graff, Sarah R. and Enrique Rodriguez-Alegria, Eds, *The Menial Art of Cooking*, Boulder: University Press of Colorado, 2012

Hale, William Harlan and Horizon Magazine, Eds, *The Horizon Cookbook and Illustrated History of Eating and Drinking Through the Ages*, [S.l.]: American Heritage Publishing, 1968

Hibi, Sadao, *Japanese Detail: Traditional Table and Kitchen Ware*, London: Thames & Hudson, 1989

Katz, Solomon H. and William W. Weaver, Eds, *Encyclopaedia of Food and Culture*, London: Thomson Gale, 2003

Kinchin, Juliet, *Counter Space*, New York: MOMA, 2011

Klippensteen, Kate, *Cool Tools: Cooking Utensils from the Japanese Kitchen*, London: Kodansha, 2006

Kness, Darlene, *The Butterick Kitchen Equipment Handbook: An Illustrated Consumer's Guide to Buying and Caring for Cookware, Utensils and Appliances*, New York: Butterick, 1977

Laudan, Rachel, *Cuisine and Empire: Cooking in World History*, London: University of California Press, 2013

Lewis, Valerie, Ed, *Miller's Kitchenware Buyer's Guide*, Kent: Miller's, 2005

London, Gloria, *Ancient Cookware from the Levant*, Equinox Publishing, 2016

Lydgate, Tony, *The Art of Elegant Wood Kitchenware*, New York: Sterling, 1996

Marshall, Jo, *Collecting for Tomorrow: Kitchenware*, London: Pitman, 1976

McFadden, Christine, *Tools for Cooks*, London: Jacqui Small, 2000

Mrs. Beeton's Household Management: A Complete Cookery Book, London: Ward, Lock & Co, 1861

Myerson, Jeremy and Slyvia Katz, Eds, *Conran Design Guides: Kitchenware*, London: Conran Octopus, 1990

Norwak, Mary, *Kitchen Antiques*, London: Ward Lock, 1975

Peachey, Stuart, *Cooking Techniques and Equipment 1580–1660*, Volume 1, Bristol: Stuart Press, 1994

Pollan, Michael, Cooked: *A Natural History of Transformation*, New York: Penguin, 2013

Sambrook, Pamela A. and Peter Brears, Eds, *The Country House Kitchen, 1650–1900*, Stroud: The History Press, 2010

Slesin, Suzanne, Daniel Rozensztroch and Stafford Cliff, Eds, *Kitchen Ceramics*, London: Abbeville, 1997

St. George, E. A., *The Cauldron Stirrer's Handbook*, London: Spook Enterprises, 2004

Snodgrass, Mary Ellen, *Encyclopedia of Kitchen History*, London: Fitzroy Dearborn, 2004

Warren, Geoffrey, *Kitchen Bygones: A Collector's Guide*, London: Souvenir Press, 1984

Watkins, Malcolm J., *A Morsel of History: Ginger in a Coffin: Food preparation and Recipes in the days of the Tudors and Stuarts*, Great Britain: Heritage Matters, 2010

Wilkinson, Jule, *The Complete Book of Cooking Equipment*, Boston: Cahners Books, 1975

Wilson, Bee, *Consider the Fork*, London: Particular Books (Penguin), 2012

Wood, Jacqui, *Prehistoric Cooking*, Stroud: Tempus, 2001

Wood, Richard, *History of Food and Cooking*, Hove: Wayland, 1996

Image Credits

Cover, object top right: Seventy deben weight, ca. 1850–1640 B.C. Rhyolite, h 9 cm ($3\frac{9}{16}$ in); w 6.5 cm ($2\frac{9}{16}$ in); d 5.5 cm ($2\frac{3}{16}$ in); weight 1 kg (2.1 lbs). The Met Museum, Rogers Fund, 1915, 15.3.233. Remaining objects and back cover, photography Corinne Mynatt. Terracotta amphora, 3rd century BCE. Terracotta, h 15¼ in (38.8 cm). The Met Museum, The Cesnola Collection, Purchased by subscription, 1874–76, 74.51.392. (p. 13). Shutterstock (p. 14). Image courtesy of Eron Johnson Antiques, Colorado. Photo: Sergio Garcia (p. 17). Image courtesy of Africa Direct, www.africadirect.com. (p. 16). Image courtesy of Salisbury Antiques Centre. h 38 cm (15 in), w 36 cm (14.2 in), d 21 cm (8.3 in), (p. 19). US Patent Office, June 2, 1947, E. S. Tupper (p. 20). Image courtesy of Noleggiocose by Andrea Moscardi (p. 21). Image courtesy of World of Bacara, www.worldofbacara.com. h 52 cm (20½ in) Top: 8.9 × 8.9 cm (3½ × 3½ in) Base: 16.5 × 16.5 cm (6½ × 6½ in), (p. 23). Image courtesy of Decorative Antiques UK, East Sussex. Janet Penny Photography. (p. 25). Top: Butter Dish, Richards and Hartley Flint Glass Co. (ca. 1870–1890), Gift of Mrs. Emily Winthrop Miles, 1946. h 7⅛ in (18.1 cm); w 5⅝ in (14.3 cm) Met Museum; Bottom: Weesper porseleinfabriek, c. 1759–1771. Rijks Museum (p. 32). Kendi, Indonesia, Eastern Java, Majapahit, 14th–15th century. Terracotta, 18.4 × 20 × 16.5 cm (7¼ × 7⅞ × 6½ in.) LACMA, Gift of James and Jane Singer, M.88.72. (p. 34). Image courtesy of Arnout Visser and Museum Boijmans van Beuningen. (p. 36). Image courtesy of trendglas Jena. (p. 37). Image courtesy of Mori Masahiro Design Studio, Saga, Japan. (p. 38). Image courtesy of Jorre van Ast. (p. 40). Batter jug, 1882–85. Stoneware, h 8¾ in (22.2 cm). The Met Museum, Gift of Miss Levantia Halsey, 1926, 26.245. (p. 41). Image courtesy of Kagedo Japanese Art. From the Seikado Collection of the Mitsubishi family. (p. 44). Teacup, 1840–1860. Porcelain, h 6.7 cm (2¾ in) d 1.2 cm (½ in) Kulturparken Småland, M 66478-1-2. Attribution International (CC BY 4.0). (p. 45).). 1) Standard kilogram, 1798. Brass, h 9 cm (3½ in) d 6 cm (2½ in). The Rijksmusuem, NG-2001-16-D-9.; 2) Weight, Dynasty 19–20, d 7 cm (2¾ in), Rogers Fund, 1915, 15.3.1023. Met Museum.; 3) Quart Measure, Boardman and Hart, 1835. Pewter, h 10 in (25.4 cm). The Met Museum, Clara L-S Weber Gift, 1979.449.; 4) Bull's-Head Weight of 2 Deben, ca. 1550–1391 B.C. Bronze or copper alloy, h 3.1 cm (1¼ in) w 4.3 cm ($1\frac{11}{16}$ in), 181.22 g 6.392 oz.). The Met Museum, Purchase, Lila Acheson Wallace, Gift, 1968, 68.139.2. 5) Seven deben weight, ca. 1850–1640 B.C. Rhyolite, h 9 cm ($3\frac{9}{16}$ in); w 6.5 cm ($2\frac{9}{16}$ in); d 5.5 cm ($2\frac{3}{16}$ in); weight 1 kg (2.1 lbs). The Met Museum, Rogers Fund, 1915,15.3.233.; 6) Six deben weight, ca. 1981–1640 B.C., h 6 cm ($2\frac{9}{16}$ in); w 4 cm ($1\frac{9}{16}$ in); d 3 cm ($1\frac{3}{16}$ in), Rogers Fund, 1934, 34.1.175. Met Museum.; 7) Weight: 40 kedets, ca. 1981–1640 B.C., From Egypt, Memphite Region, Lisht North, Cemetery, MMA excavations, 1920–22, h 6.2 cm ($2\frac{7}{16}$ in); w 3.2 cm (1¼ in); d f0.4 cm ($\frac{3}{16}$ in); weight 301 g (0.3 kg), Rogers Fund, 1915, 15.3.607. Met Museum.; 8) Measure, late 18th–early 19th century. Pewter, 4 × 2½ in (10.2 × 6.4 cm). The Met Museum, Gift of Mr. Robert M. Parmelee and Mrs. William L. Parker, 1916,16.116.101.; (p. 46–47). Image courtesy of Alessi S.p.a Crusinallo, Italy. (p. 42, 50). 2) Funnel, 19th century. Glazed earthenware, 14.6 × 24.8 cm (5¾ × 9¾ in). Brooklyn Museum, Gift of Huldah Cail Lorimer in memory of George Burford Lorimer, 57.75.20. Creative Commons-BY (Photo: Brooklyn Museum, 57.75.20.jpg); 3) Lozi. Wood Funnel, late 19th or early 20th century. Wood, 7.6 × 35.9 × 22.2 cm (3 × $14\frac{1}{16}$ × 8¾ in). Brooklyn Museum, Gift of John Hewitt, 74.33.2. Creative Commons-BY (Photo: Brooklyn Museum, 74.33.2_bw.jpg); 4) Pottery funnel of red ware, Cyprus, c. 2000 B.C. Wellcome Collection. Attribution 4.0 International (CC BY 4.0); 5)Tratt. BA 62, Föremål, Kulturparken Småland/Smålands museum, Kulturparken Småland / Smålands museum, May 12, 2020, 021028597423, Digital Museum (p. 52–53). J.Ely. Hydrometer, July 19, 1910. 964,628. (p. 54). Image courtesy of Richard Sapper Archives (p. 55). US Patent Office, August 2 1971, Jean Mantelet, Paris, Assignor to Moulinex Societe Anonyme, Bagnolet, France. (p. 64). Cassava squeezer, 2003.436, © Horniman Museum and Gardens. (p. 70). Beer Strainer, 1972.356, © Horniman Museum and Gardens (p. 71). US Patent Office, T.G Melish, Flour Sifter, No. 1,753,995, 16 June 1926. (p. 73). Collection of Salisbury and South Wiltshire Museum. Attributed to The Portable Antiquities Scheme / The Trustees of the British Museum. Photograph: Richard Henry. Attribution-ShareAlike 2.0 Generic (CC BY-SA 2.0) (p. 74). American. Apple Peeler, 19th century. Iron, wood, 27.3 × 20.3 × 16.5 cm (10¾ × 8 × 6½ in). Brooklyn Museum, Gift of Fred Tannery, 82.112.10a–b. (p. 75). Good Grips Prototype For A Peeler, 1990; Designed by Davin Stowell and Daniel Formosa; USA; carved foam, metal; h 18.5 cm ($7\frac{5}{16}$ in), w 3 cm ($1\frac{3}{16}$ in), d 2 cm ($\frac{13}{16}$ in); Cooper Hewitt, Gift of Smart Design, Inc.; 2011-50-13. ; Matt Flynn © Smithsonian Institution. New York, Cooper-Hewitt – Smithsonian Design Museum. © 2021. Cooper-Hewitt, Smithsonian Design Museum/Art Resource, NY/Scala, Florence. (p. 77–78). US Patent Office, B.F. Macy, Egg Seperator, No. 28,876. 14 June, 1898 (p. 84). Photo: Takimata, License CC BY-SA 3.0. (p. 85). Pastry Pricker, Brödpigg, XLM.06630, 20 (7¾ in) 11 cm (4⅓ in), Länsmuseet Gävleborg and Brödpick, XLM.09749, 11 cm (4⅓ in), Länsmuseet Gävleborg, Digital Museum ; Brödnagg, XLM.06630, Föremålssamling, Länsmuseet Gävleborg, Digital Museum. (p. 86). Top left, image courtesy of Puckhaber Decorative Antiques, London and Rye, UK. (p. 95). Kniv, XLM.00397, Föremålssamling, Länsmuseet Gävleborg, Digital Museum; Hackkniv XLM.02894a, Föremålssamling, Länsmuseet Gävleborg, Digital Museum; Hackkniv, XLM.15276a, Föremålssamling, Länsmuseet Gävleborg, Digital Museum (p. 95). Knives 1,2,4,7,8,9,11, courtesy of Kitchen Provisions, London. (pp. 98–99). US Patent Office, F.B. Seeberger, Frozen Food Cutter, June 2, 1953, No. 2685131. (p. 101). Whetstones courtesy of Kitchen Provisions, London. (p. 108). Image courtesy of Richard Sapper Archives. (p. 109). Image courtesy of The Antique Kitchen, Norfolk, UK. theantiquekitchen.co.uk (p. 111). Chop2Pot courtesy of Joseph Joseph. (p. 112). Benktzon, Maria (1946–) and Juhlin, Sven-Eric (b. 1940): Kitchen Knife and Cutting Board, 1973. manufacturer: AB Gustavsberg, Sweden. Design firm: Ergonomi Design Gruppen (now Veryday). New York, Museum of Modern Art (MoMA). 1 (knife): Stainless steel and polypropylene, 8.9 × 10.2 × 2.5 cm (3½ × 4 × 1 in) .2 (cutting board): plastic, 13.3 × 38.3 × 13.7 cm (5¼ × $15\frac{1}{16}$ × 5⅜ in). Gift of RFSU Rehab. Acc. no.: 437.1983.1-2. © 2021. Digital image, The Museum of Modern Art, New York/Scala, Florence (p. 113). Image courtesy of The Fancy Fox, Antiques & Collectibles, UK. (p. 92, 118). Scissors courtesy of Fiskars (p. 122). US Patent Office, E.D. Woods, Can Opener, 8.10.1901. 684,334. (p. 127). Schomburg Center for Research in Black Culture, Jean Blackwell Hutson Research and Reference Division, The New York Public Library. 'Les pileuses de couscous. -- L'horrible danse du pilon est dans toute sa vigueur. (Composition de M. le capitaine Philippe.)' The New York Public Library Digital Collections. 1890. (p. 130). A. Davey family photograph. Creative Commons license: Attribution 2.0 Generic (CC BY 2.0). (p. 131). 1) Alabaster mortar, ca. 1200–1050 B.C.,

The Cesnola Collection, Purchased by subscription, 1874–76, h 3.8 cm (1½ in); w (10.8 cm (4¼ in), 74.51.5139, Met Museum.; 2) Mortar and pestle, Gift of Mr. and Mrs. William A. Moore, 1923, 23.80.16a, b, 13.7 × 14.6 × 25.4 cm (5⅜ × 5¾ × 10 in). Met Museum.; 3) Mortar and pestle, Wedgwood and Bentley (British, Etruria, Staffordshire, 1769–1780), Gift of Dr. and Mrs. Lazarus A. Orkin, 1978, mortar: 6.7 × 14.3 cm (2⅝ × 5⅝ in) 1. 978.306.1.2 Met Museum.; 4) Wooden mortar and pestle, Europe, 1501–1800. Science Museum, London. Attribution 4.0 International (CC BY 4.0).; 5) Wooden mortar and pestle, Europe, 1501–1800, Wellcome Collection. Mortel, XLM.07258, 19 × 23 × 20 cm (7½ × 9 × 8 in), (p. 133–134). Metate with Bird Head, Costa Rica, Guanacaste-Nicoya, 300–700 CE. Basalt, 27.9 × 53.3 × 20.3 cm (11 × 21 × 8 in). LACMA, Gift of the Art Museum Council in honor of the museum's twenty-fifth anniversary, M.90.168.43. (p. 136). Poi Pounder (Pōhaku Ku'i Poi). Stone, 15.5 × 17 cm (6⅛ × 6¹¹⁄₁₆ in). Brooklyn Museum, Gift of George C. Brackett and Robert B. Woodward, 02.258.2659. (p. 137). 1) Grater, 1760–1810. Brass, iron, 2.9 × 1.15 × 0.4 cm (1 × ½ × ⅓ in). Östergötland Museum, OM.A.003657. Attrbution-Share Alike (CC BY-SA). ; 2) Grater with Handle in the Form of a Male Head, Colombia or Ecuador, Tumaco-La Tolita, Tumaco-La Tolita, 500 BCE–500 CE. Ceramic, 4.76 × 8.57 × 21.91 cm (1⅞ × 3⅜ × 8⅝ in). LACMA, The Muñoz Kramer Collection, gift of Camilla Chandler Frost and Stephen and Claudia Muñoz-Kramer (M.2007.146.578).; 3) Rivjärn, OM.A.019448.0061, Östergötlands museum (p. 139). 1, 3)Silver Nutmeg Graters, one with fishkin case, and one barrel-shaped.; Wellcome Collection. Attribution 4.0 International (CC BY 4.0); 2) Grater, ca. 1690. Cowrie shell, silver, l 5 in (12.7 cm). The Met Museum, Gift of Irwin Untermyer, 1968, 68.141.278.; (p. 145) Smörkärna (Butter churn), 19ᵗʰ century. Wood, iron, h 6.3 cm (2½ in), w 7.7 cm (3 in), d 2.5 cm (1 in). Kulturparken Småland AB, gift of Blenda Andersson, BA 103. License: Attribution. Photo: Jörgen Ludwigsson. (p. 154). Visp (whisk), 1814. Birch, 52 cm (20½ in). Gävleborg County Museum (Länsmuseet Gävleborg), XLM.02136. License: Attrbution-ShareAlike (CC BY-SA); Visp, GF2136 – Föremålet märkt, Föremålssamling, Länsmuseet Gävleborg, Länsmuseet Gävleborg, 021028351956, June 4, 2019. (p. 155). US Patent Office, C.S. Pusey. 25/10/1887. No. 327,043. (p. 156). US Patent Office, Caroline S. Pusey, Culinary or Egg Beater, 372,043, Oct 25, 1887. (p. 156). Mini-masher courtesy of Kitchen Provisions, London. (p. 161). Image courtesy of Hobson May Collection, UK, hobsonmaycollection.com (p. 162). Image courtesy of J Collins and Son Antiques, 8 Charles Avenue, Bideford, Devon, EX39 2PH. (p. 170, 171). Image courtesy of Alessi S.p.a., Crusinallo, Italy (p. 175). French Chrome Duck Press From the Estate of Anthony Bourdain Image Courtesy of Lark Mason Associates and iGavel Auctions, New York. (p. 181). Image courtesy of Marcato (p. 182). Image courtesy of Pal-Ed. (p. 184). Image courtesy of Appleby Antiques. (p. 189). Pastry cutter, 16ᵗʰ century, Brass, L 13.70 centimetres. Brass, L 13.70 centimetres. The British Museum, 1877,0802.14. © The Trustees of the British Museum. (p. 190). US Patent Office, N.Waterman, Egg Pan and Cake Baker, 23, 517. (p. 194). Image courtesy of Ivan Day. (p. 198). Smörform, XLM.05485, GM5485 - Föremålet märkt, Föremålssamling, Länsmuseet Gävleborg, 021028367386, Digital Museum.; Stämpel, XLM.07529c, Föremålssamling, Länsmuseet Gävleborg Digital Museum. (p. 202). Shutterstock (p. 205). Images courtesy of The Springerle Baker thespringerlebaker.com : Clockwise from top left: Crafters mould, location unknown, 18th century; Property of a Franconian (Central German) bakery, 1800; Stuttgart, late 1700s; Stuttgart, Biedermeier period, carved 1814–1836. (pp. 206–207). Image courtesy of Appleby Antiques. (p. 208). Form, tin plate, 14 × 17 cm / 5½ × 6¾ in (upper diameter) × 11.5 cm / 4½ in (lower diameter). Gävleborg County Museum, gift of Sigrid Lenbäck, XLM.18481a. (p. 209). Image courtesy of Nisbets. (p. 212). Skewer, early 18ᵗʰ century, iron, 560 mm. Kulturparken Småland / Smålands museum, gift of Blenda Andersson, BA 146. (p. 216). Broaching or toasting fork, 17ᵗʰ century, l 102.9 cm (40½ in), Rogers Fund, 1907, 07.52.8, Met Museum (p. 217). Image courtesy of Trish Hayward and the Antique Metalware Society. (p. 219). Cooking pot, before 1613. Iron, h 24 × d 26.5 cm (9½ × 10½ in). The Rijksmuseum, NG-1977-195-W. (p. 220). Image courtesy of English Salvage, Herefordshire. (p. 221). Image courtesy of Walpole Antiques, London. (p. 222). Henry Wigstead. Remarks on a Tour to North and South Wales: in the year 1797, No, 40 Charing Cross, London: W. Wigstead 1799. pp. 52–53. Collection of the British Library. (p. 223). Image courtesy of Alessi S.p.a., Crusinallo, Italy. (p. 225). Image courtesy of Parade Antiques, www.paradeantiques.co.uk. Photo: Jon Cooney, @iamjoncooney. (pp. 226-7). Shutterstock. (p. 228). Image courtesy of Habitat, UK. (p. 232). Molcajete courtesy of Milagros, London. (p. 236). Image courtesy of littala. (p. 235). Potta (pot), 1850s. Iron, h 2.4 cm, l 2.7 cm. Kulturparken Småland / Smålands Museum. Photo: Jörgen Ludwigsson. Attribution (CC BY). (p. 237). Shutterstock (p. 239). US Patent Office, W. J Russell. Pressure Cooker, Jan 14, 1947. Des. 146,235 (p. 244). ; US Patent Office, J. H. Jacobs. Pressure Cooker Lock, December 19, 1922. 1,439,000. (p. 244). Halter (Gridiron), date unknown. Iron, h 10 cm (4 in), d 2.7 cm (1 in), l 5.9 cm (2⅓ in). Nordic Museum, Skansen, SKANM.0122225. Photo: Attribution-ShareAlike (CC BY-SA) (p. 247). 32.5 cm (12½ in), 2.3 cm (¾ in), XLM.17913, Länsmuseet Gävleborg, Länsmuseet Gävleborg, Föremålssamling, January 11, 2020, Digital Museum (p. 249). Image courtesy of Native & Co, London, www.nativeandco.com. (p. 254). US Patent Office, Vegetable Steamer, Gerald M. Feld. Feb 13, 1979. 4,138,939. (p. 256). Shutterstock (p. 264). BA 227, Föremål, Kulturparken Småland / Smålands museum, July 1, 2020, Digital Museum (p. 268). Ice Cream Slicer and 10 Ice Cream Spoons, ca. 1863. Silver and silver gilt, l 23.8 cm (9⅜ in). The Met, Gift of D. Frederick Baker from the Baker/Pisano Collection, 2016.533.8.1–.11. (p. 272). Kelly, Sherman. Service Portion Gatherer. US 2,210,623. 28 April 1939. (p. 273). Image courtesy of Marion Harris, Art and Antiques, Park Avenue, New York. (p. 274). Image courtesy of Bharbjt Cheese Tools, www.bharbjt.com. (p. 275). Image courtesy of Alessi S.p.a., Crusinallo, Italy. (p. 276). Left: Logkvast (Broom), 1800–1899. Birch, 1050.0 mm. Kulturparken Småland AB, BA 212. Photo: Ludwigsson, Jörgen. Attribution (CC BY). (p. 284). Dough Board Scraper, 1800–1830. Iron, 6.4 × 11.4 × 9.5 cm (2½ × 4½ × 3¾ in). The Met, Gift of Mrs. J. Insley Blair, 1937, 37.134.10 and 37.134.9. (p. 288). US Patent Office, P.E. Hitzigrath. September 18, 1928. 1,684,734. (p. 293). E. Chancrin and F. Faideau Eds. Larousse ménager illustré. Paris: Librairie Larousse, 1926, p1029, (p. 294).

Published in 2021 by Hardie Grant Books,
an imprint of Hardie Grant Publishing

Hardie Grant Books (London)
5th & 6th Floors
52–54 Southwark Street
London SE1 1UN

Hardie Grant Books (Melbourne)
Building 1, 658 Church Street
Richmond, Victoria 3121

hardiegrantbooks.com

British Library Cataloguing-in-Publication Data. A catalogue
record for this book is available from the British Library.

Tools for Food by Corinne Mynatt
ISBN: 978-1-78488-404-8

10 9 8 7 6 5 4 3 2 1

Publisher: Kajal Mistry
Commissioning Editor: Eve Marleau
Copy-editor: Caroline West
Indexer: Vanessa Bird
Design: A Practice for Everyday Life
Production Controller: Nikolaus Ginelli

Colour reproduction by p2d
Printed and bound in China by Leo Paper Products Ltd.